the complete

geisha™

by andi watson

book design by
Keith Wood

edited by
Jamie S. Rich

*This book collects issues 1-4 of the
Oni Press comic book series* Geisha,
the Geisha *One-shot, and the short story
from the* Oni Press Summer Vacation
Supercolor Fun Special.

Published by Oni Press, Inc.
Joe Nozemack, publisher
James Lucas Jones, associate editor

ONI PRESS, INC.
6336 SE Milwaukie Avenue, PMB30
Portland, OR 97202
USA

www.onipress.com
www.andiwatson.com

First edition: May 2003
ISBN 1-929998-51-1

1 3 5 7 9 10 8 6 4 2
PRINTED IN CANADA

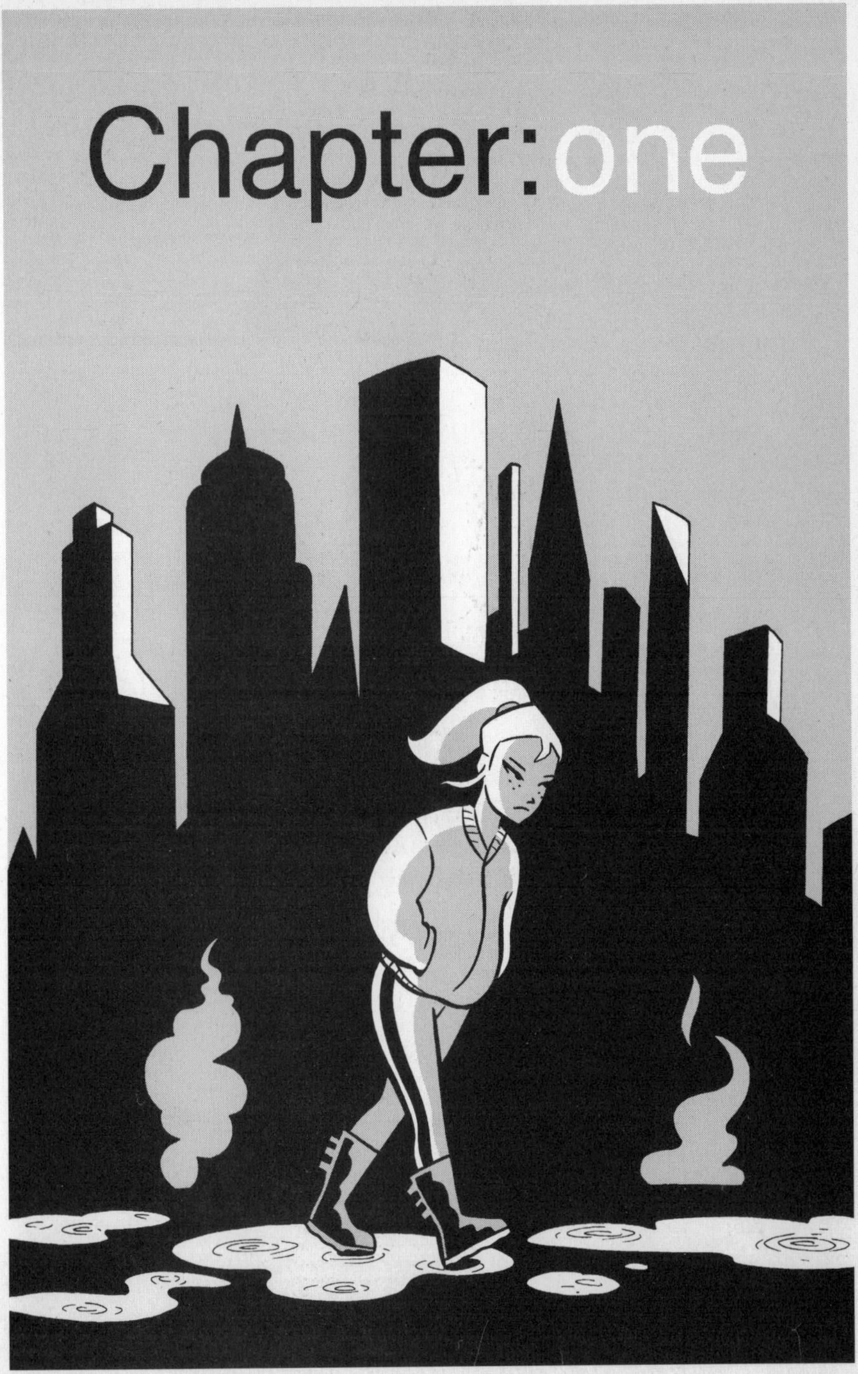
Chapter:one

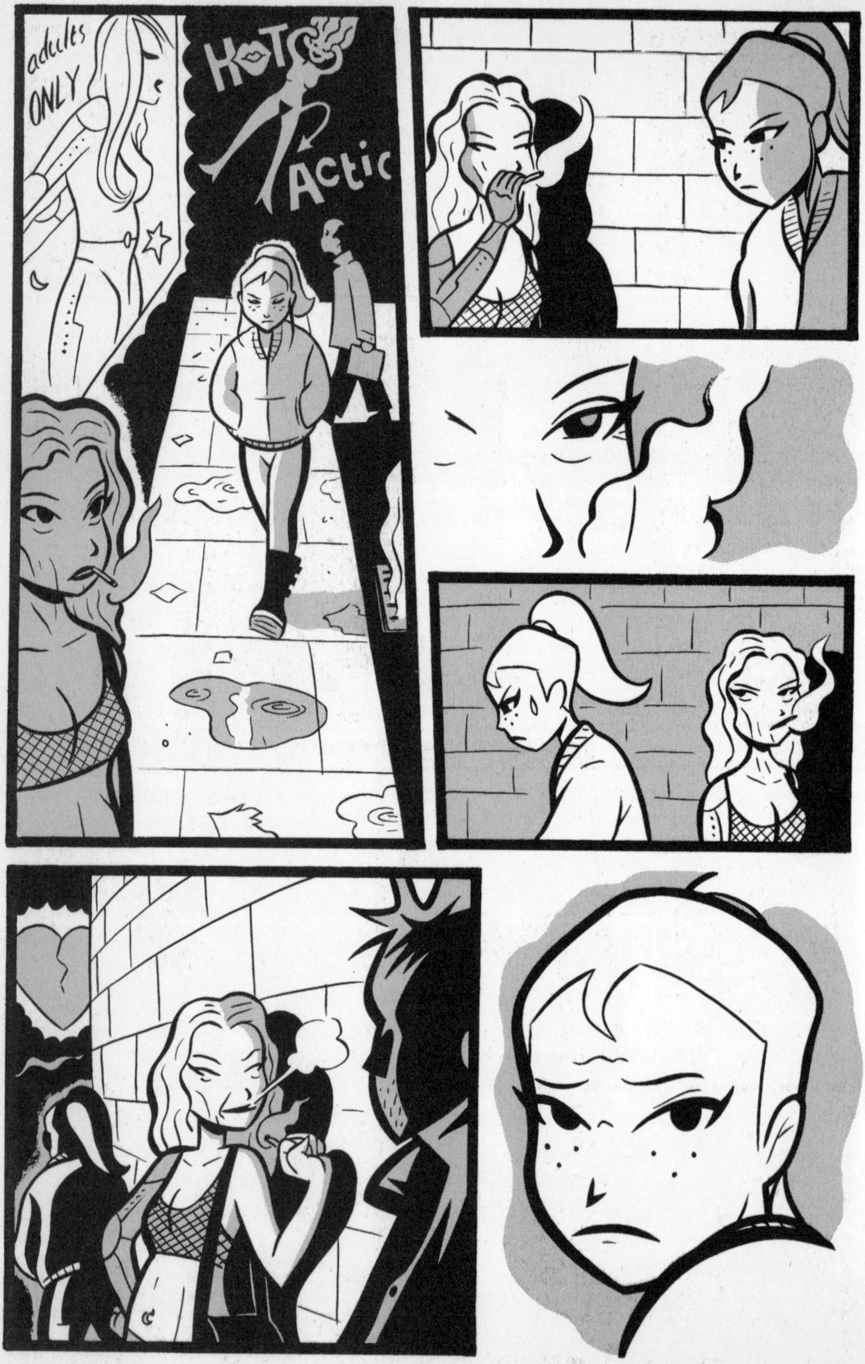
adults ONLY
HoT Actic

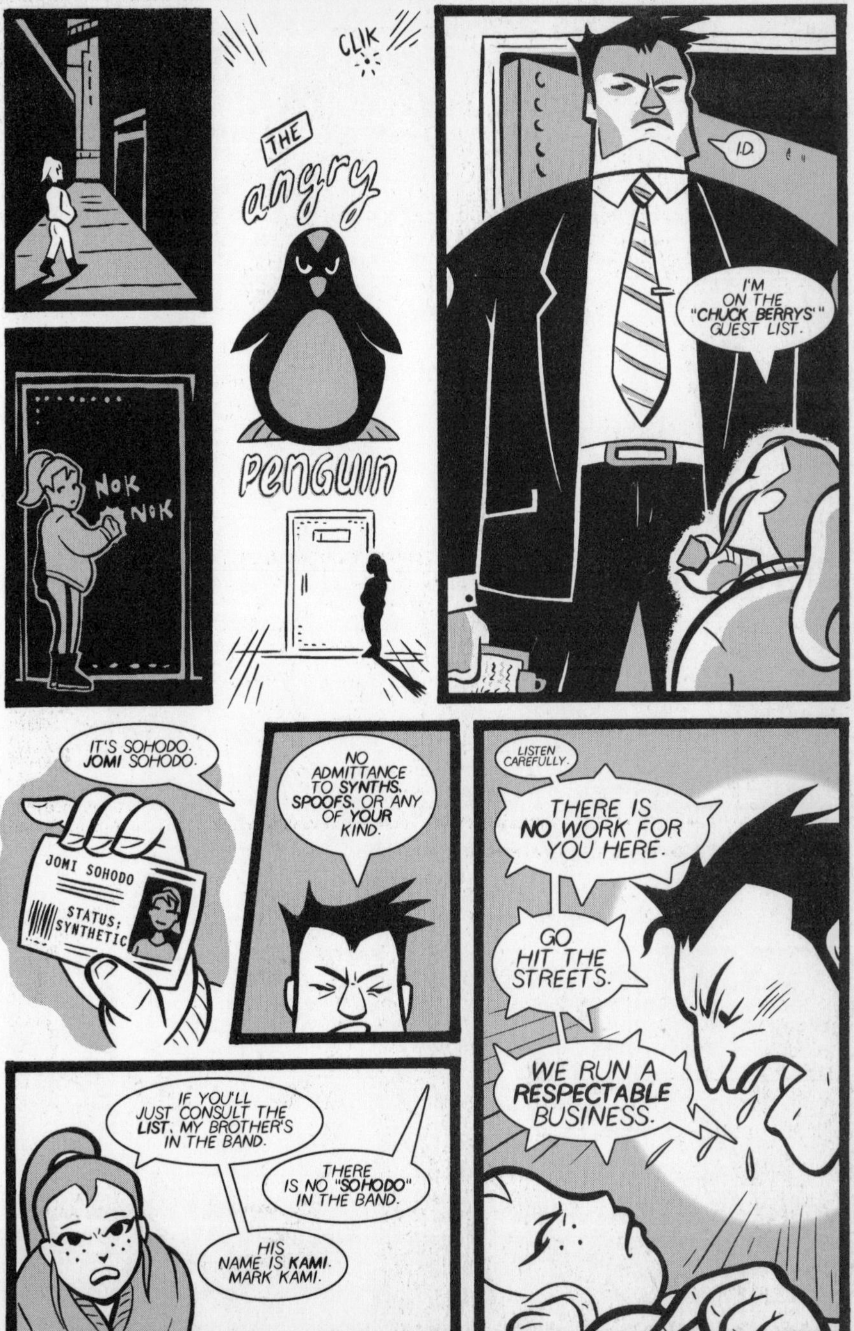
CLIK
THE angry PENGUIN
NOK NOK
I.D.
I'M ON THE "CHUCK BERRYS" GUEST LIST.
IT'S SOHODO. JOMI SOHODO.
JOMI SOHODO
STATUS: SYNTHETIC
NO ADMITTANCE TO SYNTHS, SPOOFS, OR ANY OF YOUR KIND.
IF YOU'LL JUST CONSULT THE LIST, MY BROTHER'S IN THE BAND.
THERE IS NO "SOHODO" IN THE BAND.
HIS NAME IS KAMI. MARK KAMI.
LISTEN CAREFULLY.
THERE IS NO WORK FOR YOU HERE.
GO HIT THE STREETS.
WE RUN A RESPECTABLE BUSINESS.

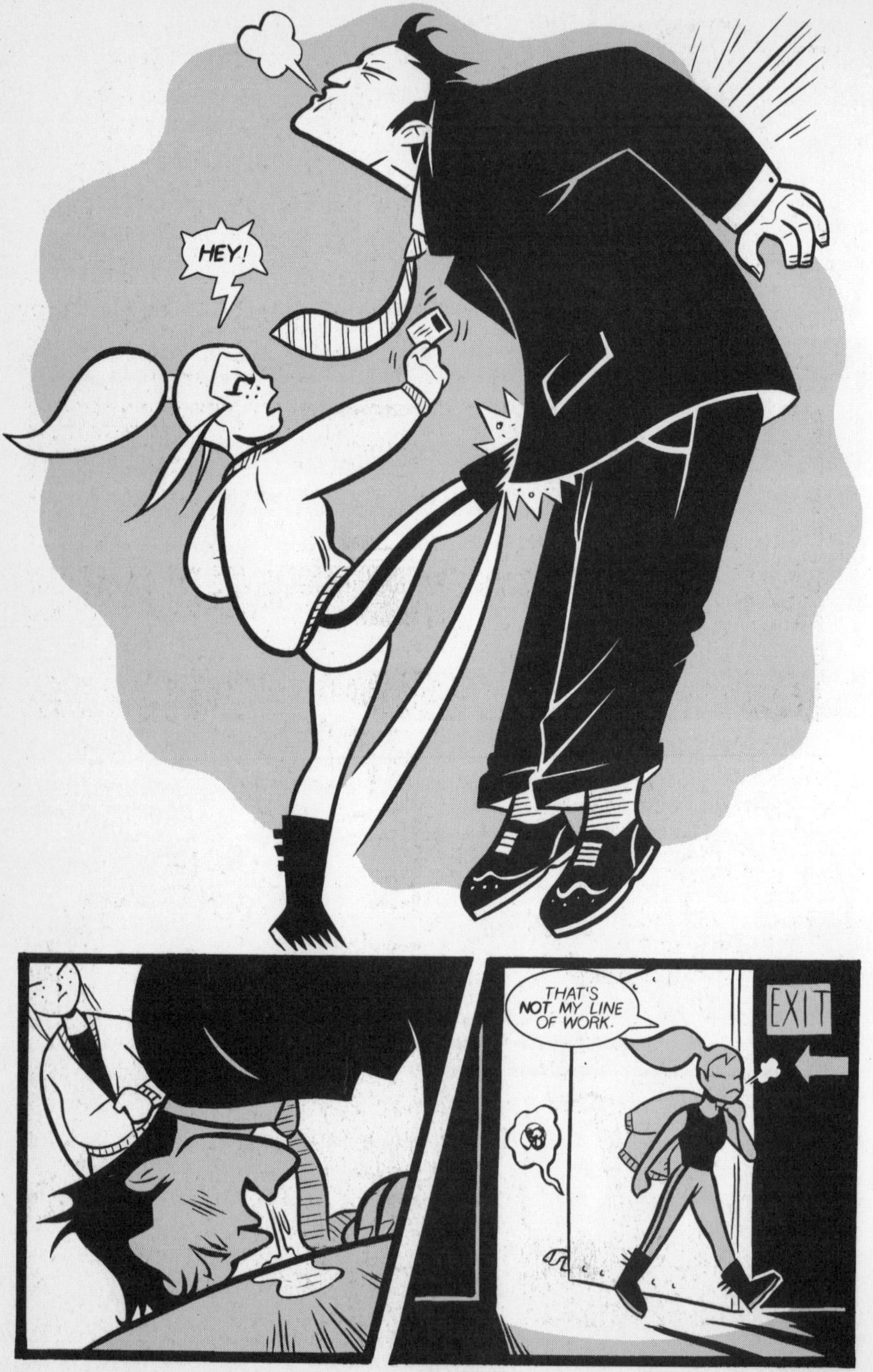
HEY!
THAT'S NOT MY LINE OF WORK.
EXIT

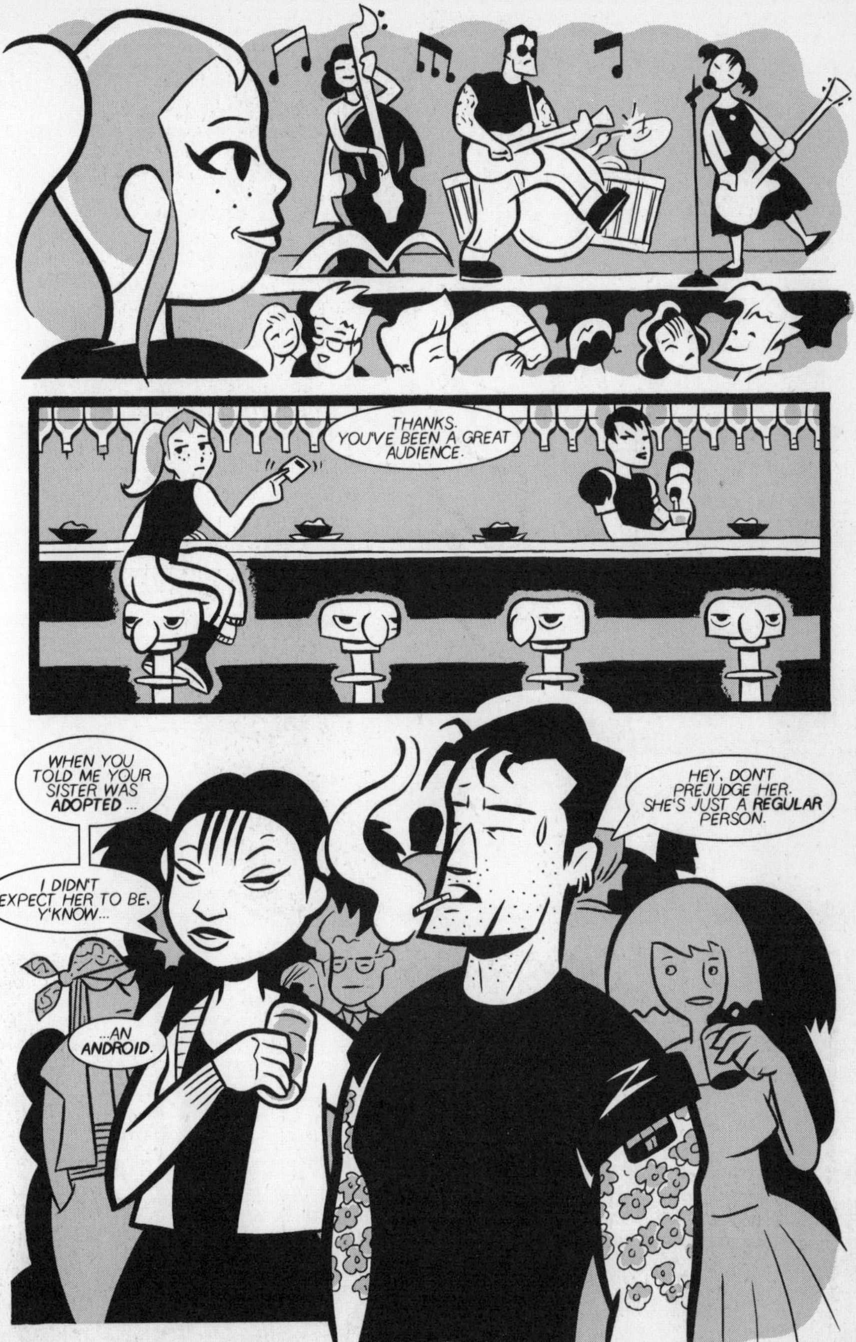
THANKS. YOU'VE BEEN A GREAT AUDIENCE.
WHEN YOU TOLD ME YOUR SISTER WAS **ADOPTED** ...
I DIDN'T EXPECT HER TO BE, Y'KNOW...
...AN **ANDROID**.
HEY, DON'T PREJUDGE HER. SHE'S JUST A **REGULAR** PERSON.

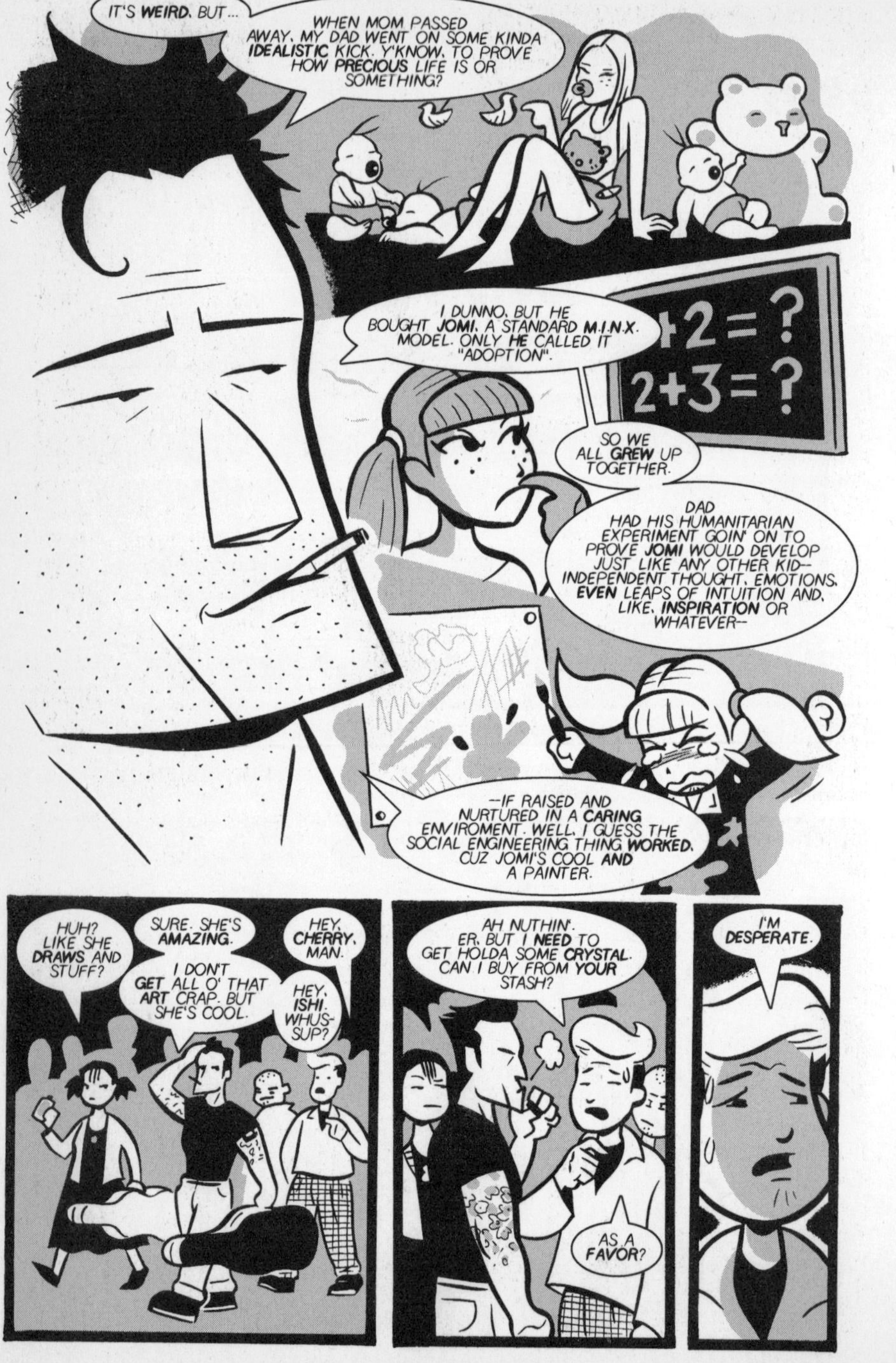

IT'S WEIRD, BUT...
WHEN MOM PASSED AWAY, MY DAD WENT ON SOME KINDA IDEALISTIC KICK. Y'KNOW, TO PROVE HOW PRECIOUS LIFE IS OR SOMETHING?
I DUNNO, BUT HE BOUGHT JOMI, A STANDARD M.I.N.X. MODEL. ONLY HE CALLED IT "ADOPTION".
+2=?
2+3=?
SO WE ALL GREW UP TOGETHER.
DAD HAD HIS HUMANITARIAN EXPERIMENT GOIN' ON TO PROVE JOMI WOULD DEVELOP JUST LIKE ANY OTHER KID-- INDEPENDENT THOUGHT, EMOTIONS, EVEN LEAPS OF INTUITION AND, LIKE, INSPIRATION OR WHATEVER--
--IF RAISED AND NURTURED IN A CARING ENVIROMENT. WELL, I GUESS THE SOCIAL ENGINEERING THING WORKED, CUZ JOMI'S COOL AND A PAINTER.
HUH? LIKE SHE DRAWS AND STUFF?
SURE. SHE'S AMAZING.
I DON'T GET ALL O' THAT ART CRAP. BUT SHE'S COOL.
HEY, CHERRY, MAN.
HEY, ISHI. WHUS-SUP?
AH NUTHIN'. ER, BUT I NEED TO GET HOLDA SOME CRYSTAL. CAN I BUY FROM YOUR STASH?
AS A FAVOR?
I'M DESPERATE.

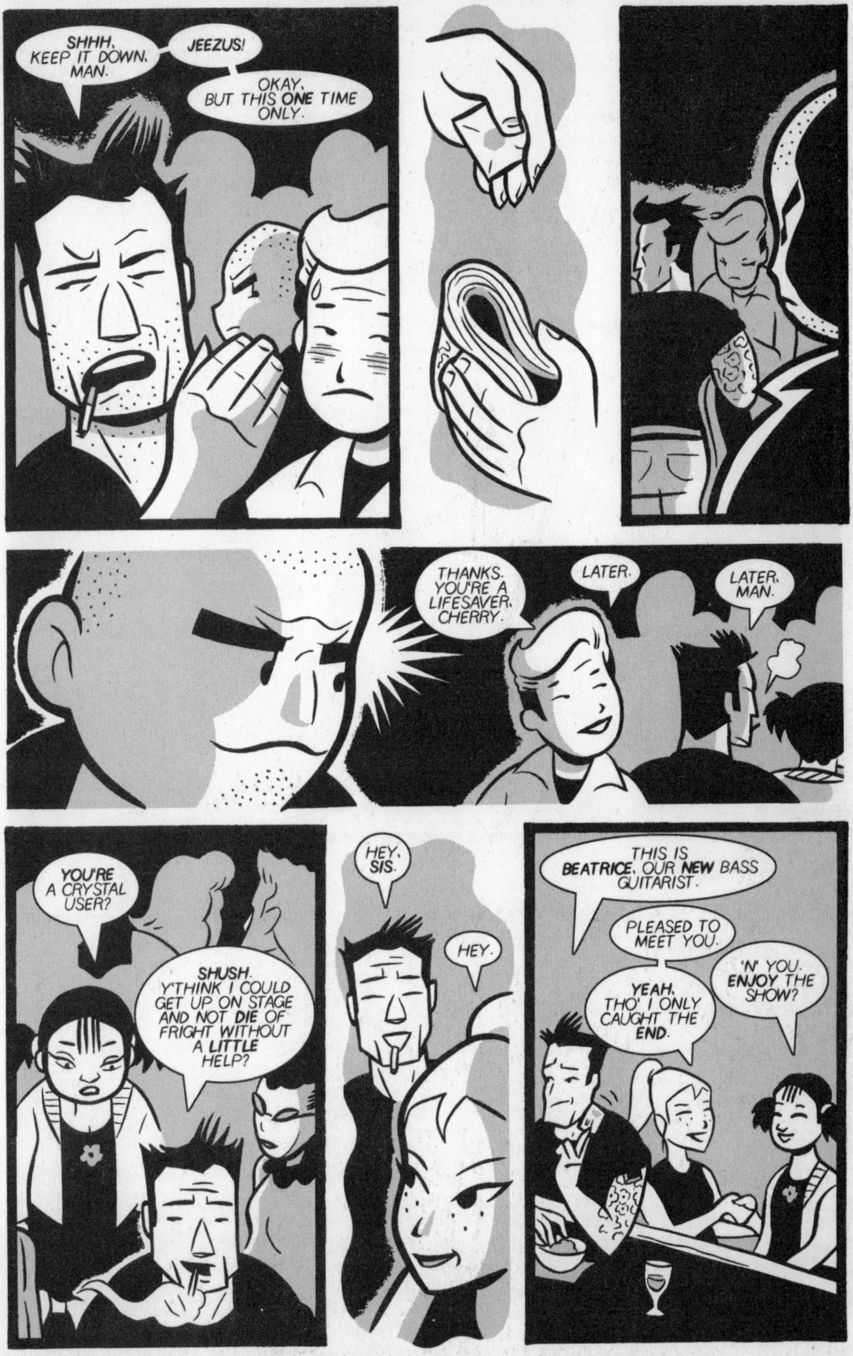
SHHH. KEEP IT DOWN, MAN.
JEEZUS!
OKAY, BUT THIS ONE TIME ONLY.
THANKS. YOU'RE A LIFESAVER, CHERRY.
LATER.
LATER, MAN.
YOU'RE A CRYSTAL USER?
SHUSH. Y'THINK I COULD GET UP ON STAGE AND NOT DIE OF FRIGHT WITHOUT A LITTLE HELP?
HEY, SIS.
HEY.
THIS IS BEATRICE, OUR NEW BASS GUITARIST.
PLEASED TO MEET YOU.
YEAH, THO' I ONLY CAUGHT THE END.
'N' YOU. ENJOY THE SHOW?

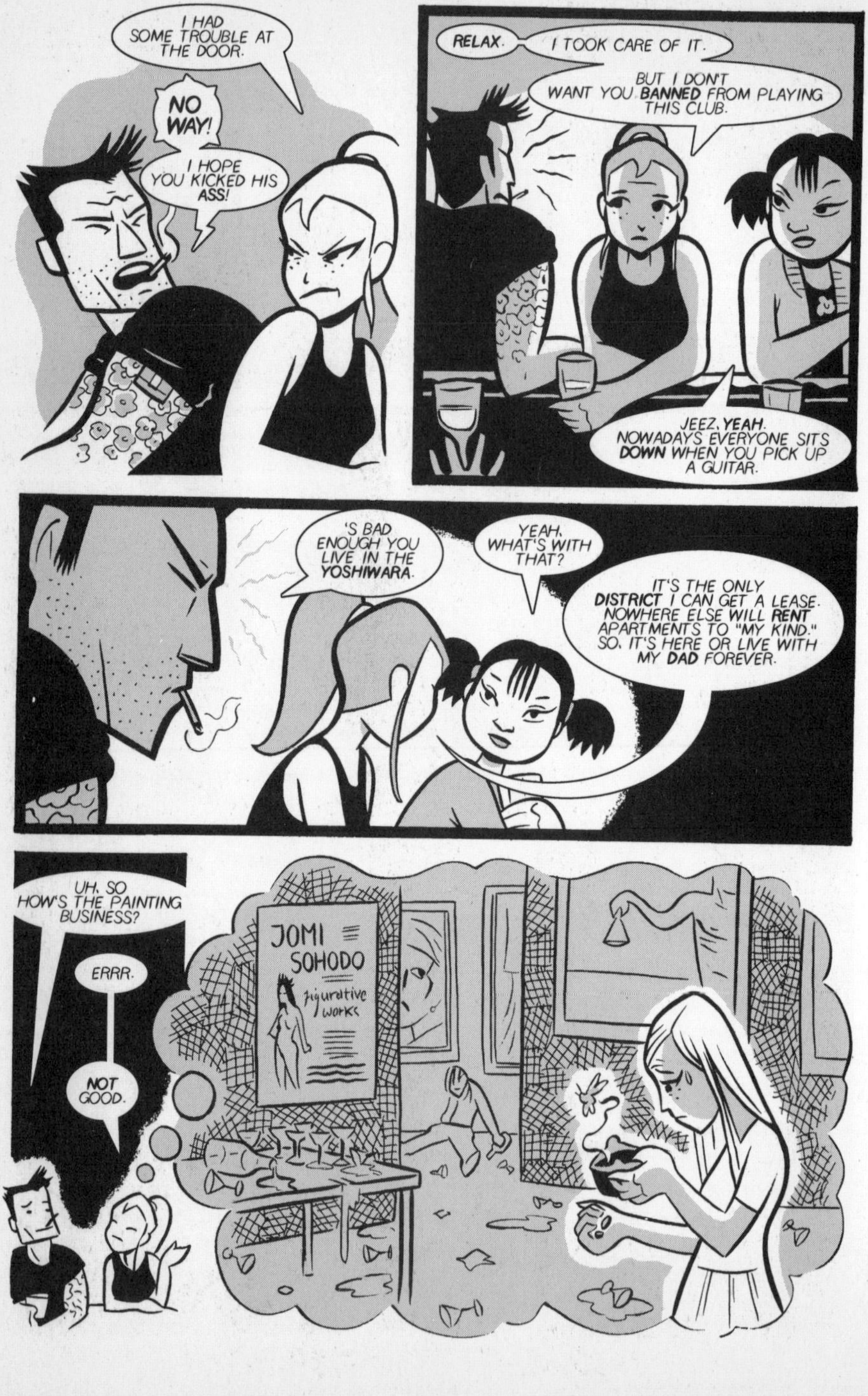
I HAD SOME TROUBLE AT THE DOOR.
NO WAY!
I HOPE YOU KICKED HIS ASS!
RELAX.
I TOOK CARE OF IT.
BUT I DON'T WANT YOU BANNED FROM PLAYING THIS CLUB.
JEEZ, YEAH. NOWADAYS EVERYONE SITS DOWN WHEN YOU PICK UP A GUITAR.
'S BAD ENOUGH YOU LIVE IN THE YOSHIWARA.
YEAH, WHAT'S WITH THAT?
IT'S THE ONLY DISTRICT I CAN GET A LEASE. NOWHERE ELSE WILL RENT APARTMENTS TO "MY KIND." SO, IT'S HERE OR LIVE WITH MY DAD FOREVER.
UH, SO HOW'S THE PAINTING BUSINESS?
ERRR.
NOT GOOD.
JOMI SOHODO
figurative works

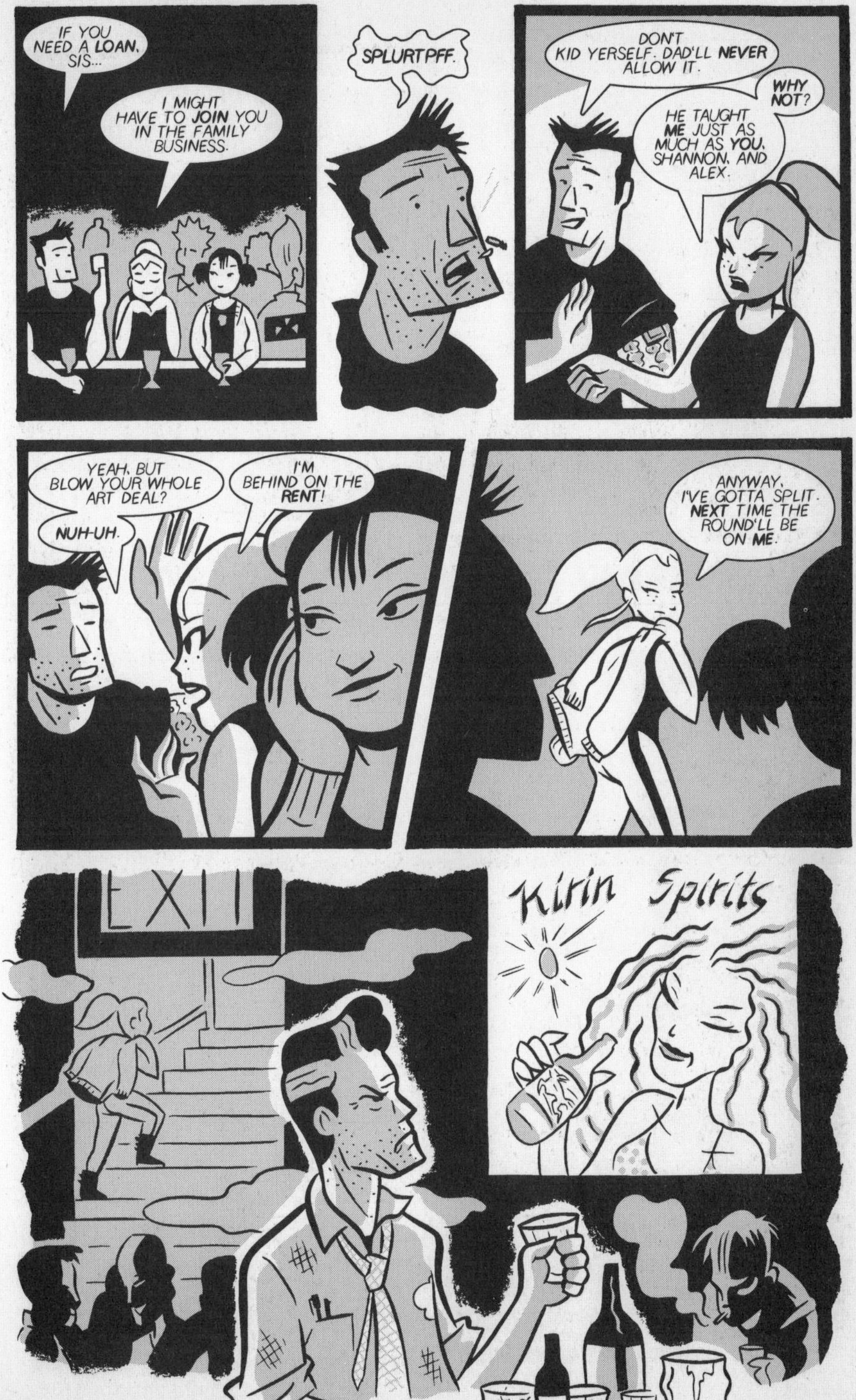
IF YOU NEED A LOAN, SIS...
I MIGHT HAVE TO JOIN YOU IN THE FAMILY BUSINESS.
SPLURTPFF.
DON'T KID YERSELF. DAD'LL NEVER ALLOW IT.
WHY NOT?
HE TAUGHT ME JUST AS MUCH AS YOU, SHANNON, AND ALEX.
YEAH, BUT BLOW YOUR WHOLE ART DEAL?
NUH-UH.
I'M BEHIND ON THE RENT!
ANYWAY, I'VE GOTTA SPLIT. NEXT TIME THE ROUND'LL BE ON ME.
EXIT
Kirin Spirits

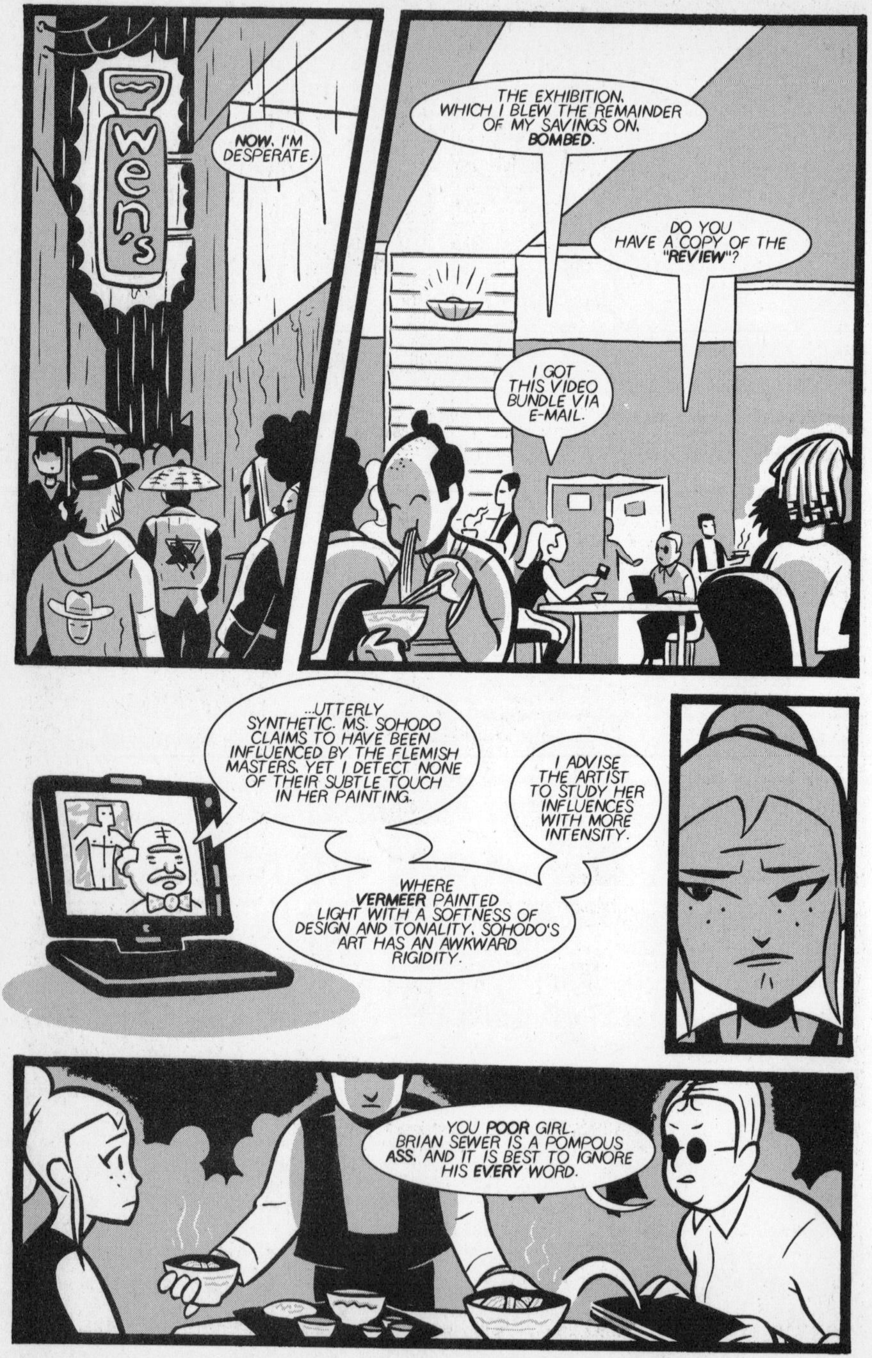

wen's
NOW, I'M DESPERATE.
THE EXHIBITION, WHICH I BLEW THE REMAINDER OF MY SAVINGS ON, BOMBED.
DO YOU HAVE A COPY OF THE "REVIEW"?
I GOT THIS VIDEO BUNDLE VIA E-MAIL.
...UTTERLY SYNTHETIC. MS. SOHODO CLAIMS TO HAVE BEEN INFLUENCED BY THE FLEMISH MASTERS, YET I DETECT NONE OF THEIR SUBTLE TOUCH IN HER PAINTING.
I ADVISE THE ARTIST TO STUDY HER INFLUENCES WITH MORE INTENSITY.
WHERE VERMEER PAINTED LIGHT WITH A SOFTNESS OF DESIGN AND TONALITY, SOHODO'S ART HAS AN AWKWARD RIGIDITY.
YOU POOR GIRL. BRIAN SEWER IS A POMPOUS ASS, AND IT IS BEST TO IGNORE HIS EVERY WORD.

THE PROBLEM IS THAT FIGURATIVE WORK ISN'T FASHIONABLE RIGHT NOW. HOLOGRAPHY IS THE *NEW*, HOT MARKET. STACEY ERMIN'S "BIVOUAC" WAS SOLD TO THE SCRAATCHI SISTERS FOR OVER A MILLION LAST MONTH.

YOU NEED TO TAKE ERMIN'S LEAD. SPEND *LESS* TIME ON THE WORK AND *MORE* TIME ON THE MARKETING.

...I DUNNO...

MAYBE SEWER'S RIGHT, *REUBEN*. MAYBE I JUST *DON'T* HAVE THE TALENT.

NONSENSE.

SURE, MAYBE I HAVE ALL THE *TECHNICAL* ASPECTS TOGETHER. BUT WHAT IF BEING WHO I AM MEANS I CAN *NEVER* GAIN THAT UNIQUE *SPARK* OF INSPIRATION.

I NEVER EXPECTED TO HEAR *YOU* RECITE *RACIST* DOGMA.

I'LL CONTINUE TO KEEP MY EARS OPEN FOR *PATRONS*. IT IS SIMPLY A MATTER OF *LUCK* AND TIMING.

AND... WORKING AN ANGLE.

ON SECOND THOUGHT, BEST AVOID THE SCRAATCHI SISTERS. THEY'LL SELL OFF ERMIN'S WORK IN A YEAR. AND OL' STACEY WILL BE BACK ON THE WHISKEY MOUTHWASH.

HE DIED YOUNG. A *JUNKIE*.

UM, YES.

YOU'RE A GOOD FRIEND, *REUBEN*. BUT THERE'S NO TALKING TO YOU IN *AD-MAN* MODE. LATER.

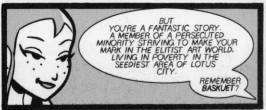

BUT YOU'RE A FANTASTIC STORY. A MEMBER OF A PERSECUTED MINORITY STRIVING TO MAKE YOUR MARK IN THE ELITIST ART WORLD, LIVING IN POVERTY IN THE SEEDIEST AREA OF LOTUS CITY.

REMEMBER BASKUET?

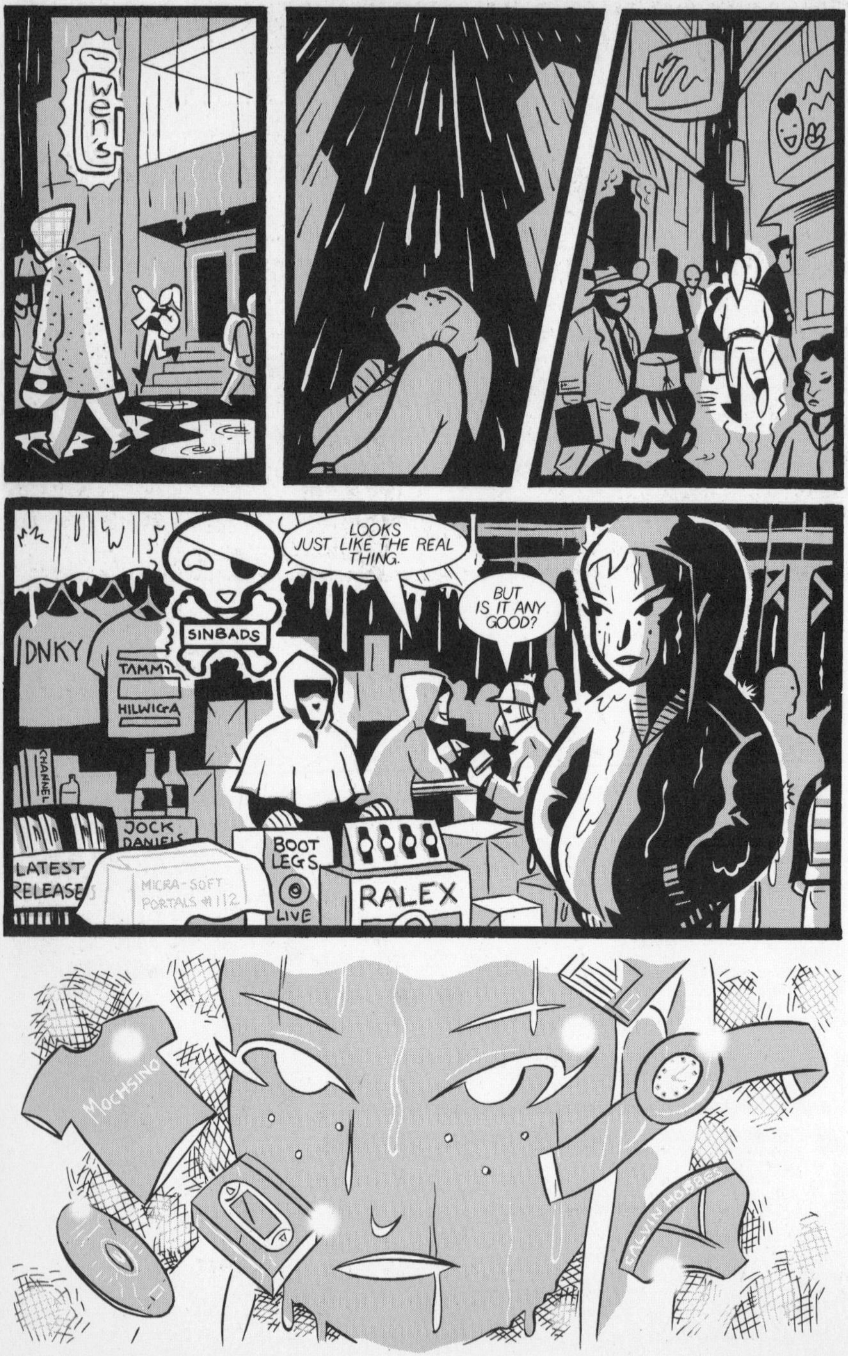

wen's
SINBADS
LOOKS JUST LIKE THE REAL THING.
BUT IS IT ANY GOOD?
DNKY
TAMMY
HILWIGA
CHANNEL
JOCK DANIELS
LATEST RELEASES
MICRA-SOFT PORTALS #112
BOOT LEGS
LIVE
RALEX
MOCHSINO
CALVIN HOBBES

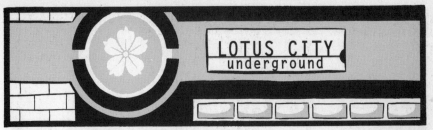

LOTUS CITY
underground

...AND SHE HAS THE LITTLE ONES.

THEY'RE QUITE A HANDFUL, I CAN TELL YOU.

Kirin Spiri

DRAWING IS ABOUT TRYING TO MAKE SENSE OF THE WORLD.

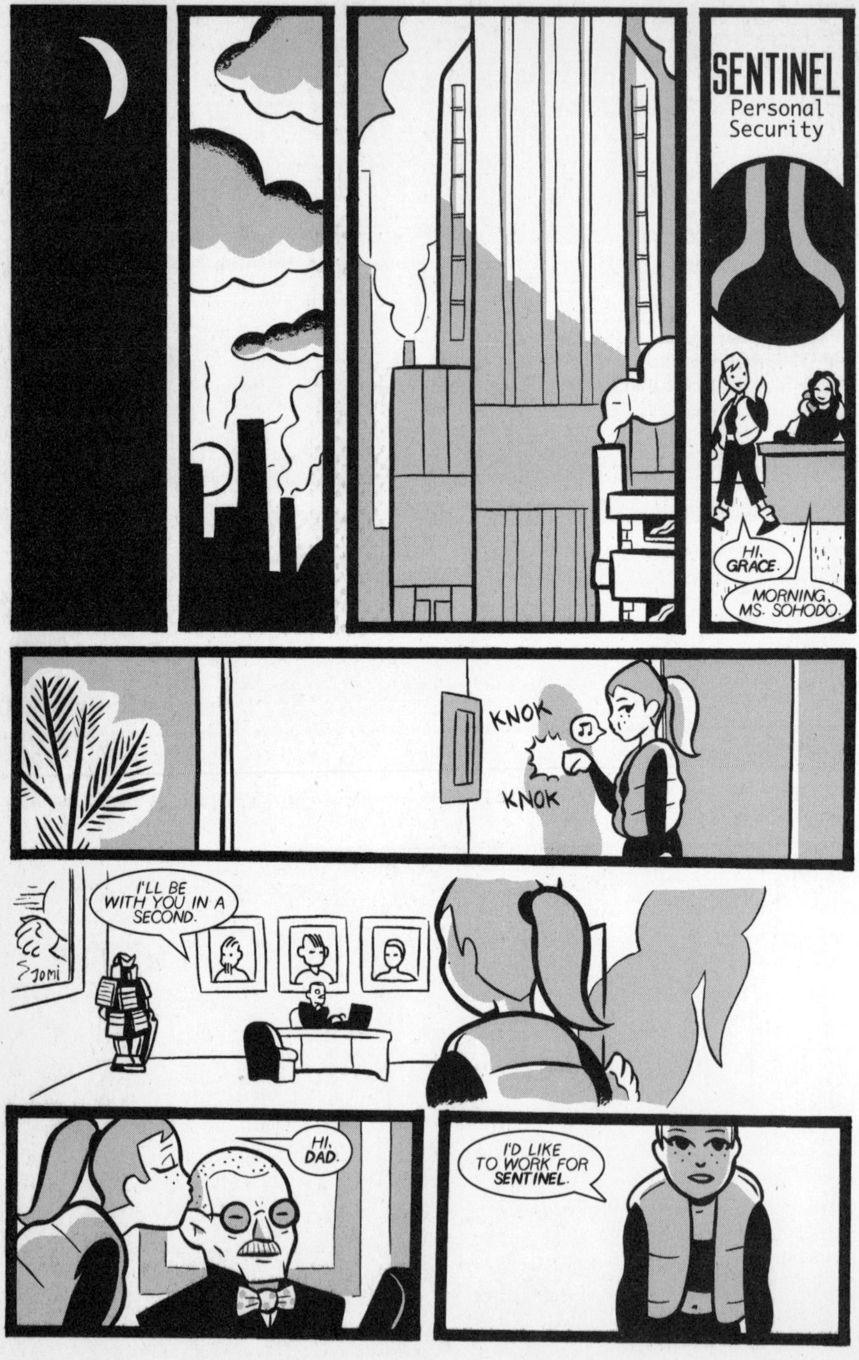
SENTINEL
Personal Security
HI, GRACE.
MORNING, MS. SOHODO.
KNOK
KNOK
I'LL BE WITH YOU IN A SECOND.
JOMI
HI, DAD.
I'D LIKE TO WORK FOR SENTINEL.

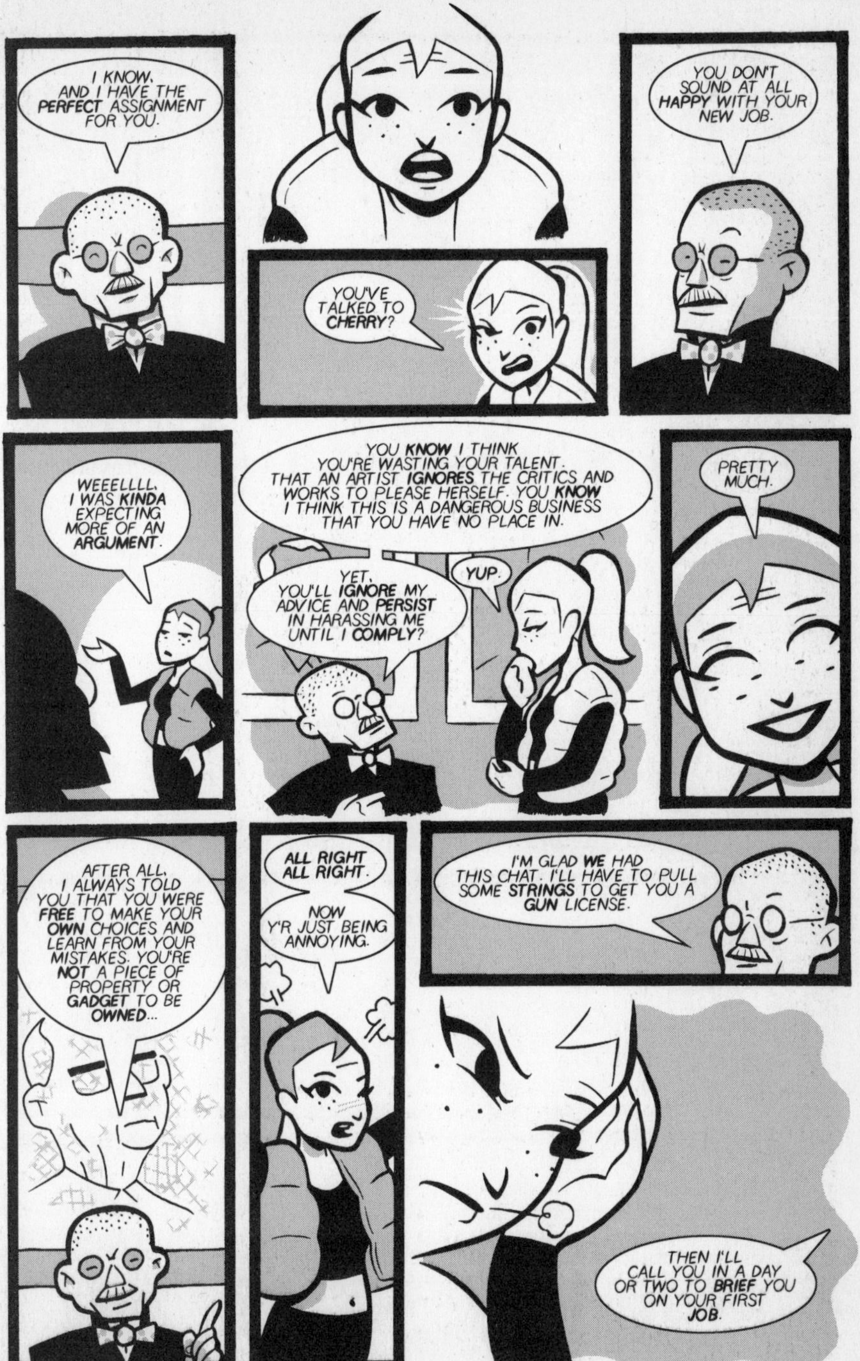
I KNOW, AND I HAVE THE PERFECT ASSIGNMENT FOR YOU.
YOU'VE TALKED TO CHERRY?
YOU DON'T SOUND AT ALL HAPPY WITH YOUR NEW JOB.
WEEELLLL, I WAS KINDA EXPECTING MORE OF AN ARGUMENT.
YOU KNOW I THINK YOU'RE WASTING YOUR TALENT. THAT AN ARTIST IGNORES THE CRITICS AND WORKS TO PLEASE HERSELF. YOU KNOW I THINK THIS IS A DANGEROUS BUSINESS THAT YOU HAVE NO PLACE IN.
YET, YOU'LL IGNORE MY ADVICE AND PERSIST IN HARASSING ME UNTIL I COMPLY?
YUP.
PRETTY MUCH.
AFTER ALL, I ALWAYS TOLD YOU THAT YOU WERE FREE TO MAKE YOUR OWN CHOICES AND LEARN FROM YOUR MISTAKES. YOU'RE NOT A PIECE OF PROPERTY OR GADGET TO BE OWNED...
ALL RIGHT ALL RIGHT.
NOW Y'R JUST BEING ANNOYING.
I'M GLAD WE HAD THIS CHAT. I'LL HAVE TO PULL SOME STRINGS TO GET YOU A GUN LICENSE.
THEN I'LL CALL YOU IN A DAY OR TWO TO BRIEF YOU ON YOUR FIRST JOB.

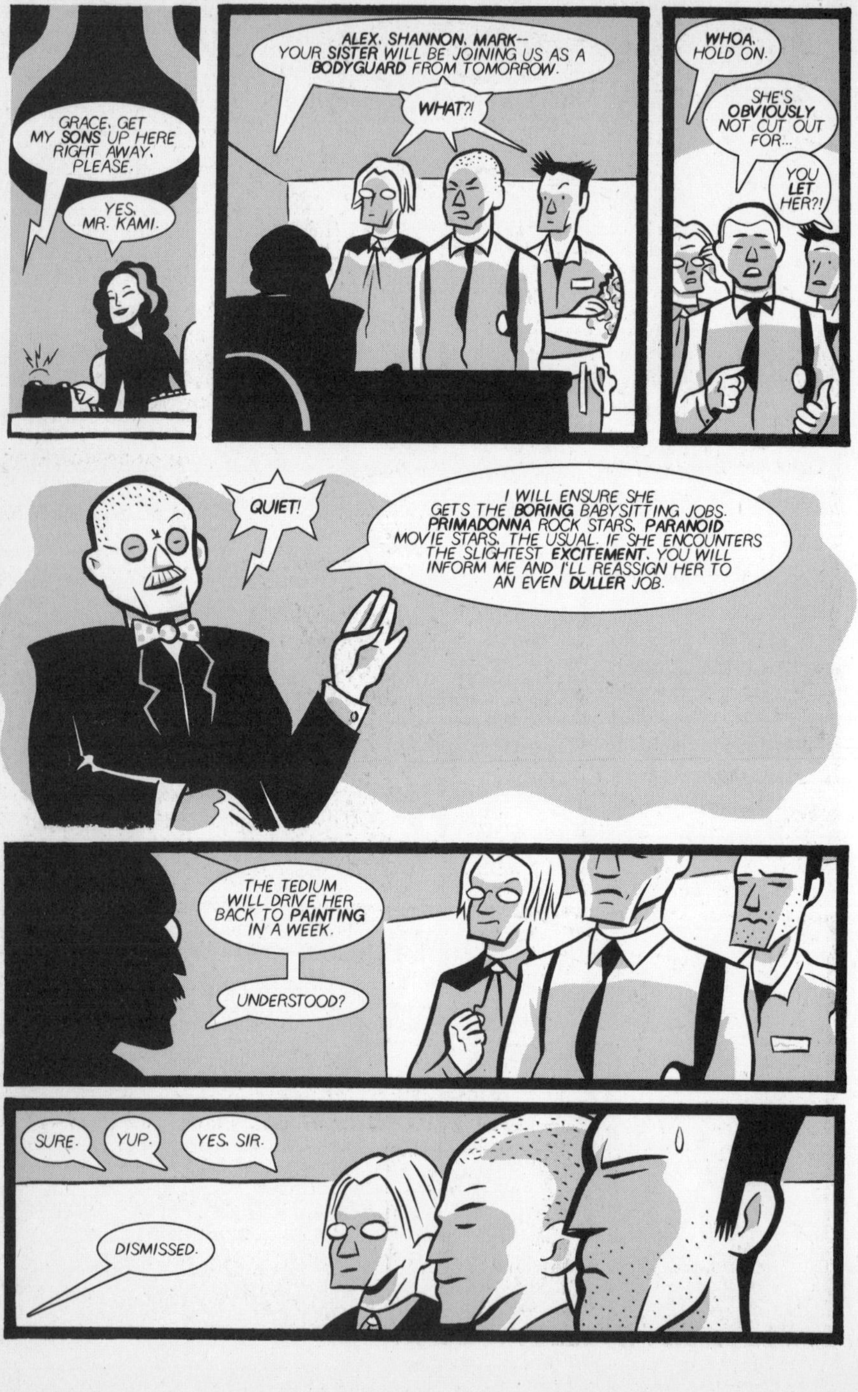
GRACE, GET MY SONS UP HERE RIGHT AWAY, PLEASE.
YES, MR. KAMI.
ALEX, SHANNON, MARK-- YOUR SISTER WILL BE JOINING US AS A BODYGUARD FROM TOMORROW.
WHAT?!
WHOA, HOLD ON.
SHE'S OBVIOUSLY NOT CUT OUT FOR...
YOU LET HER?!
QUIET!
I WILL ENSURE SHE GETS THE BORING BABYSITTING JOBS. PRIMADONNA ROCK STARS, PARANOID MOVIE STARS, THE USUAL. IF SHE ENCOUNTERS THE SLIGHTEST EXCITEMENT, YOU WILL INFORM ME AND I'LL REASSIGN HER TO AN EVEN DULLER JOB.
THE TEDIUM WILL DRIVE HER BACK TO PAINTING IN A WEEK.
UNDERSTOOD?
SURE.
YUP.
YES, SIR.
DISMISSED.

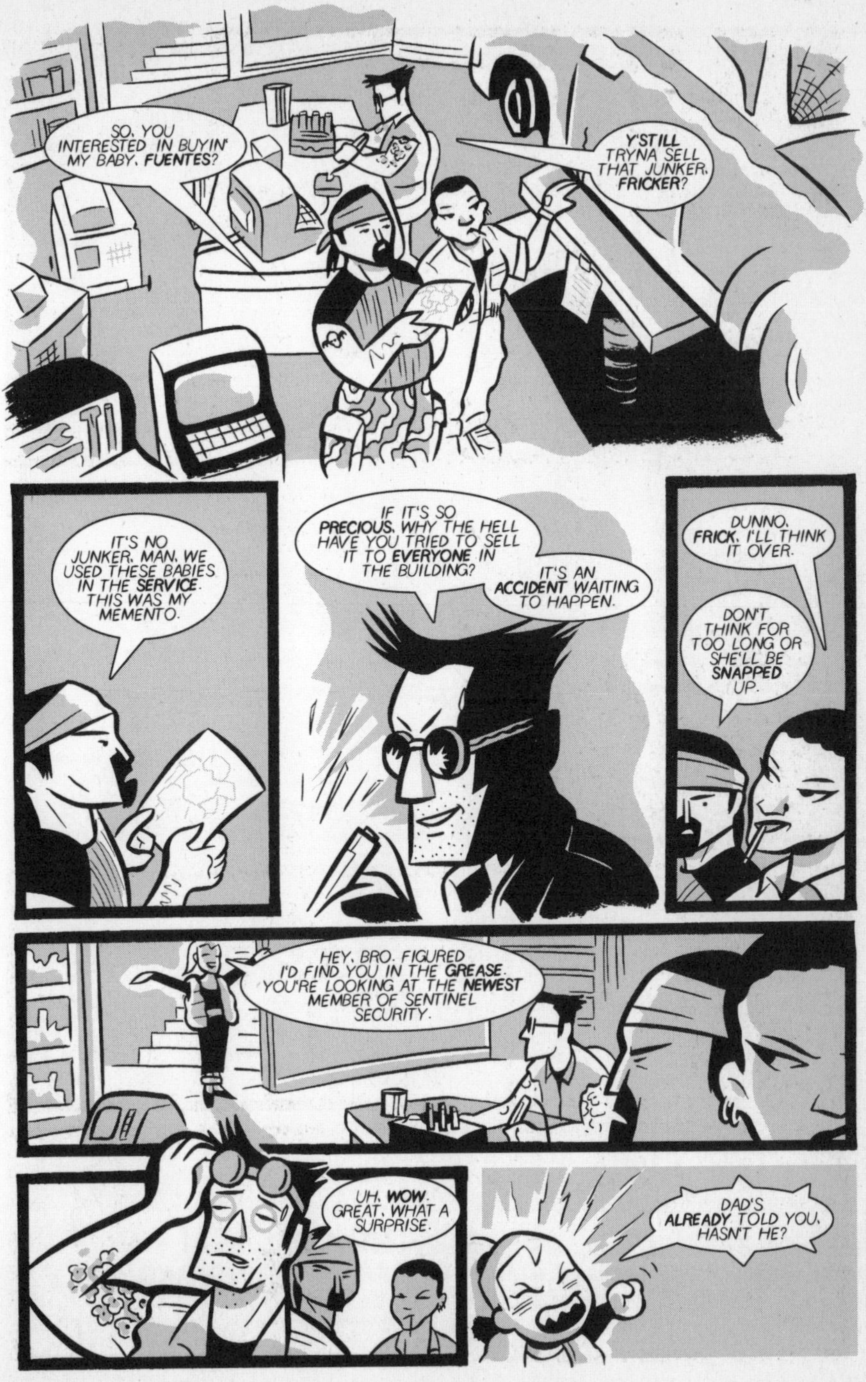
SO, YOU INTERESTED IN BUYIN' MY BABY, FUENTES?
Y'STILL TRYNA SELL THAT JUNKER, FRICKER?
IT'S NO JUNKER, MAN. WE USED THESE BABIES IN THE SERVICE. THIS WAS MY MEMENTO.
IF IT'S SO PRECIOUS, WHY THE HELL HAVE YOU TRIED TO SELL IT TO EVERYONE IN THE BUILDING?
IT'S AN ACCIDENT WAITING TO HAPPEN.
DUNNO, FRICK, I'LL THINK IT OVER.
DON'T THINK FOR TOO LONG OR SHE'LL BE SNAPPED UP.
HEY, BRO. FIGURED I'D FIND YOU IN THE GREASE. YOU'RE LOOKING AT THE NEWEST MEMBER OF SENTINEL SECURITY.
UH, WOW. GREAT. WHAT A SURPRISE.
DAD'S ALREADY TOLD YOU, HASN'T HE?

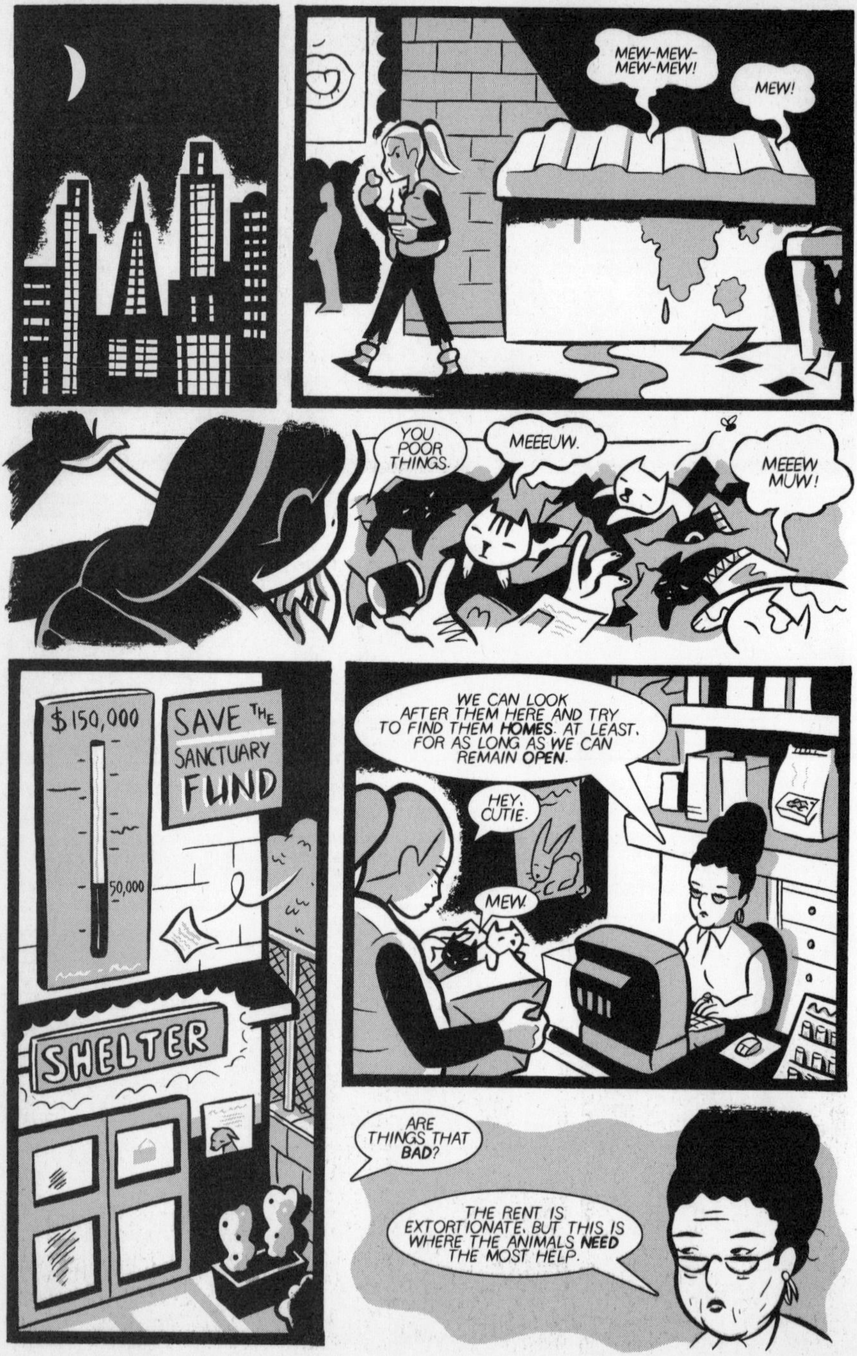
MEW-MEW-MEW-MEW!
MEW!
YOU POOR THINGS.
MEEEUW.
MEEEW MUW!
$150,000
50,000
SAVE THE SANCTUARY FUND
SHELTER
WE CAN LOOK AFTER THEM HERE AND TRY TO FIND THEM **HOMES**. AT LEAST, FOR AS LONG AS WE CAN REMAIN **OPEN**.
HEY, CUTIE.
MEW.
ARE THINGS THAT **BAD**?
THE RENT IS EXTORTIONATE, BUT THIS IS WHERE THE ANIMALS **NEED** THE MOST HELP.

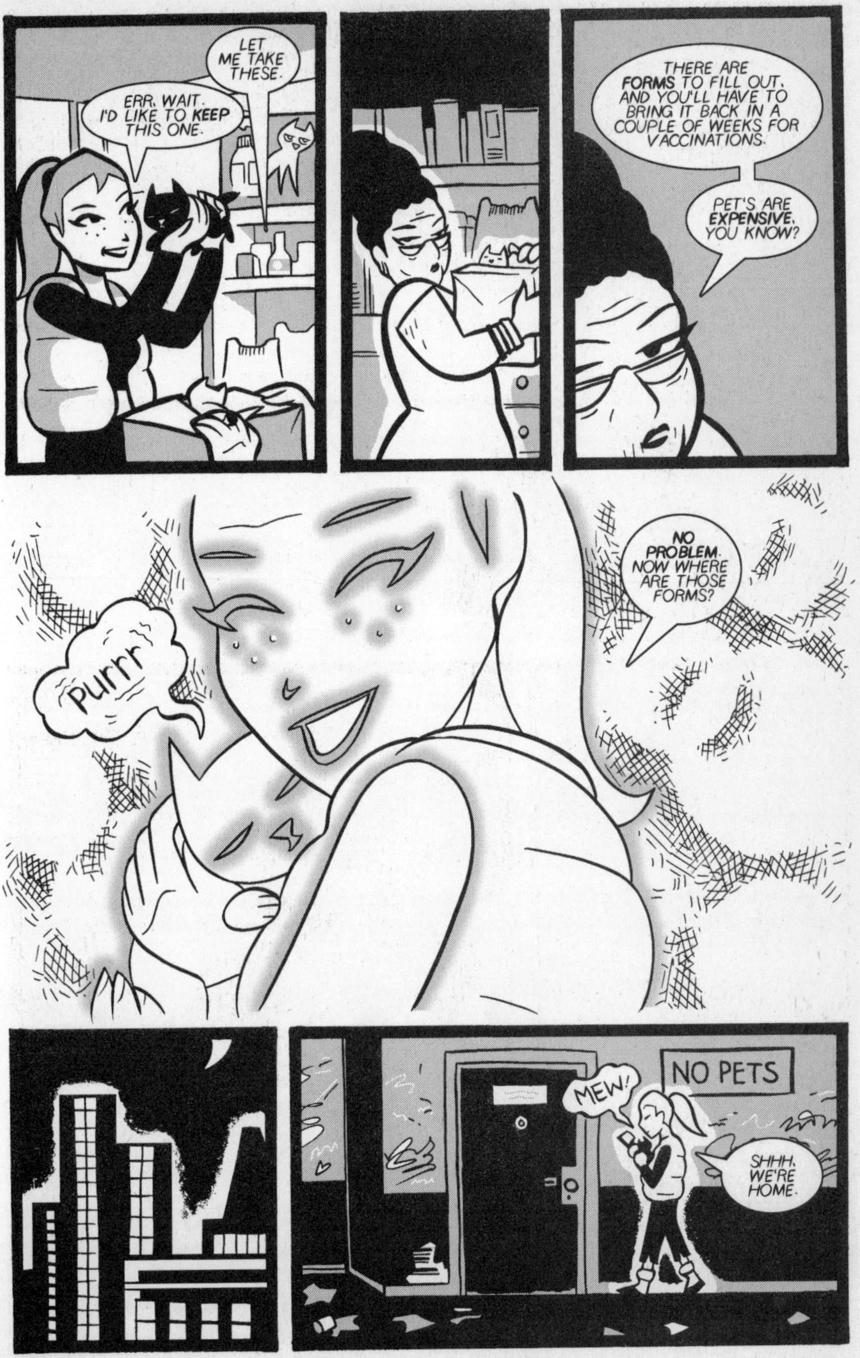
LET ME TAKE THESE.
ERR, WAIT. I'D LIKE TO **KEEP** THIS ONE.
THERE ARE **FORMS** TO FILL OUT, AND YOU'LL HAVE TO BRING IT BACK IN A COUPLE OF WEEKS FOR VACCINATIONS.
PET'S ARE **EXPENSIVE**, YOU KNOW?
Purrr
NO PROBLEM. NOW WHERE ARE THOSE FORMS?
NO PETS
MEW!
SHHH, WE'RE HOME.

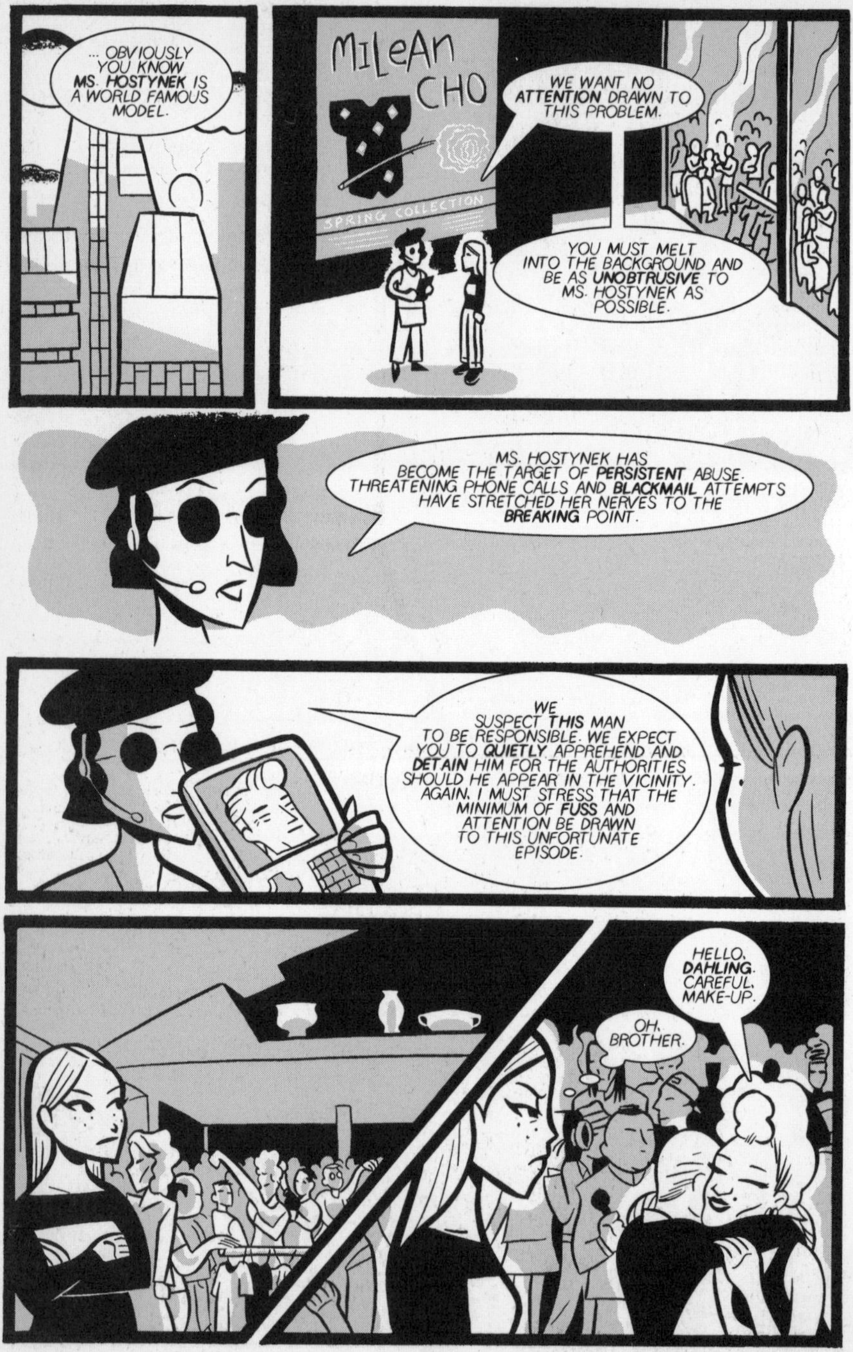

...OBVIOUSLY YOU KNOW MS. HOSTYNEK IS A WORLD FAMOUS MODEL.
MILEAN CHO
SPRING COLLECTION
WE WANT NO ATTENTION DRAWN TO THIS PROBLEM.
YOU MUST MELT INTO THE BACKGROUND AND BE AS UNOBTRUSIVE TO MS. HOSTYNEK AS POSSIBLE.
MS. HOSTYNEK HAS BECOME THE TARGET OF PERSISTENT ABUSE. THREATENING PHONE CALLS AND BLACKMAIL ATTEMPTS HAVE STRETCHED HER NERVES TO THE BREAKING POINT.
WE SUSPECT THIS MAN TO BE RESPONSIBLE. WE EXPECT YOU TO QUIETLY APPREHEND AND DETAIN HIM FOR THE AUTHORITIES SHOULD HE APPEAR IN THE VICINITY. AGAIN, I MUST STRESS THAT THE MINIMUM OF FUSS AND ATTENTION BE DRAWN TO THIS UNFORTUNATE EPISODE.
HELLO, DAHLING. CAREFUL, MAKE-UP.
OH, BROTHER.

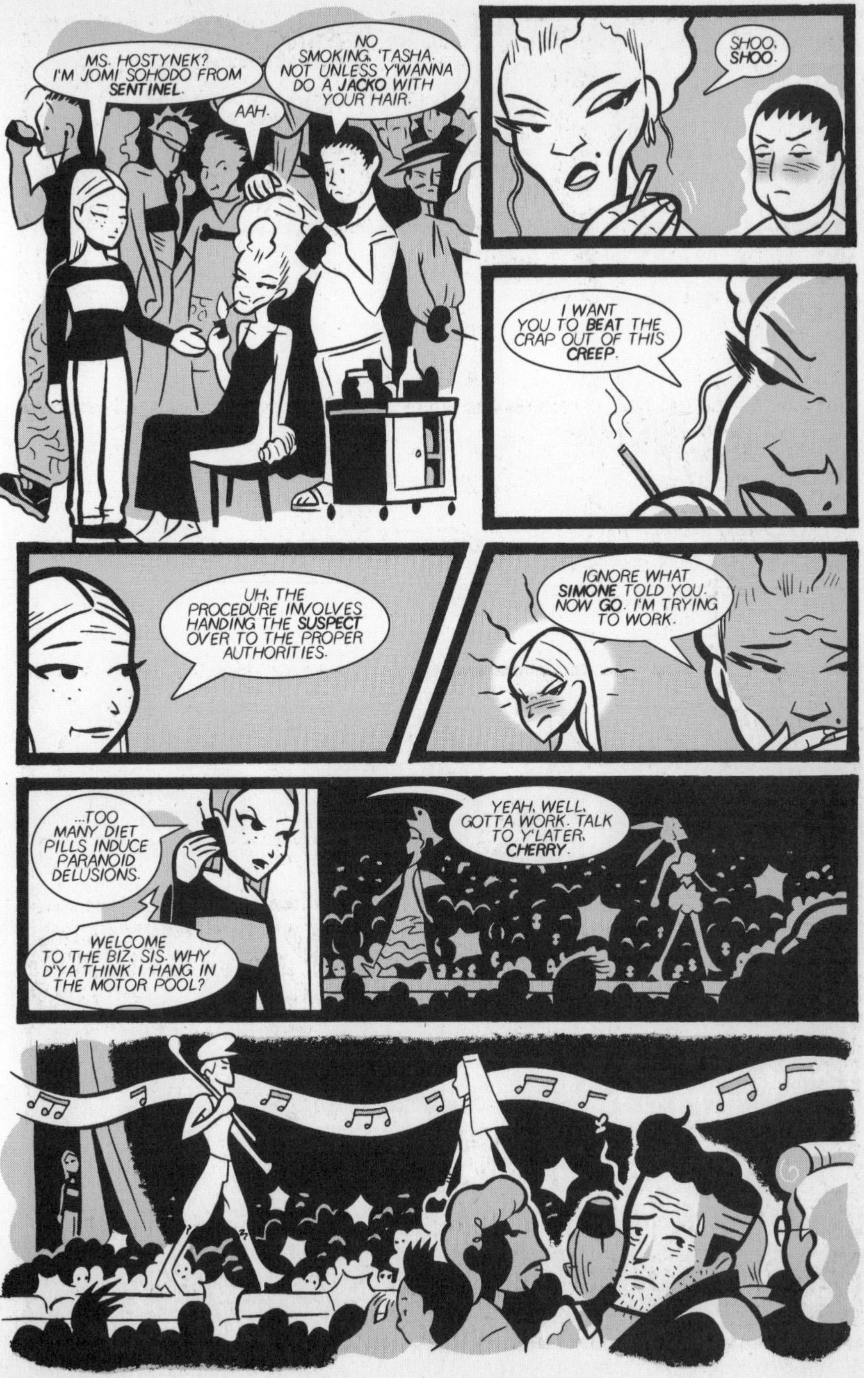
MS. HOSTYNEK? I'M JOMI SOHODO FROM SENTINEL.
AAH.
NO SMOKING, 'TASHA. NOT UNLESS Y'WANNA DO A JACKO WITH YOUR HAIR.
SHOO, SHOO.
I WANT YOU TO BEAT THE CRAP OUT OF THIS CREEP.
UH, THE PROCEDURE INVOLVES HANDING THE SUSPECT OVER TO THE PROPER AUTHORITIES.
IGNORE WHAT SIMONE TOLD YOU. NOW GO. I'M TRYING TO WORK.
...TOO MANY DIET PILLS INDUCE PARANOID DELUSIONS.
WELCOME TO THE BIZ, SIS. WHY D'YA THINK I HANG IN THE MOTOR POOL?
YEAH, WELL, GOTTA WORK. TALK TO Y'LATER, CHERRY.

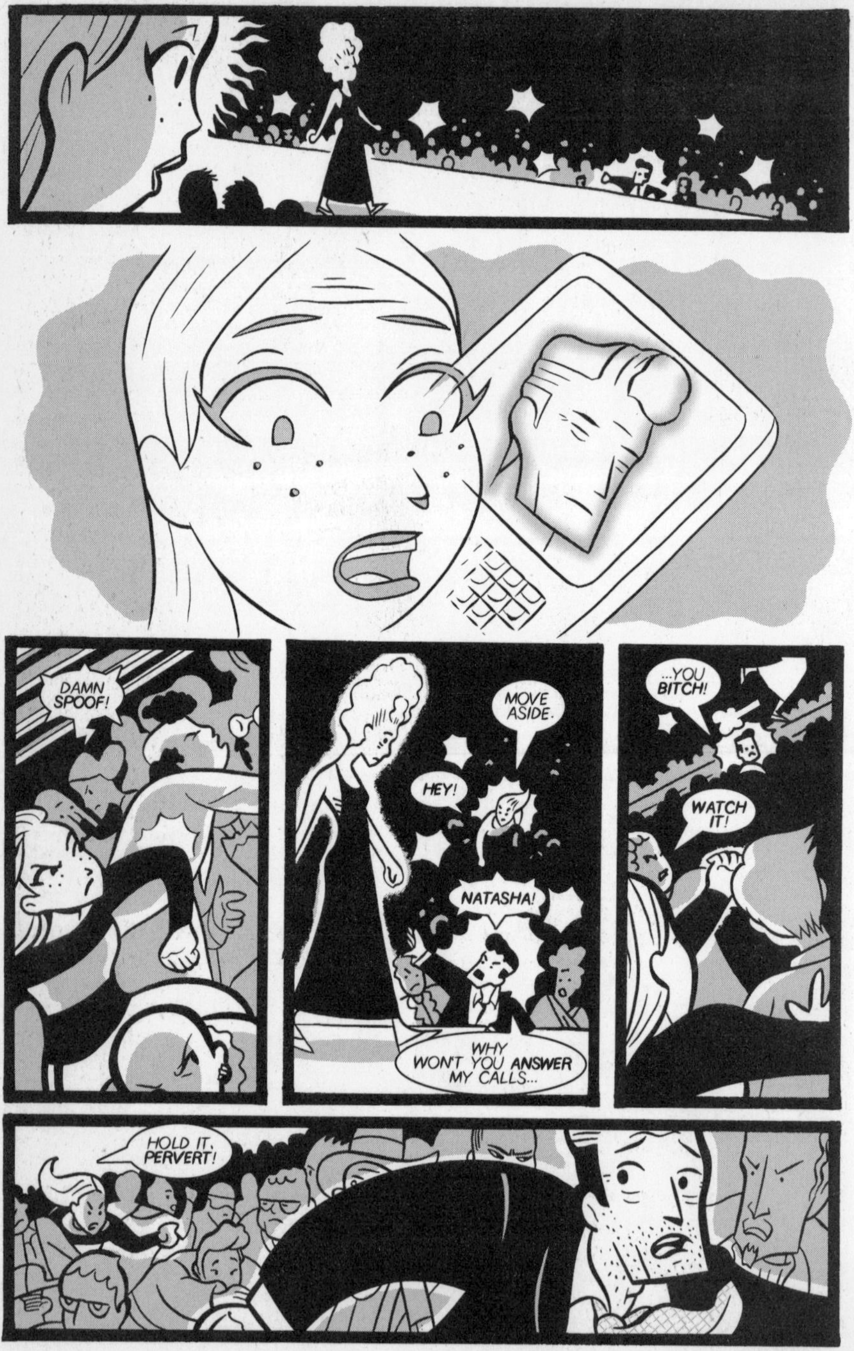
DAMN SPOOF!
MOVE ASIDE.
HEY!
NATASHA!
WHY WON'T YOU ANSWER MY CALLS...
...YOU BITCH!
WATCH IT!
HOLD IT, PERVERT!

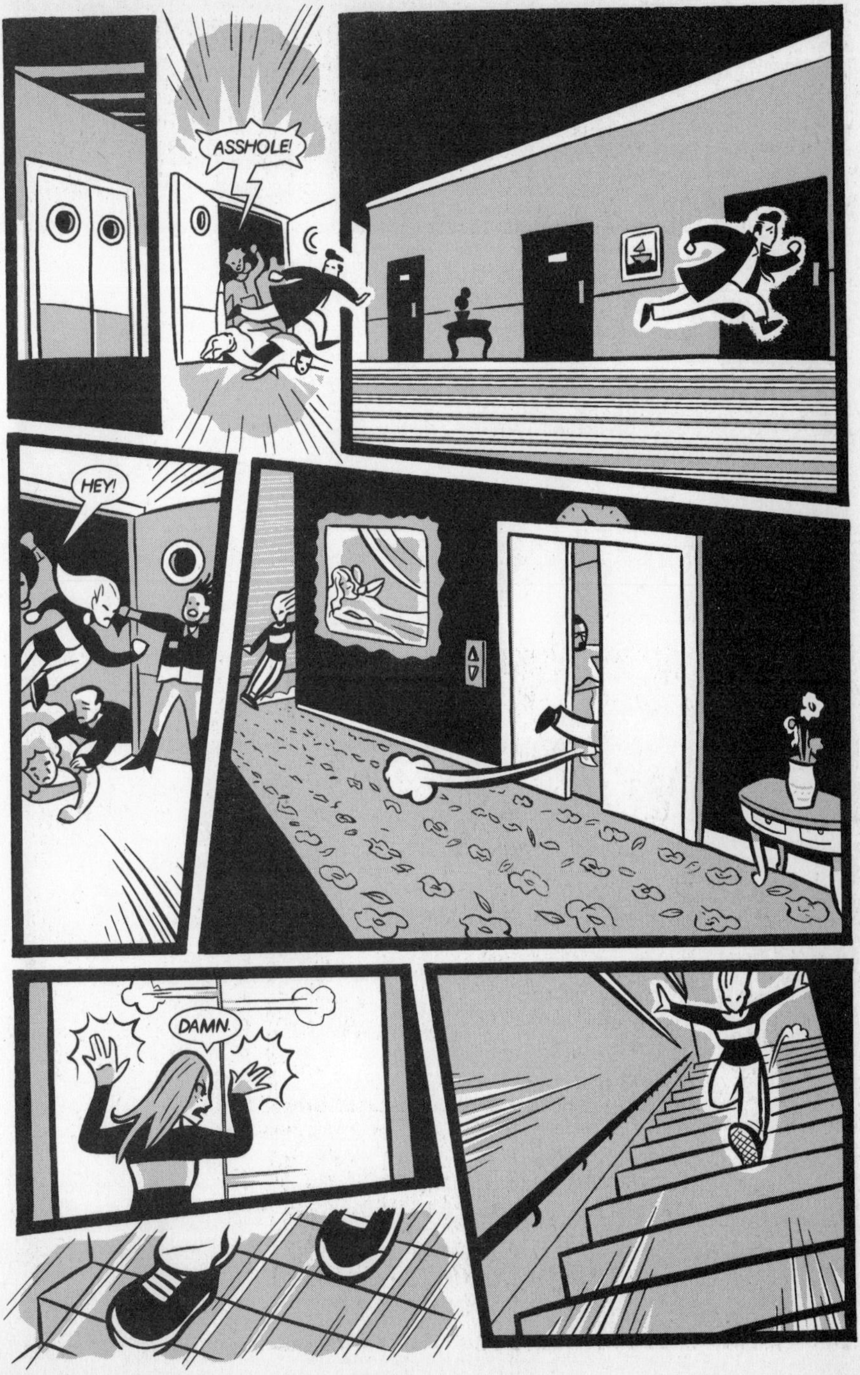

ASSHOLE!
HEY!
DAMN.

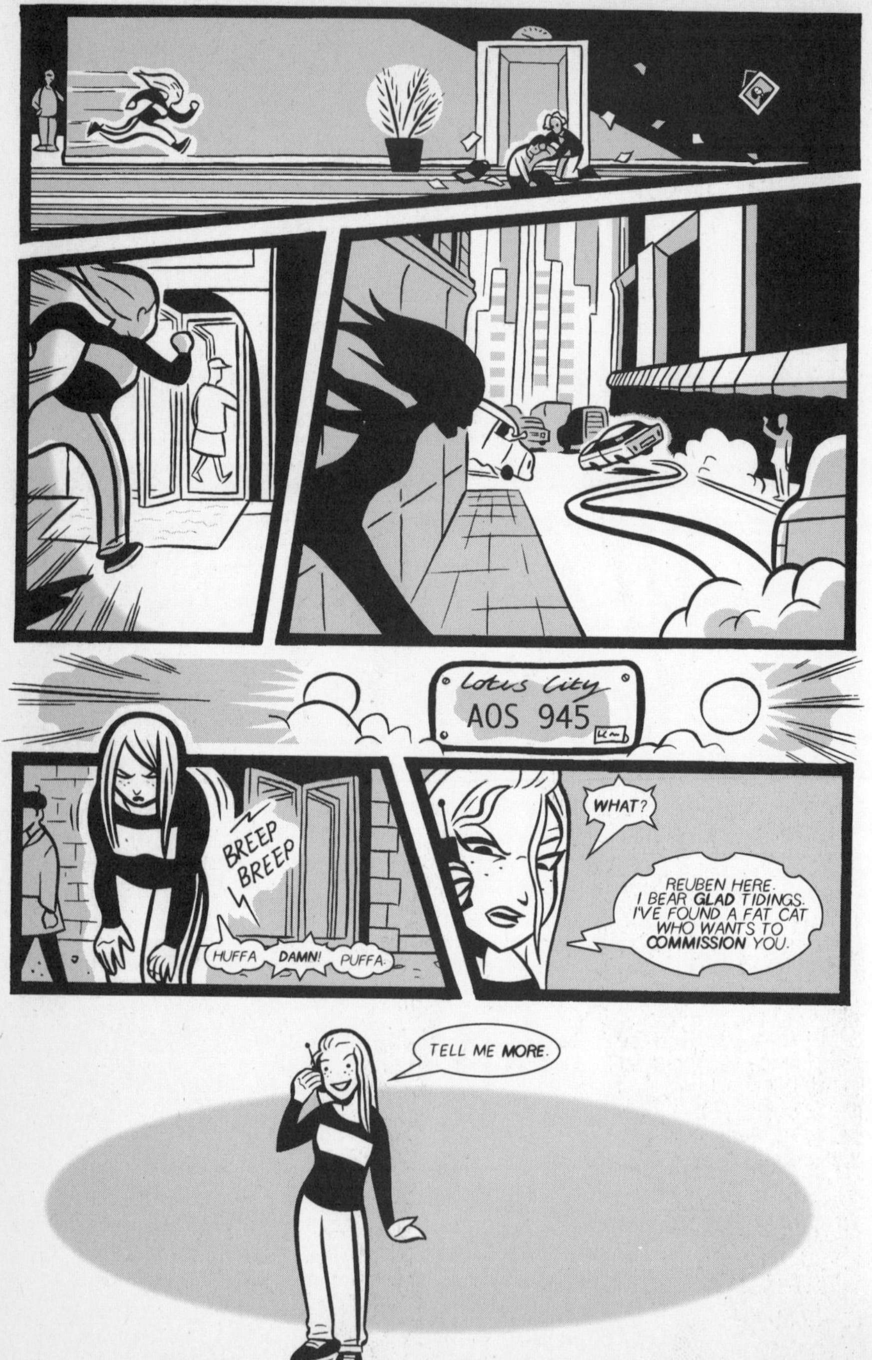

Lotus City
AOS 945
BREEP BREEP
HUFFA
DAMN!
PUFFA.
WHAT?
REUBEN HERE. I BEAR GLAD TIDINGS. I'VE FOUND A FAT CAT WHO WANTS TO COMMISSION YOU.
TELL ME MORE.

Chapter: two

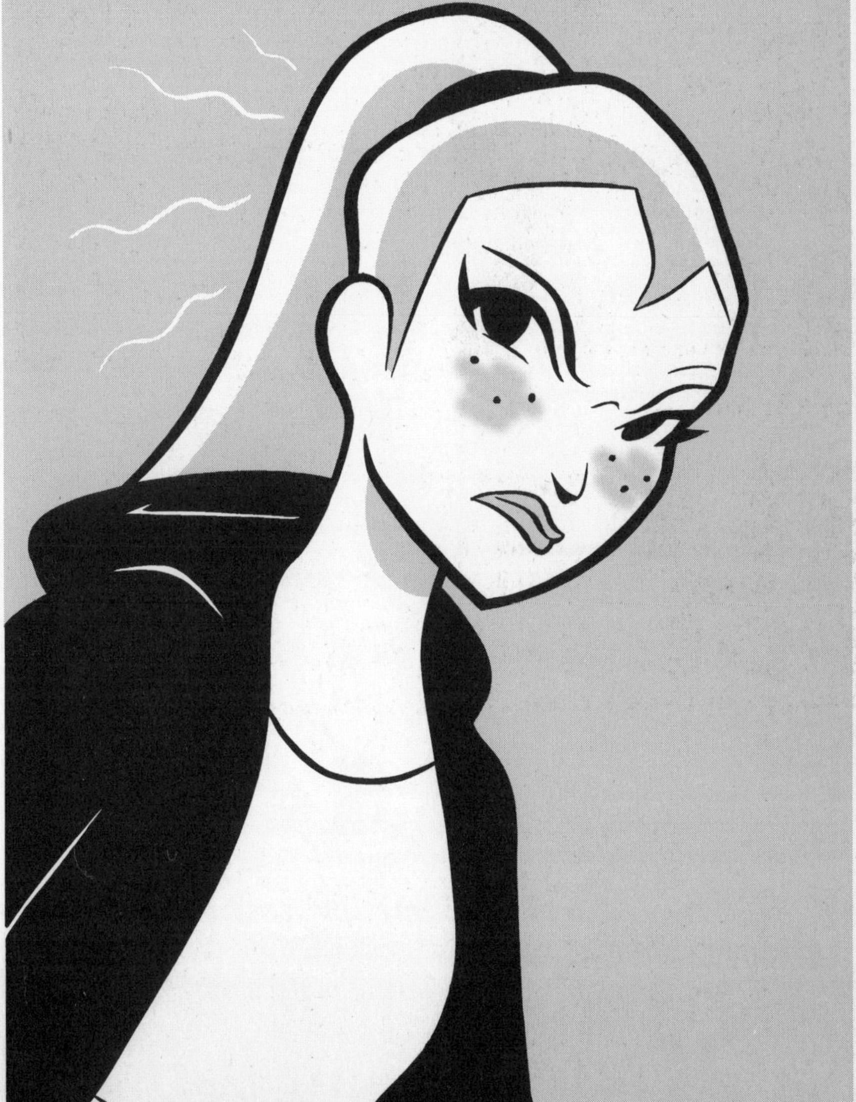

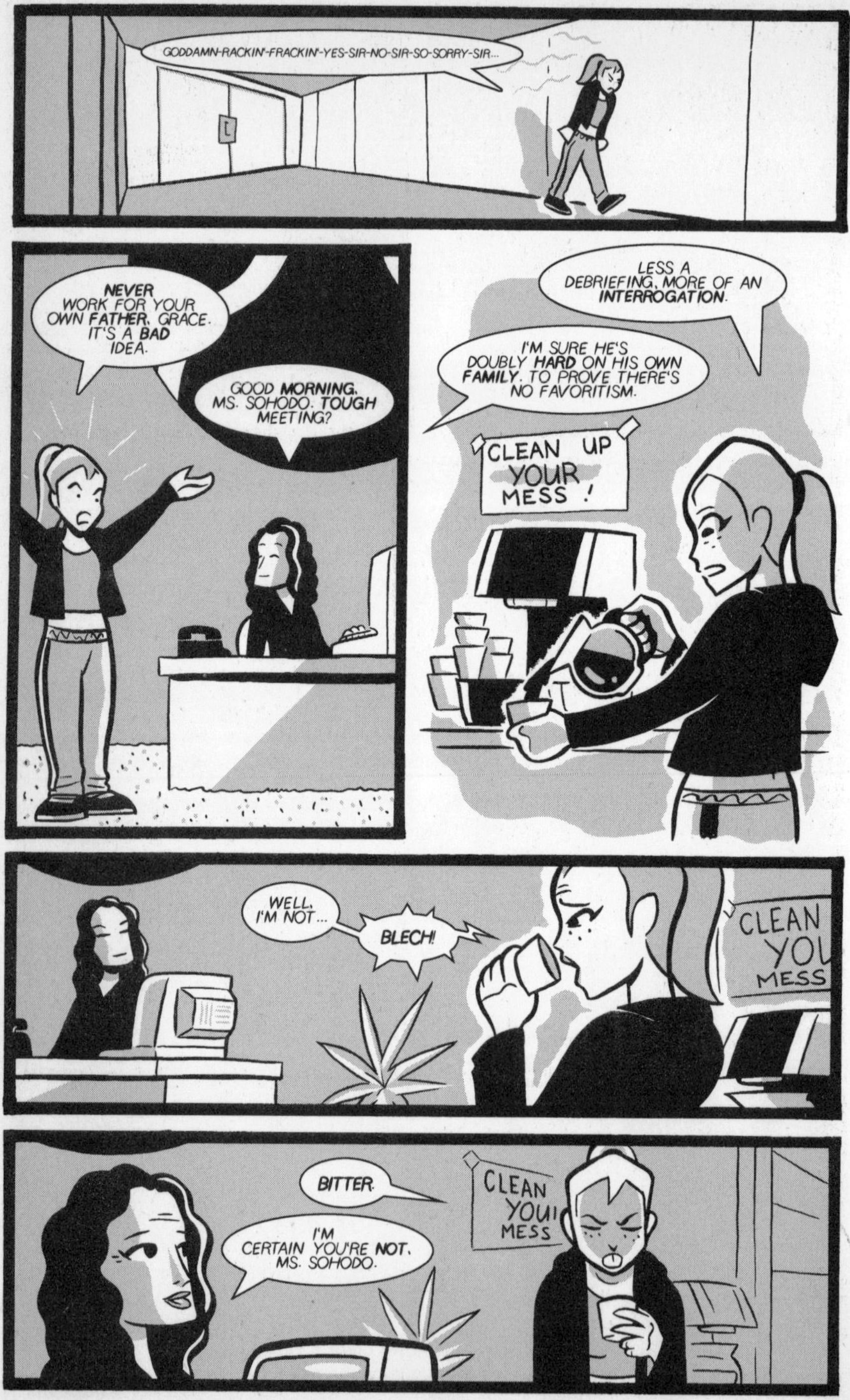
GODDAMN-RACKIN'-FRACKIN'-YES-SIR-NO-SIR-SO-SORRY-SIR...
NEVER WORK FOR YOUR OWN FATHER, GRACE. IT'S A BAD IDEA.
GOOD MORNING, MS. SOHODO. TOUGH MEETING?
LESS A DEBRIEFING, MORE OF AN INTERROGATION.
I'M SURE HE'S DOUBLY HARD ON HIS OWN FAMILY, TO PROVE THERE'S NO FAVORITISM.
CLEAN UP YOUR MESS!
WELL, I'M NOT...
BLECH!
BITTER.
I'M CERTAIN YOU'RE NOT, MS. SOHODO.

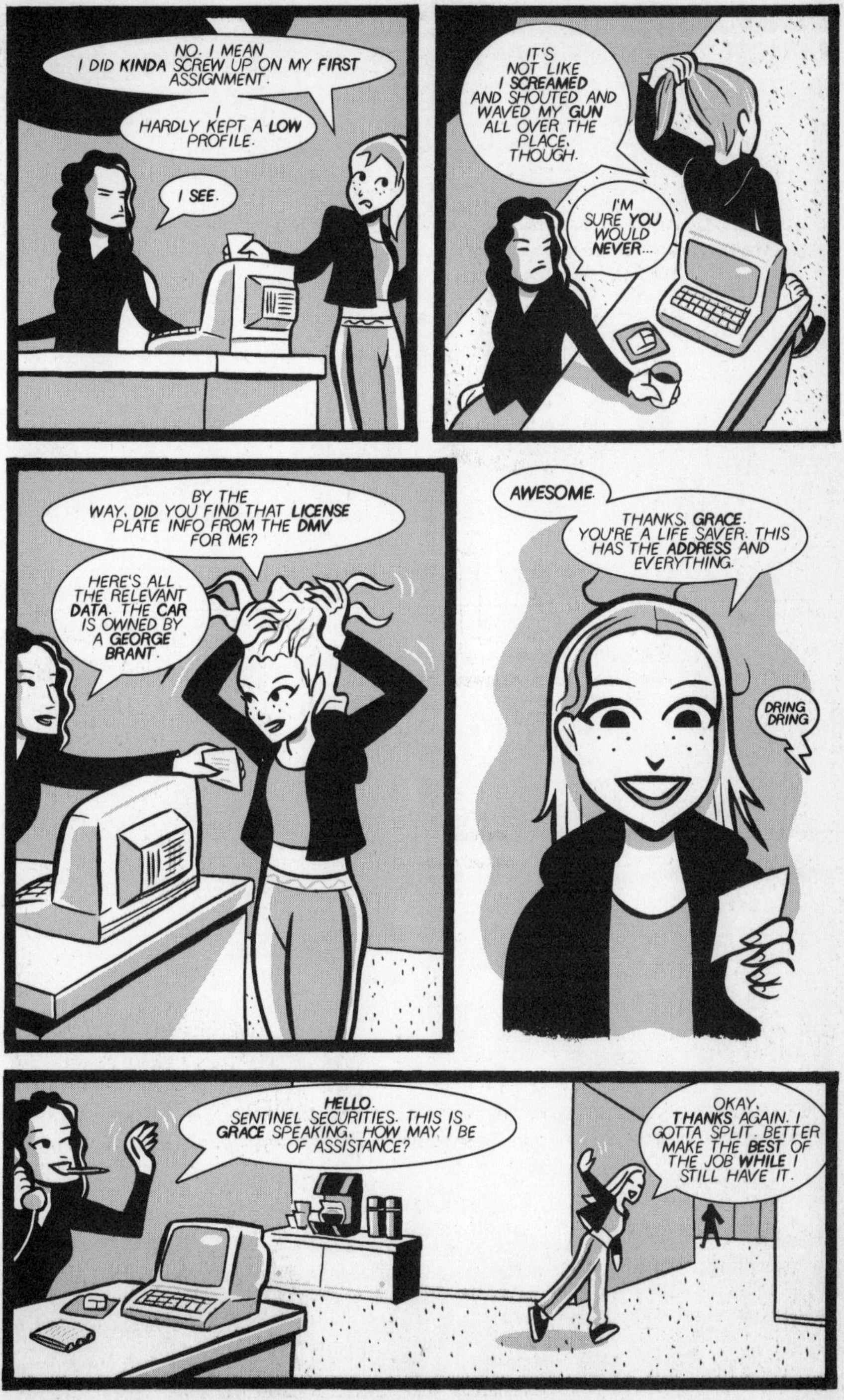
NO. I MEAN I DID KINDA SCREW UP ON MY FIRST ASSIGNMENT.
I HARDLY KEPT A LOW PROFILE.
I SEE.
IT'S NOT LIKE I SCREAMED AND SHOUTED AND WAVED MY GUN ALL OVER THE PLACE, THOUGH.
I'M SURE YOU WOULD NEVER...
BY THE WAY, DID YOU FIND THAT LICENSE PLATE INFO FROM THE DMV FOR ME?
HERE'S ALL THE RELEVANT DATA. THE CAR IS OWNED BY A GEORGE BRANT.
AWESOME.
THANKS, GRACE. YOU'RE A LIFE SAVER. THIS HAS THE ADDRESS AND EVERYTHING.
DRING DRING
HELLO. SENTINEL SECURITIES. THIS IS GRACE SPEAKING. HOW MAY I BE OF ASSISTANCE?
OKAY. THANKS AGAIN. I GOTTA SPLIT. BETTER MAKE THE BEST OF THE JOB WHILE I STILL HAVE IT.

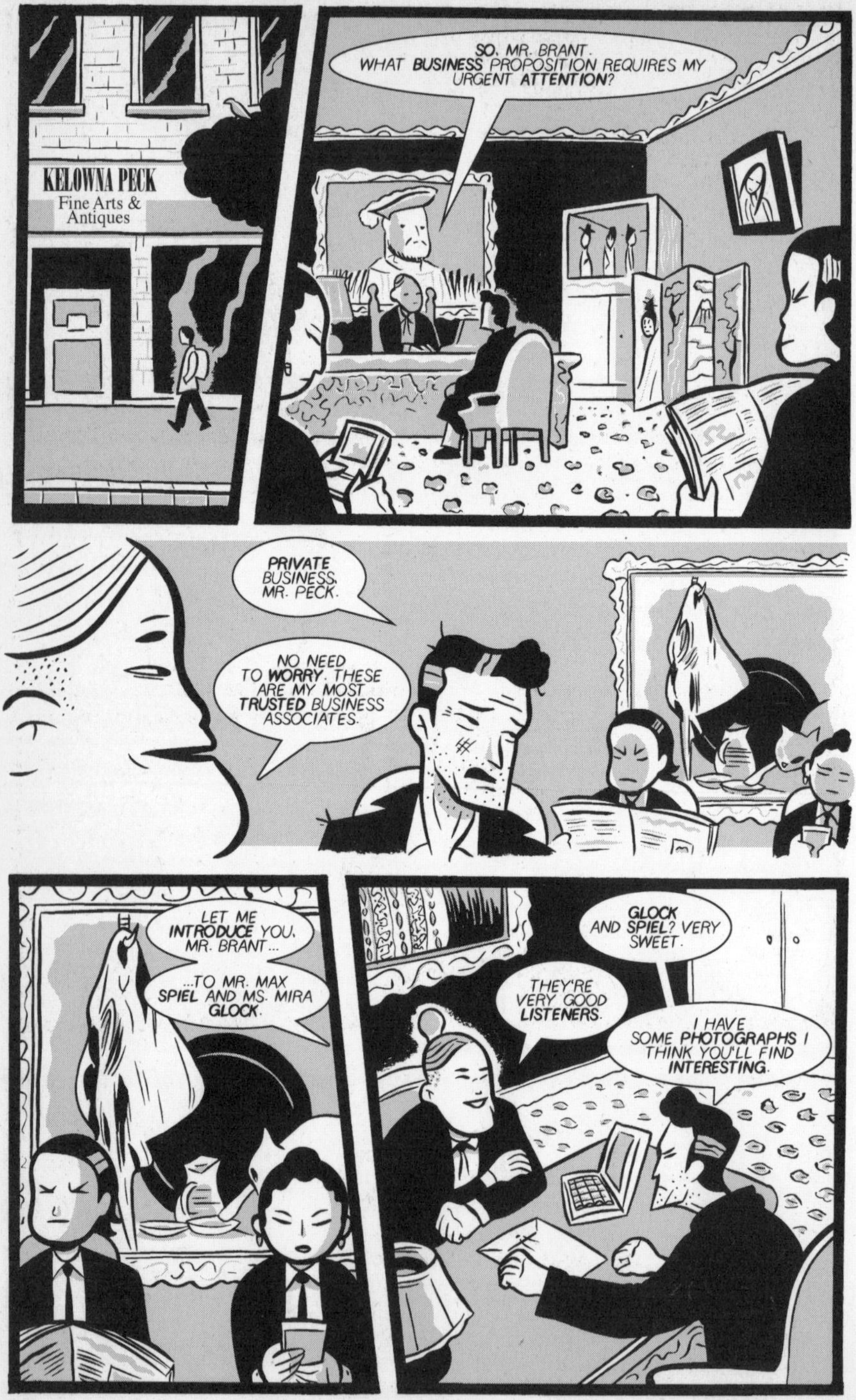
KELOWNA PECK
Fine Arts &
Antiques
SO, MR. BRANT. WHAT BUSINESS PROPOSITION REQUIRES MY URGENT ATTENTION?
PRIVATE BUSINESS, MR. PECK.
NO NEED TO WORRY. THESE ARE MY MOST TRUSTED BUSINESS ASSOCIATES.
LET ME INTRODUCE YOU, MR. BRANT...
...TO MR. MAX SPIEL AND MS. MIRA GLOCK.
GLOCK AND SPIEL? VERY SWEET.
THEY'RE VERY GOOD LISTENERS.
I HAVE SOME PHOTOGRAPHS I THINK YOU'LL FIND INTERESTING.

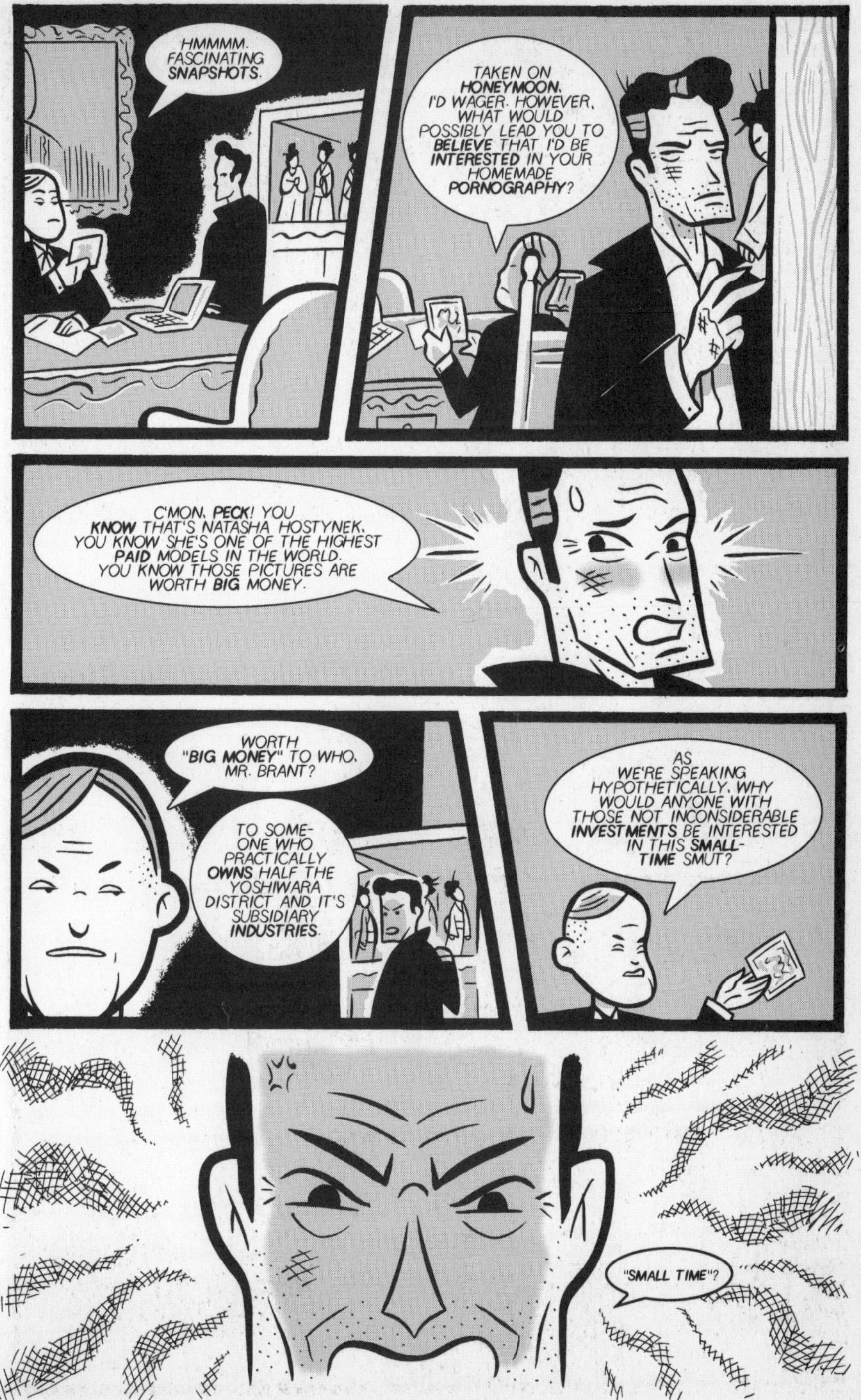
HMMMM. FASCINATING SNAPSHOTS.
TAKEN ON HONEYMOON, I'D WAGER. HOWEVER, WHAT WOULD POSSIBLY LEAD YOU TO BELIEVE THAT I'D BE INTERESTED IN YOUR HOMEMADE PORNOGRAPHY?
C'MON, PECK! YOU KNOW THAT'S NATASHA HOSTYNEK. YOU KNOW SHE'S ONE OF THE HIGHEST PAID MODELS IN THE WORLD. YOU KNOW THOSE PICTURES ARE WORTH BIG MONEY.
WORTH "BIG MONEY" TO WHO, MR. BRANT?
TO SOMEONE WHO PRACTICALLY OWNS HALF THE YOSHIWARA DISTRICT AND IT'S SUBSIDIARY INDUSTRIES.
AS WE'RE SPEAKING HYPOTHETICALLY, WHY WOULD ANYONE WITH THOSE NOT INCONSIDERABLE INVESTMENTS BE INTERESTED IN THIS SMALL-TIME SMUT?
"SMALL TIME"?

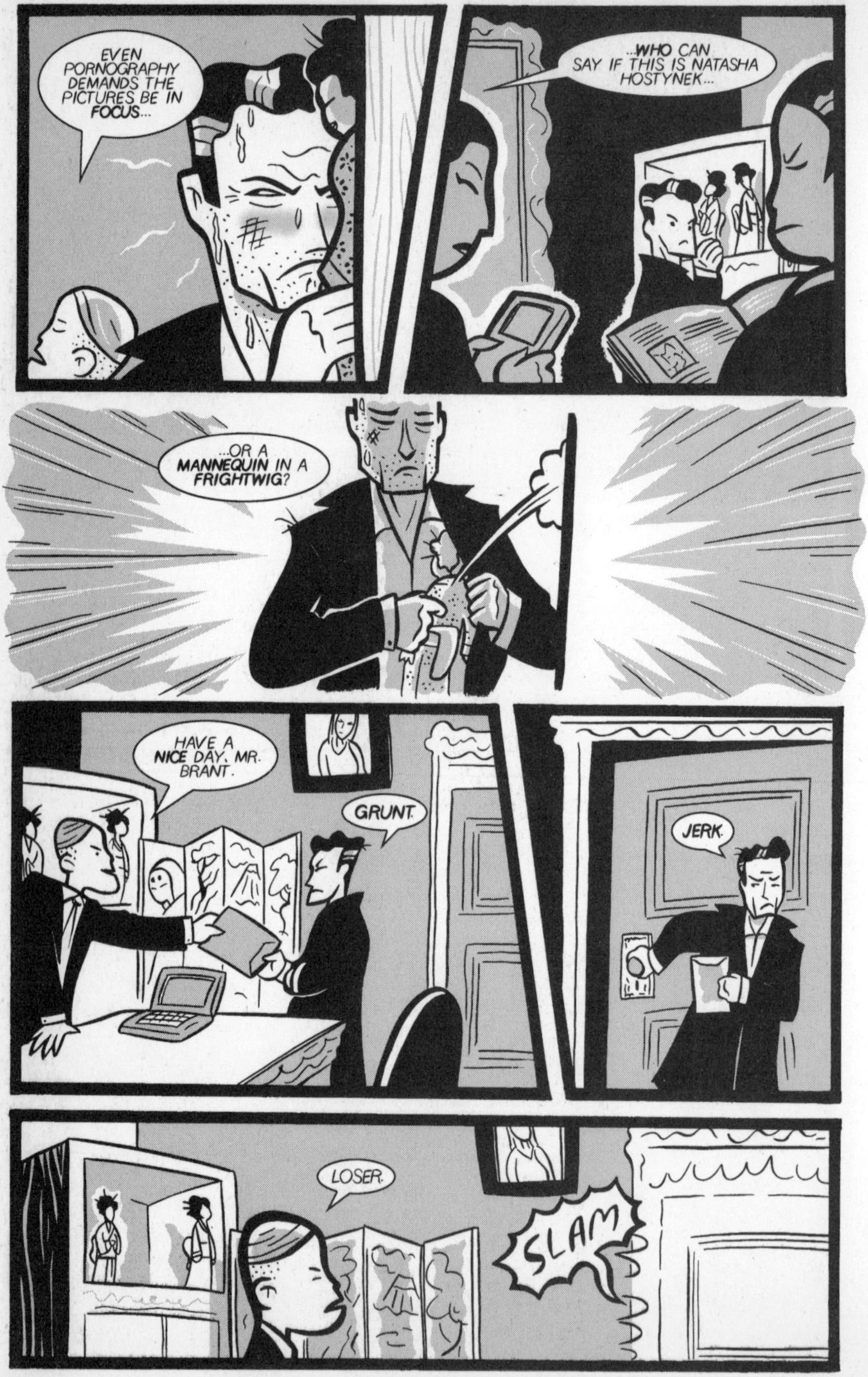
EVEN PORNOGRAPHY DEMANDS THE PICTURES BE IN FOCUS...
...WHO CAN SAY IF THIS IS NATASHA HOSTYNEK...
...OR A MANNEQUIN IN A FRIGHTWIG?
HAVE A NICE DAY, MR. BRANT.
GRUNT.
JERK.
LOSER.
SLAM

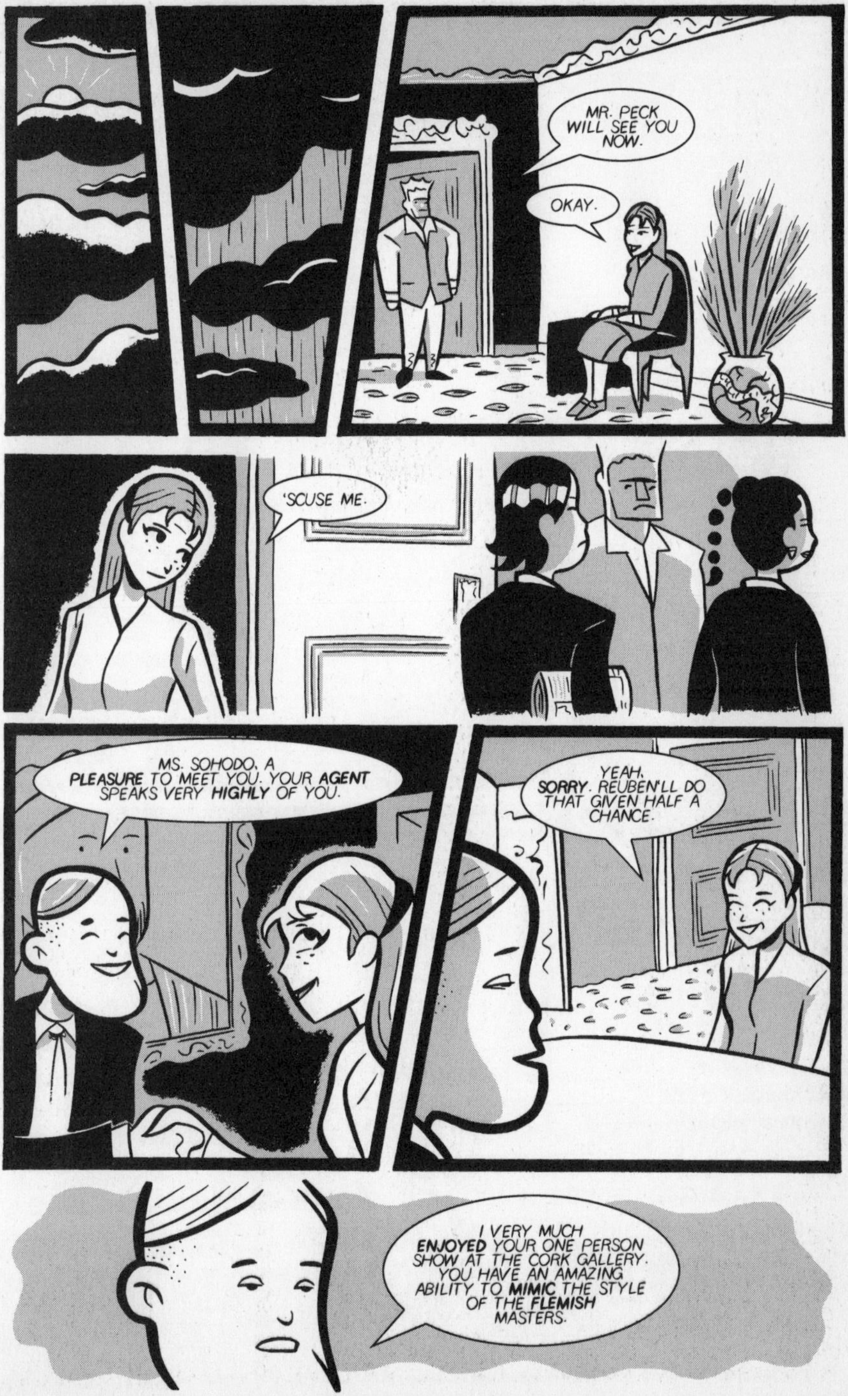
MR. PECK WILL SEE YOU NOW.
OKAY.
'SCUSE ME.
MS. SOHODO, A **PLEASURE** TO MEET YOU. YOUR **AGENT** SPEAKS VERY **HIGHLY** OF YOU.
YEAH, **SORRY**. REUBEN'LL DO THAT GIVEN HALF A CHANCE.
I VERY MUCH **ENJOYED** YOUR ONE PERSON SHOW AT THE CORK GALLERY. YOU HAVE AN AMAZING ABILITY TO **MIMIC** THE STYLE OF THE **FLEMISH** MASTERS.

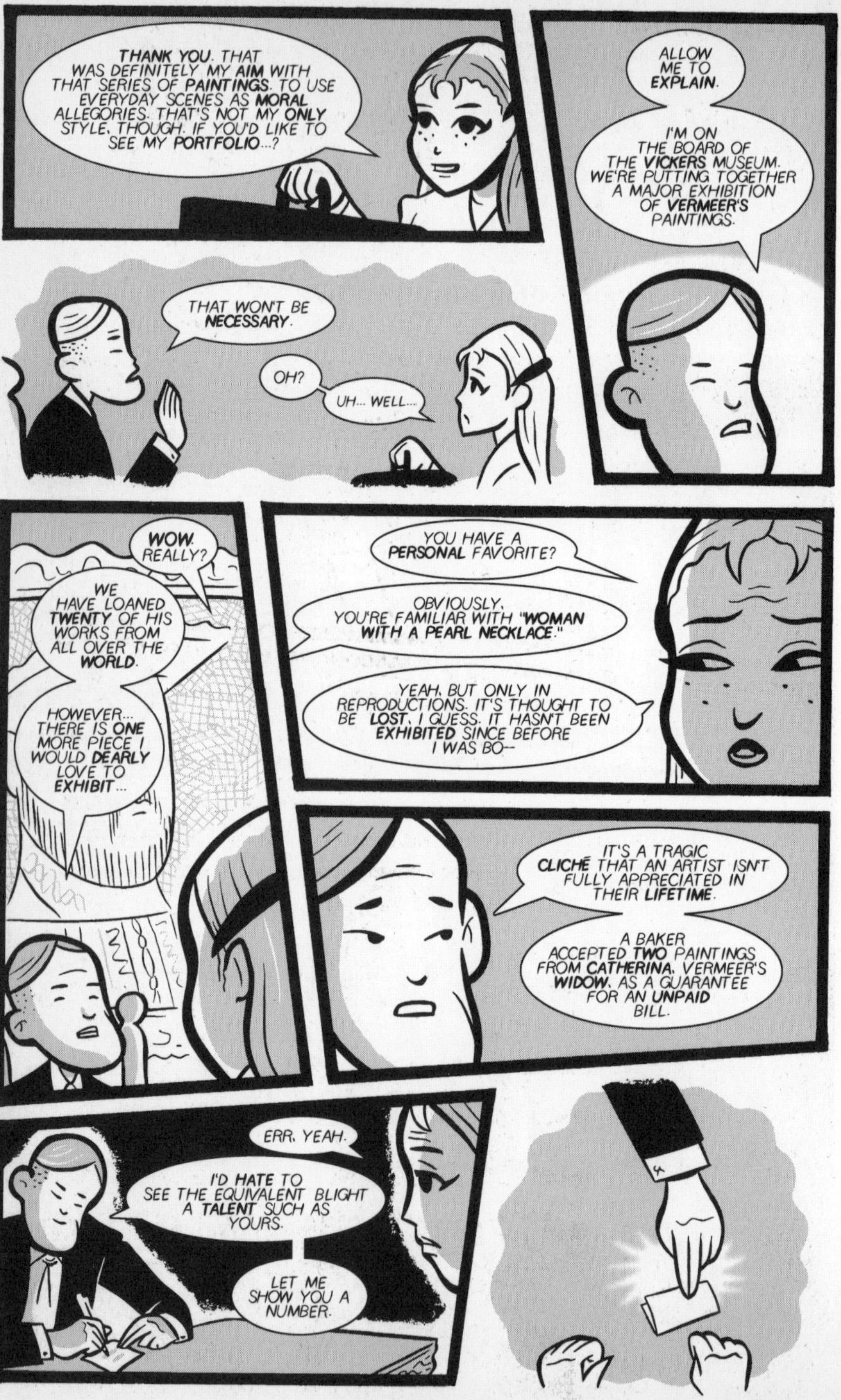
THANK YOU. THAT WAS DEFINITELY MY AIM WITH THAT SERIES OF PAINTINGS. TO USE EVERYDAY SCENES AS MORAL ALLEGORIES. THAT'S NOT MY ONLY STYLE, THOUGH. IF YOU'D LIKE TO SEE MY PORTFOLIO...?
THAT WON'T BE NECESSARY.
OH?
UH... WELL...
ALLOW ME TO EXPLAIN.
I'M ON THE BOARD OF THE VICKERS MUSEUM. WE'RE PUTTING TOGETHER A MAJOR EXHIBITION OF VERMEER'S PAINTINGS.
WOW. REALLY?
WE HAVE LOANED TWENTY OF HIS WORKS FROM ALL OVER THE WORLD.
HOWEVER... THERE IS ONE MORE PIECE I WOULD DEARLY LOVE TO EXHIBIT...
YOU HAVE A PERSONAL FAVORITE?
OBVIOUSLY, YOU'RE FAMILIAR WITH "WOMAN WITH A PEARL NECKLACE."
YEAH, BUT ONLY IN REPRODUCTIONS. IT'S THOUGHT TO BE LOST, I GUESS. IT HASN'T BEEN EXHIBITED SINCE BEFORE I WAS BO--
IT'S A TRAGIC CLICHÉ THAT AN ARTIST ISN'T FULLY APPRECIATED IN THEIR LIFETIME.
A BAKER ACCEPTED TWO PAINTINGS FROM CATHERINA, VERMEER'S WIDOW, AS A GUARANTEE FOR AN UNPAID BILL.
ERR, YEAH.
I'D HATE TO SEE THE EQUIVALENT BLIGHT A TALENT SUCH AS YOURS.
LET ME SHOW YOU A NUMBER.

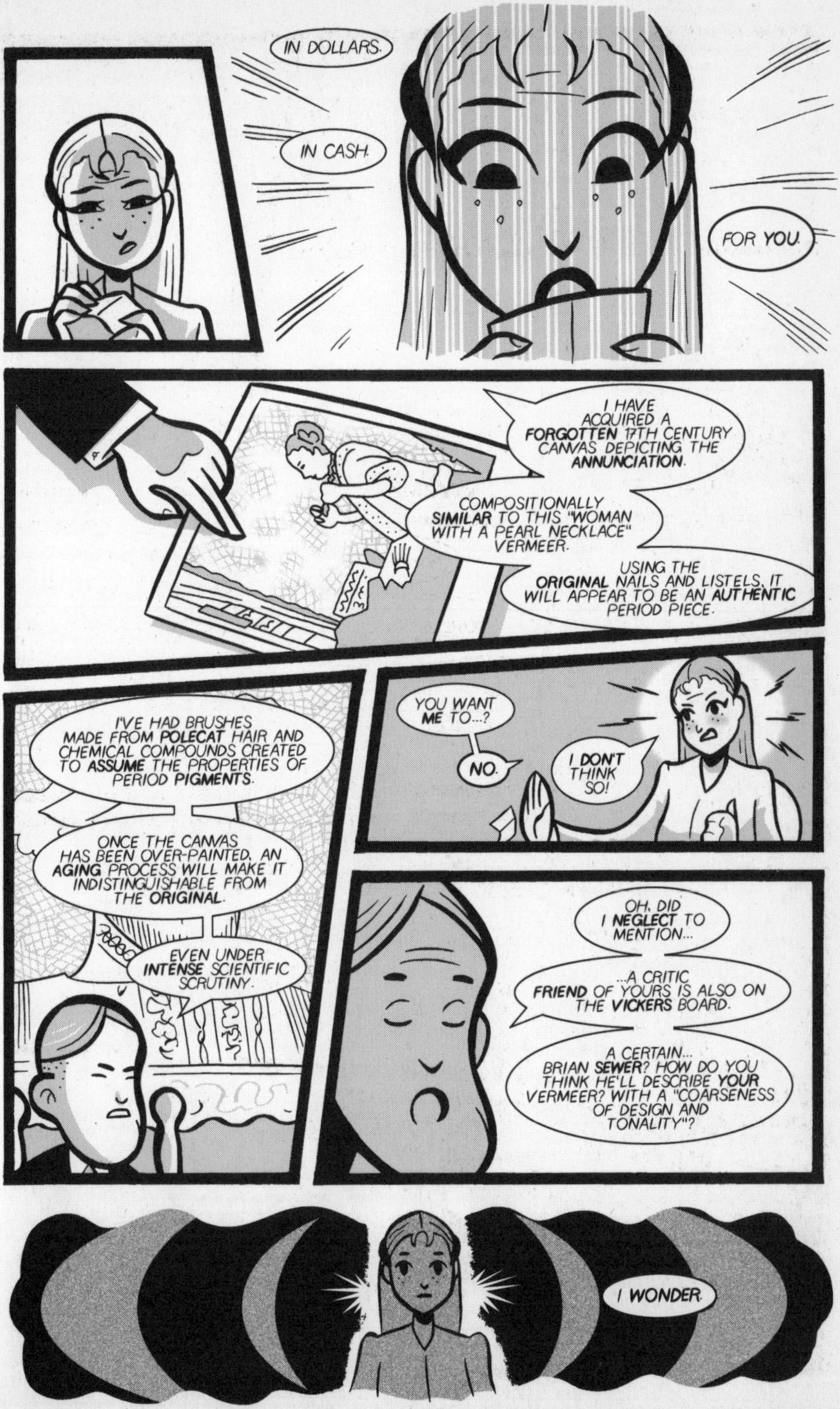
IN DOLLARS.
IN CASH.
FOR YOU.
I HAVE ACQUIRED A FORGOTTEN 17TH CENTURY CANVAS DEPICTING THE ANNUNCIATION.
COMPOSITIONALLY SIMILAR TO THIS "WOMAN WITH A PEARL NECKLACE" VERMEER.
USING THE ORIGINAL NAILS AND LISTELS, IT WILL APPEAR TO BE AN AUTHENTIC PERIOD PIECE.
I'VE HAD BRUSHES MADE FROM POLECAT HAIR AND CHEMICAL COMPOUNDS CREATED TO ASSUME THE PROPERTIES OF PERIOD PIGMENTS.
ONCE THE CANVAS HAS BEEN OVER-PAINTED, AN AGING PROCESS WILL MAKE IT INDISTINGUISHABLE FROM THE ORIGINAL.
EVEN UNDER INTENSE SCIENTIFIC SCRUTINY.
YOU WANT ME TO...?
NO.
I DON'T THINK SO!
OH, DID I NEGLECT TO MENTION...
...A CRITIC FRIEND OF YOURS IS ALSO ON THE VICKERS BOARD.
A CERTAIN... BRIAN SEWER? HOW DO YOU THINK HE'LL DESCRIBE YOUR VERMEER? WITH A "COARSENESS OF DESIGN AND TONALITY"?
I WONDER.

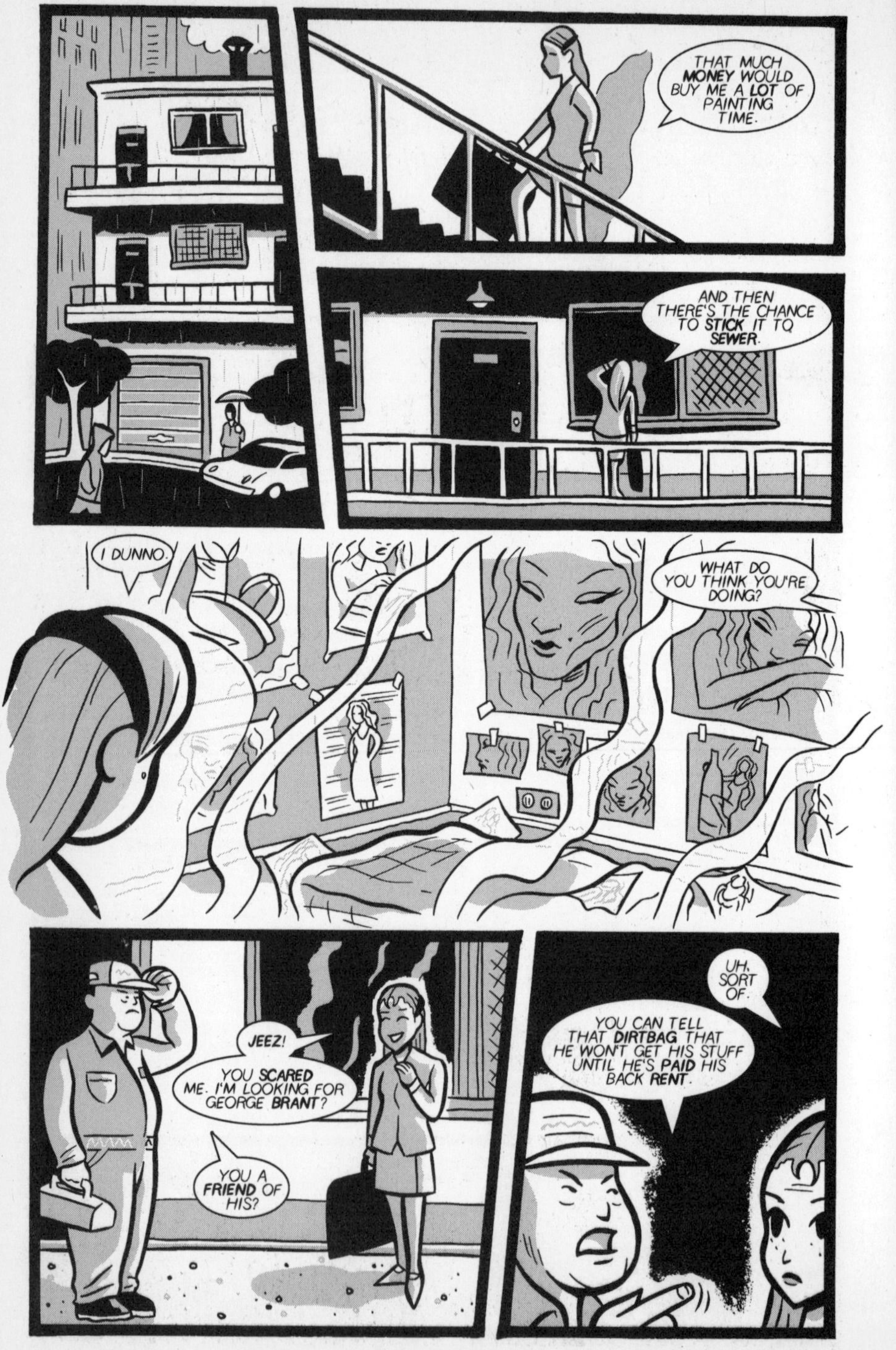

THAT MUCH MONEY WOULD BUY ME A LOT OF PAINTING TIME.
AND THEN THERE'S THE CHANCE TO STICK IT TO SEWER.
WHAT DO YOU THINK YOU'RE DOING?
I DUNNO.
JEEZ!
YOU SCARED ME. I'M LOOKING FOR GEORGE BRANT?
YOU A FRIEND OF HIS?
UH. SORT OF.
YOU CAN TELL THAT DIRTBAG THAT HE WON'T GET HIS STUFF UNTIL HE'S PAID HIS BACK RENT.

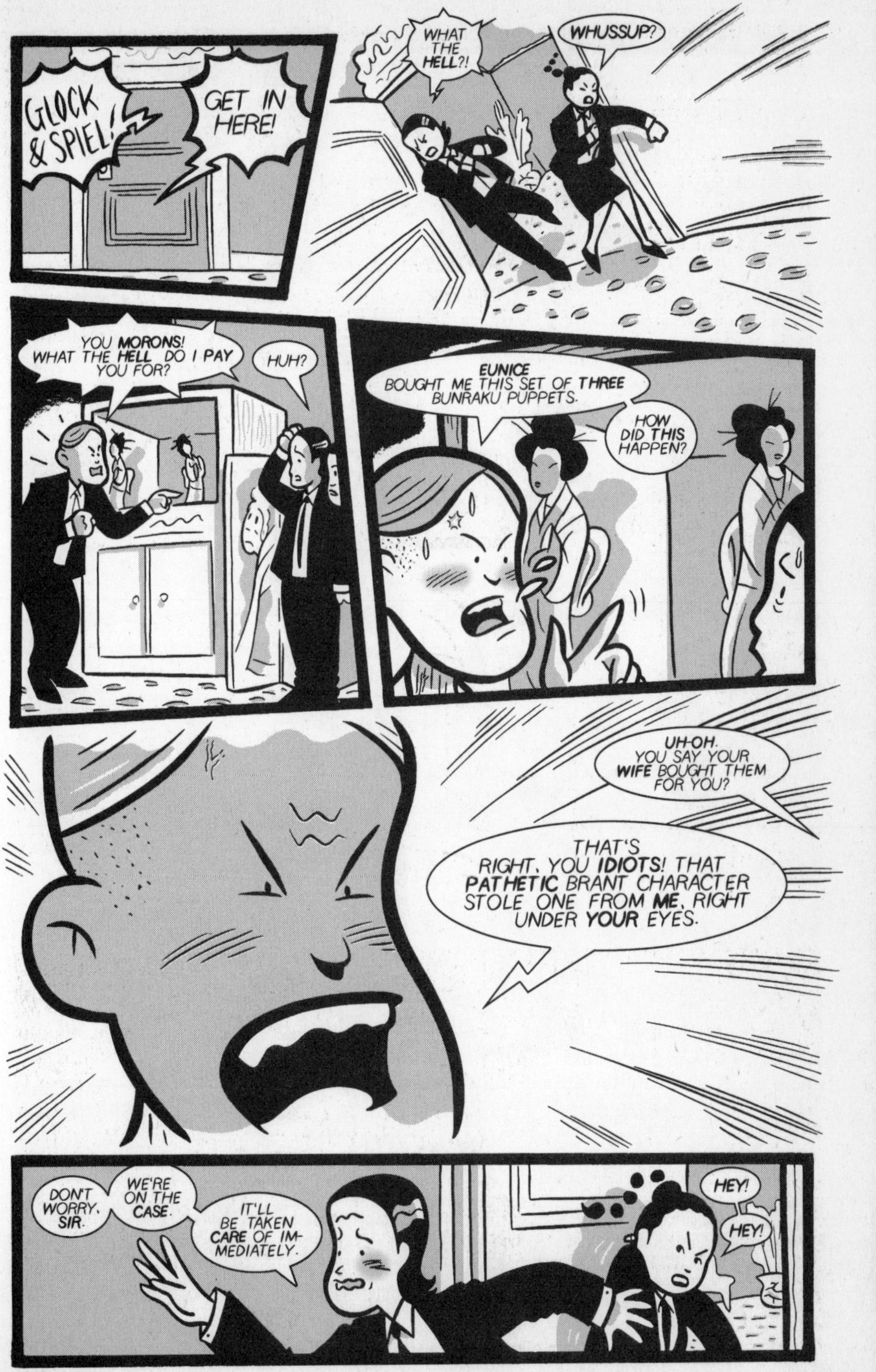
GLOCK & SPIEL!
GET IN HERE!
WHAT THE HELL?!
WHUSSUP?
YOU MORONS! WHAT THE HELL DO I PAY YOU FOR?
HUH?
EUNICE BOUGHT ME THIS SET OF THREE BUNRAKU PUPPETS.
HOW DID THIS HAPPEN?
UH-OH. YOU SAY YOUR WIFE BOUGHT THEM FOR YOU?
THAT'S RIGHT, YOU IDIOTS! THAT PATHETIC BRANT CHARACTER STOLE ONE FROM ME, RIGHT UNDER YOUR EYES.
DON'T WORRY, SIR.
WE'RE ON THE CASE.
IT'LL BE TAKEN CARE OF IMMEDIATELY.
HEY!
HEY!

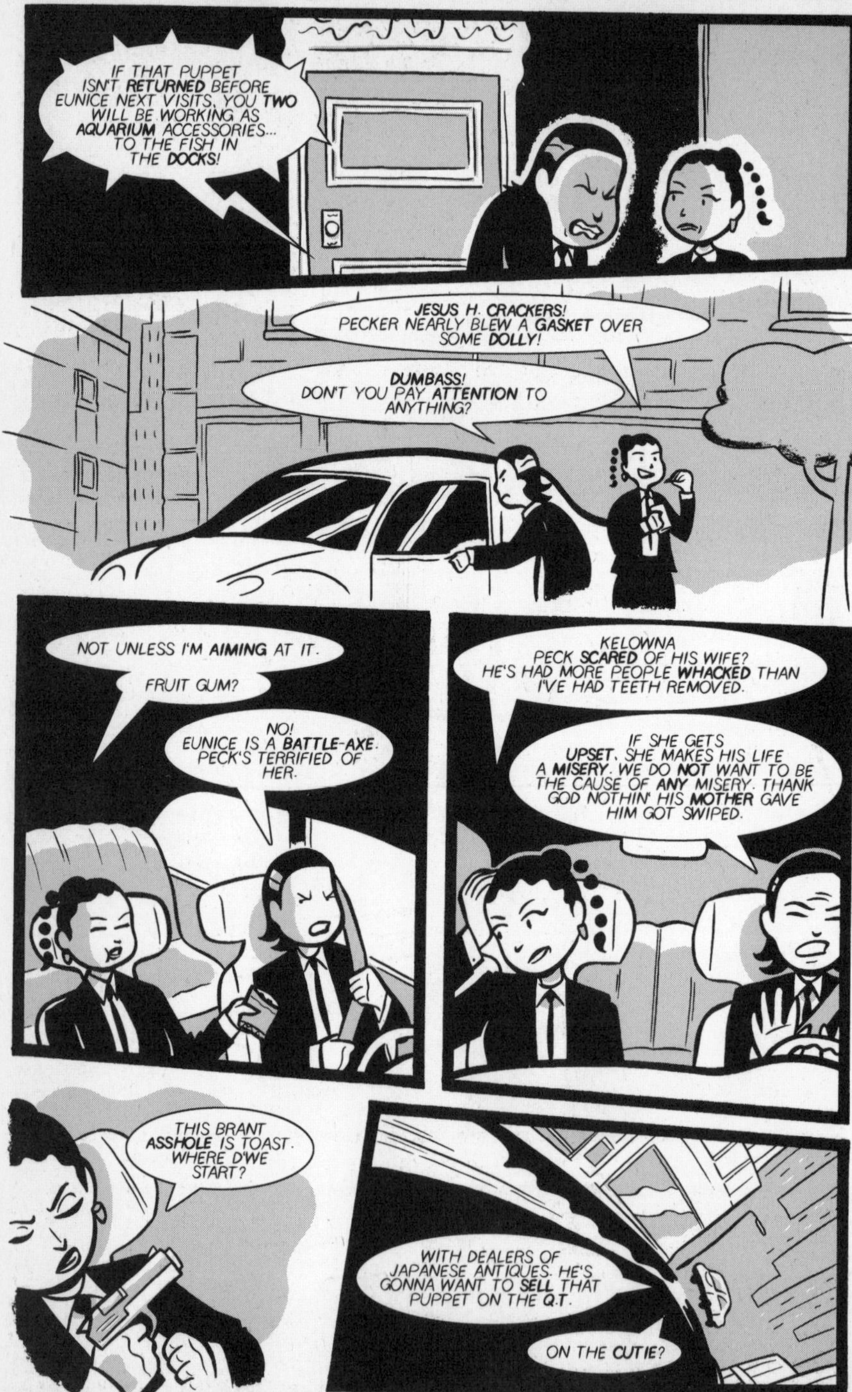
IF THAT PUPPET ISN'T RETURNED BEFORE EUNICE NEXT VISITS, YOU TWO WILL BE WORKING AS AQUARIUM ACCESSORIES... TO THE FISH IN THE DOCKS!
JESUS H. CRACKERS! PECKER NEARLY BLEW A GASKET OVER SOME DOLLY!
DUMBASS! DON'T YOU PAY ATTENTION TO ANYTHING?
NOT UNLESS I'M AIMING AT IT.
FRUIT GUM?
NO! EUNICE IS A BATTLE-AXE. PECK'S TERRIFIED OF HER.
KELOWNA PECK SCARED OF HIS WIFE? HE'S HAD MORE PEOPLE WHACKED THAN I'VE HAD TEETH REMOVED.
IF SHE GETS UPSET, SHE MAKES HIS LIFE A MISERY. WE DO NOT WANT TO BE THE CAUSE OF ANY MISERY. THANK GOD NOTHIN' HIS MOTHER GAVE HIM GOT SWIPED.
THIS BRANT ASSHOLE IS TOAST. WHERE D'WE START?
WITH DEALERS OF JAPANESE ANTIQUES. HE'S GONNA WANT TO SELL THAT PUPPET ON THE Q.T.
ON THE CUTIE?

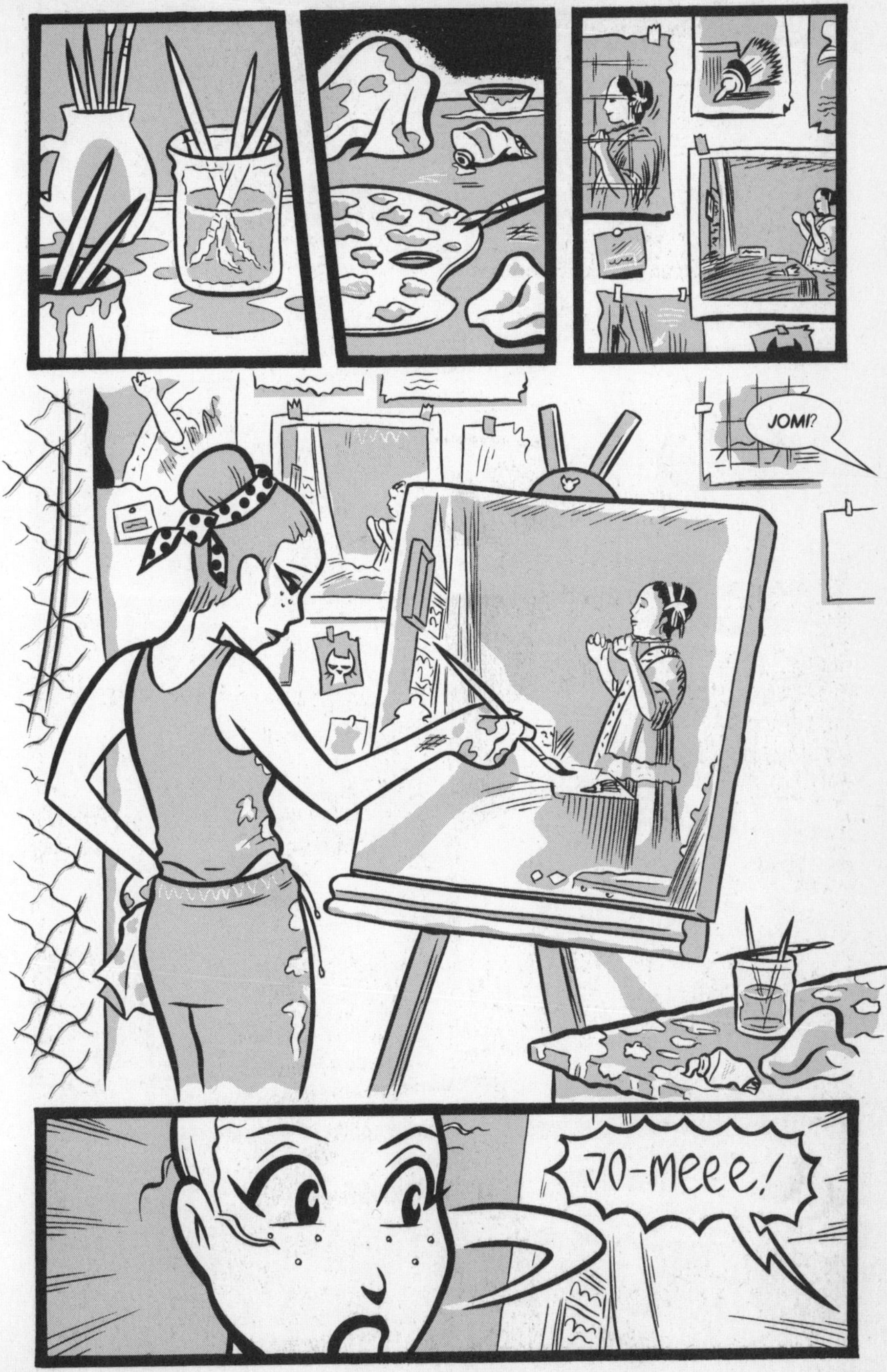
JOMI?
JO-MEEE!

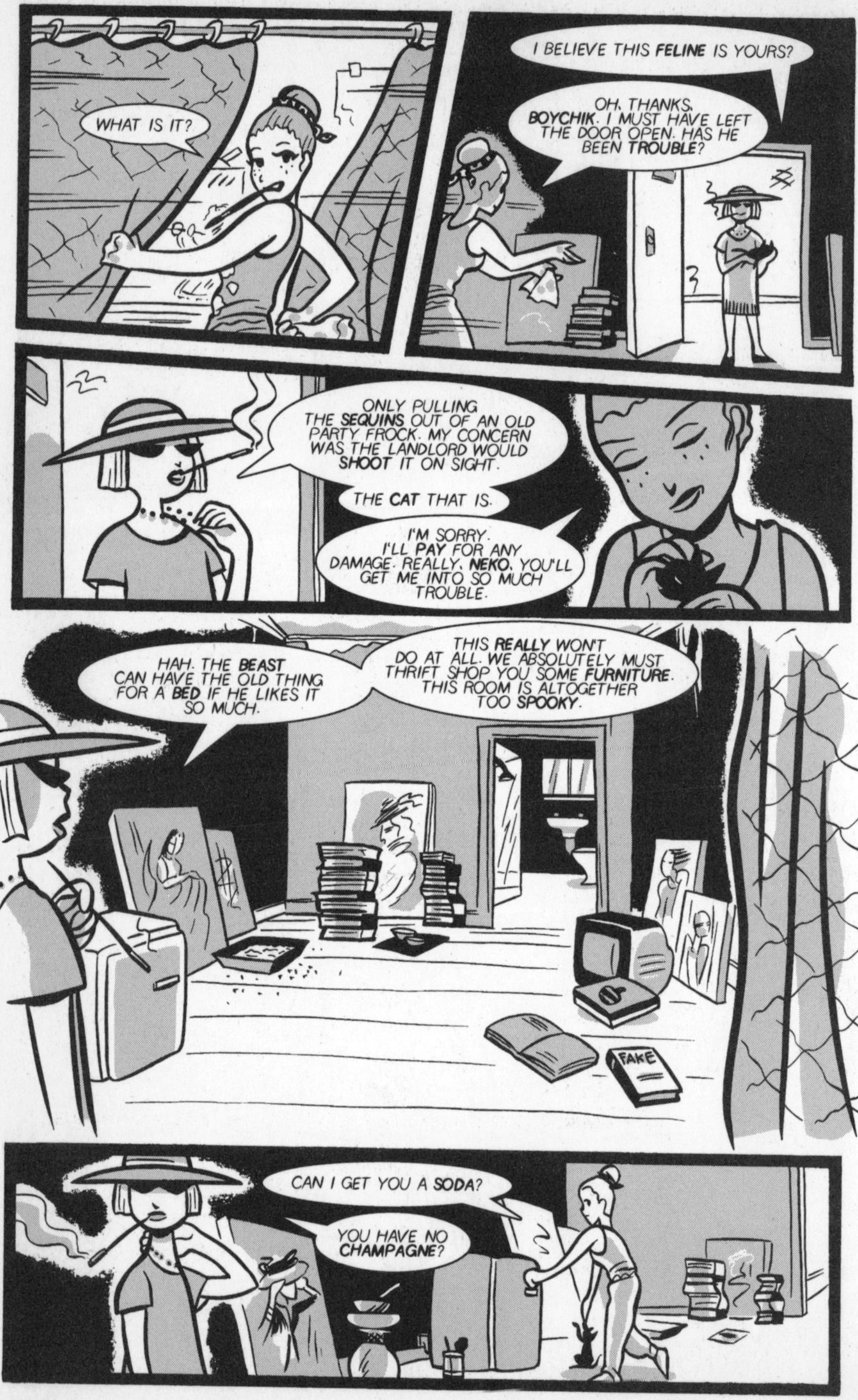
WHAT IS IT?
I BELIEVE THIS FELINE IS YOURS?
OH. THANKS, BOYCHIK. I MUST HAVE LEFT THE DOOR OPEN. HAS HE BEEN TROUBLE?
ONLY PULLING THE SEQUINS OUT OF AN OLD PARTY FROCK. MY CONCERN WAS THE LANDLORD WOULD SHOOT IT ON SIGHT.
THE CAT THAT IS.
I'M SORRY. I'LL PAY FOR ANY DAMAGE. REALLY, NEKO, YOU'LL GET ME INTO SO MUCH TROUBLE.
HAH. THE BEAST CAN HAVE THE OLD THING FOR A BED IF HE LIKES IT SO MUCH.
THIS REALLY WON'T DO AT ALL. WE ABSOLUTELY MUST THRIFT SHOP YOU SOME FURNITURE. THIS ROOM IS ALTOGETHER TOO SPOOKY.
FAKE
CAN I GET YOU A SODA?
YOU HAVE NO CHAMPAGNE?

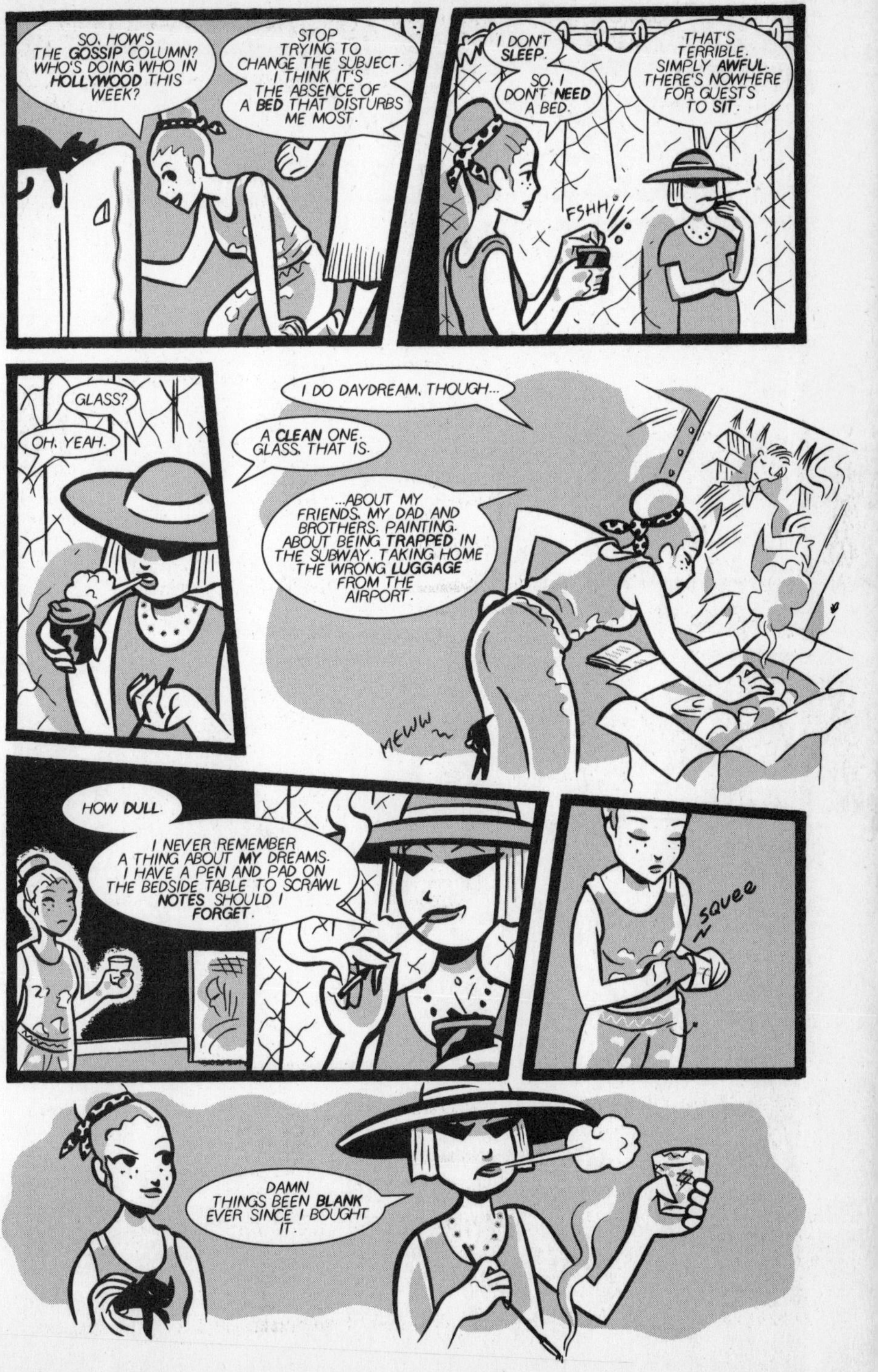
SO, HOW'S THE GOSSIP COLUMN? WHO'S DOING WHO IN HOLLYWOOD THIS WEEK?
STOP TRYING TO CHANGE THE SUBJECT. I THINK IT'S THE ABSENCE OF A BED THAT DISTURBS ME MOST.
I DON'T SLEEP.
SO, I DON'T NEED A BED.
THAT'S TERRIBLE. SIMPLY AWFUL. THERE'S NOWHERE FOR GUESTS TO SIT.
FSHH
GLASS?
OH, YEAH.
A CLEAN ONE. GLASS, THAT IS.
I DO DAYDREAM, THOUGH...
...ABOUT MY FRIENDS, MY DAD AND BROTHERS. PAINTING. ABOUT BEING TRAPPED IN THE SUBWAY. TAKING HOME THE WRONG LUGGAGE FROM THE AIRPORT.
MEWW
HOW DULL.
I NEVER REMEMBER A THING ABOUT MY DREAMS. I HAVE A PEN AND PAD ON THE BEDSIDE TABLE TO SCRAWL NOTES SHOULD I FORGET.
SQUEE
DAMN THINGS BEEN BLANK EVER SINCE I BOUGHT IT.

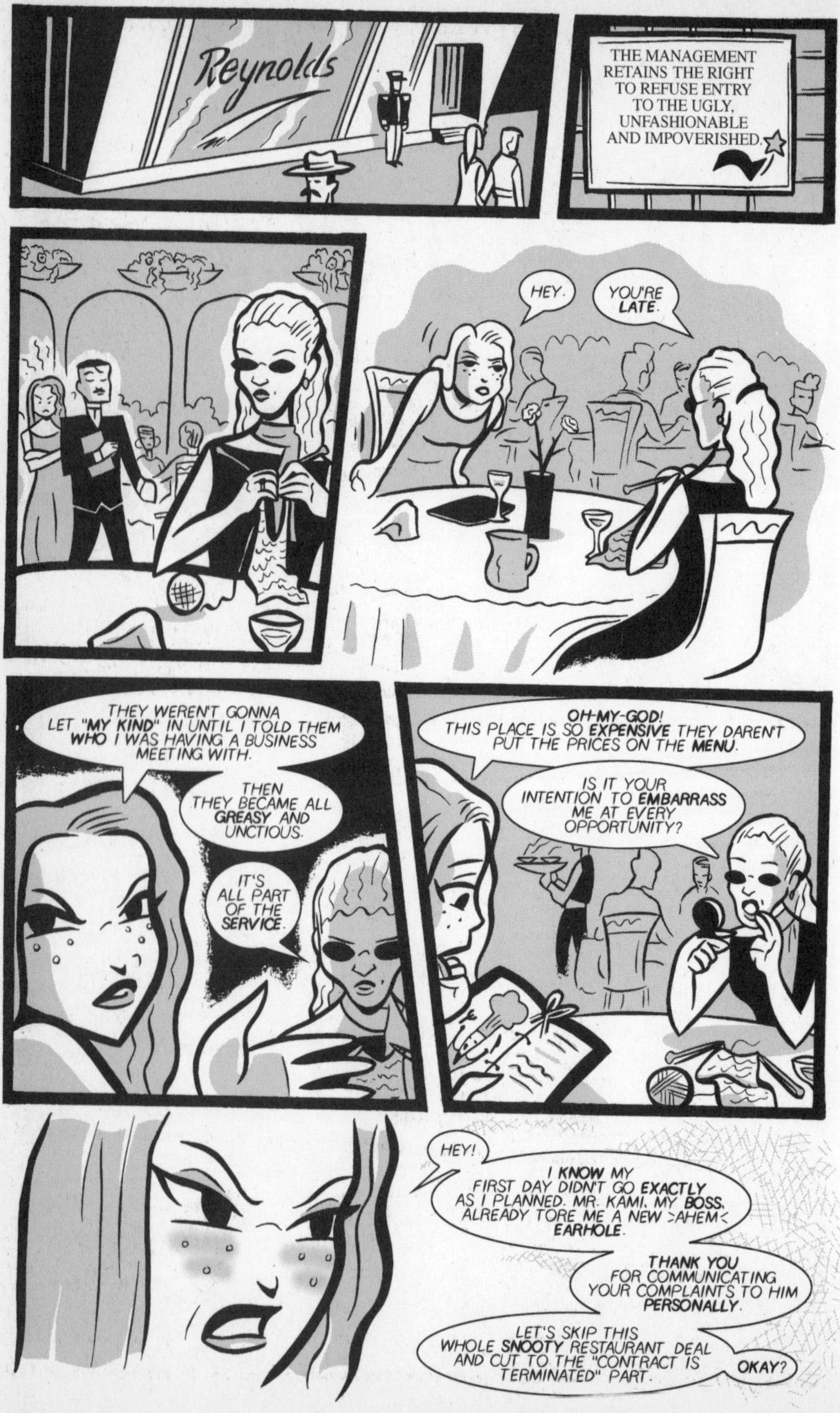
Reynolds
THE MANAGEMENT RETAINS THE RIGHT TO REFUSE ENTRY TO THE UGLY, UNFASHIONABLE AND IMPOVERISHED.
HEY.
YOU'RE LATE.
THEY WEREN'T GONNA LET "MY KIND" IN UNTIL I TOLD THEM WHO I WAS HAVING A BUSINESS MEETING WITH.
THEN THEY BECAME ALL GREASY AND UNCTIOUS.
IT'S ALL PART OF THE SERVICE.
OH-MY-GOD! THIS PLACE IS SO EXPENSIVE THEY DAREN'T PUT THE PRICES ON THE MENU.
IS IT YOUR INTENTION TO EMBARRASS ME AT EVERY OPPORTUNITY?
HEY!
I KNOW MY FIRST DAY DIDN'T GO EXACTLY AS I PLANNED. MR. KAMI, MY BOSS, ALREADY TORE ME A NEW >AHEM< EARHOLE.
THANK YOU FOR COMMUNICATING YOUR COMPLAINTS TO HIM PERSONALLY.
LET'S SKIP THIS WHOLE SNOOTY RESTAURANT DEAL AND CUT TO THE "CONTRACT IS TERMINATED" PART.
OKAY?

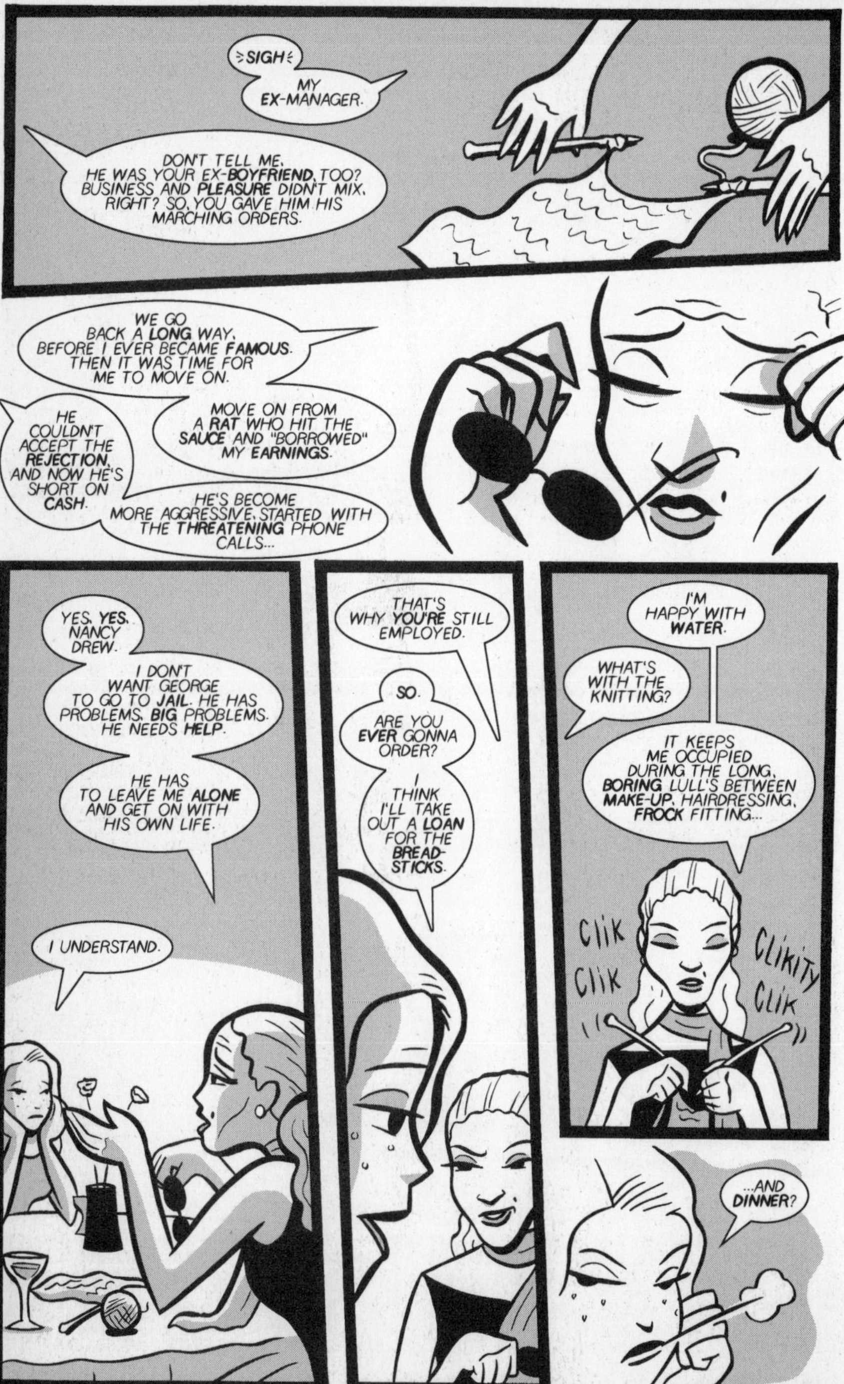

SIGH
MY EX-MANAGER.
DON'T TELL ME. HE WAS YOUR EX-BOYFRIEND, TOO? BUSINESS AND PLEASURE DIDN'T MIX, RIGHT? SO, YOU GAVE HIM HIS MARCHING ORDERS.
WE GO BACK A LONG WAY, BEFORE I EVER BECAME FAMOUS. THEN IT WAS TIME FOR ME TO MOVE ON.
MOVE ON FROM A RAT WHO HIT THE SAUCE AND "BORROWED" MY EARNINGS.
HE COULDN'T ACCEPT THE REJECTION, AND NOW HE'S SHORT ON CASH.
HE'S BECOME MORE AGGRESSIVE, STARTED WITH THE THREATENING PHONE CALLS...
YES, YES, NANCY DREW.
I DON'T WANT GEORGE TO GO TO JAIL. HE HAS PROBLEMS. BIG PROBLEMS. HE NEEDS HELP.
HE HAS TO LEAVE ME ALONE AND GET ON WITH HIS OWN LIFE.
I UNDERSTAND.
THAT'S WHY YOU'RE STILL EMPLOYED.
SO.
ARE YOU EVER GONNA ORDER?
I THINK I'LL TAKE OUT A LOAN FOR THE BREAD-STICKS.
I'M HAPPY WITH WATER.
WHAT'S WITH THE KNITTING?
IT KEEPS ME OCCUPIED DURING THE LONG, BORING LULL'S BETWEEN MAKE-UP, HAIRDRESSING, FROCK FITTING...
CLIK
CLIK
CLIKITY
CLIK
...AND DINNER?

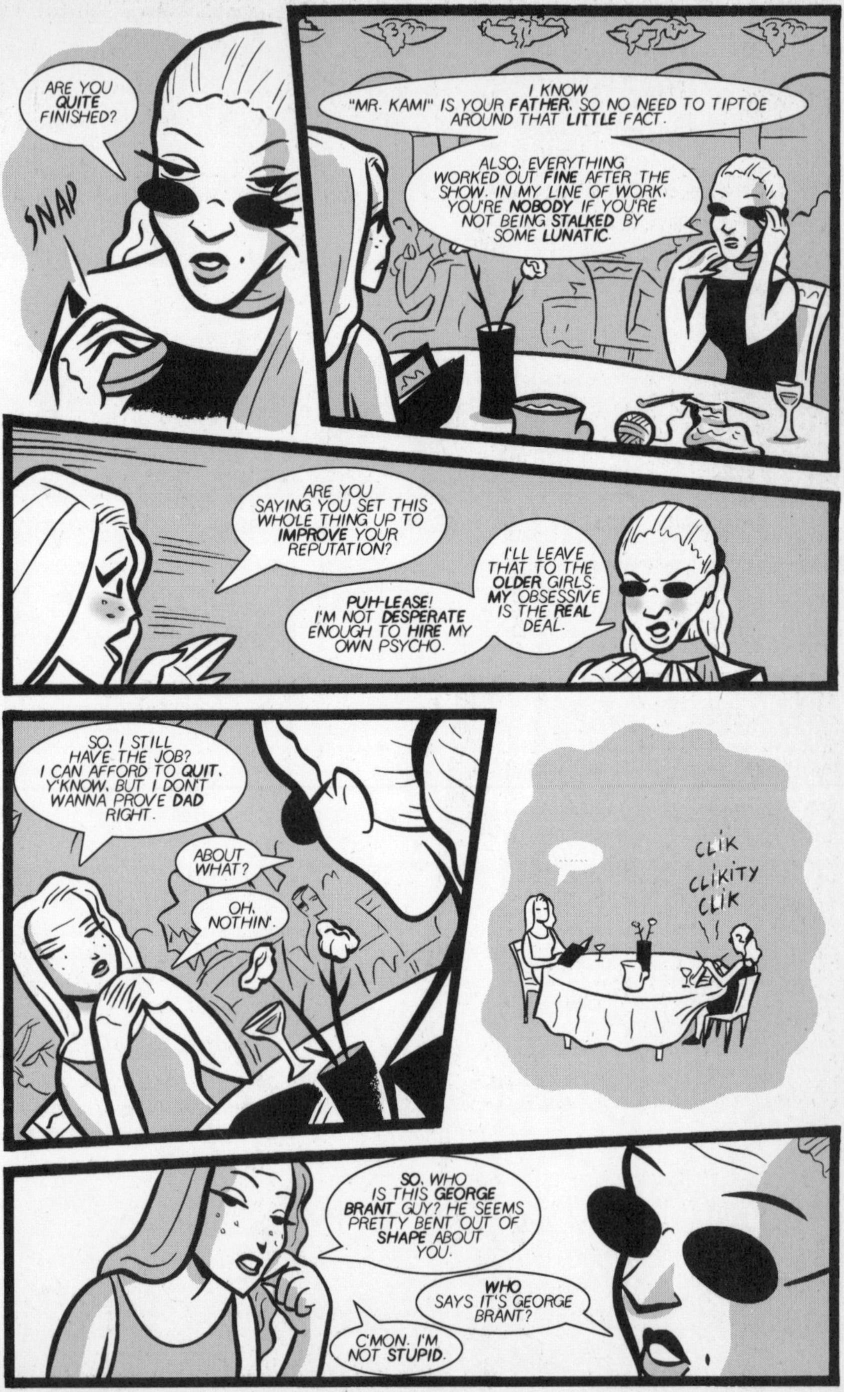
ARE YOU QUITE FINISHED?
SNAP
I KNOW "MR. KAMI" IS YOUR FATHER, SO NO NEED TO TIPTOE AROUND THAT LITTLE FACT.
ALSO, EVERYTHING WORKED OUT FINE AFTER THE SHOW. IN MY LINE OF WORK, YOU'RE NOBODY IF YOU'RE NOT BEING STALKED BY SOME LUNATIC.
ARE YOU SAYING YOU SET THIS WHOLE THING UP TO IMPROVE YOUR REPUTATION?
PUH-LEASE! I'M NOT DESPERATE ENOUGH TO HIRE MY OWN PSYCHO.
I'LL LEAVE THAT TO THE OLDER GIRLS. MY OBSESSIVE IS THE REAL DEAL.
SO, I STILL HAVE THE JOB? I CAN AFFORD TO QUIT, Y'KNOW, BUT I DON'T WANNA PROVE DAD RIGHT.
ABOUT WHAT?
OH, NOTHIN'.
......
CLIK
CLIKITY
CLIK
SO, WHO IS THIS GEORGE BRANT GUY? HE SEEMS PRETTY BENT OUT OF SHAPE ABOUT YOU.
WHO SAYS IT'S GEORGE BRANT?
C'MON. I'M NOT STUPID.

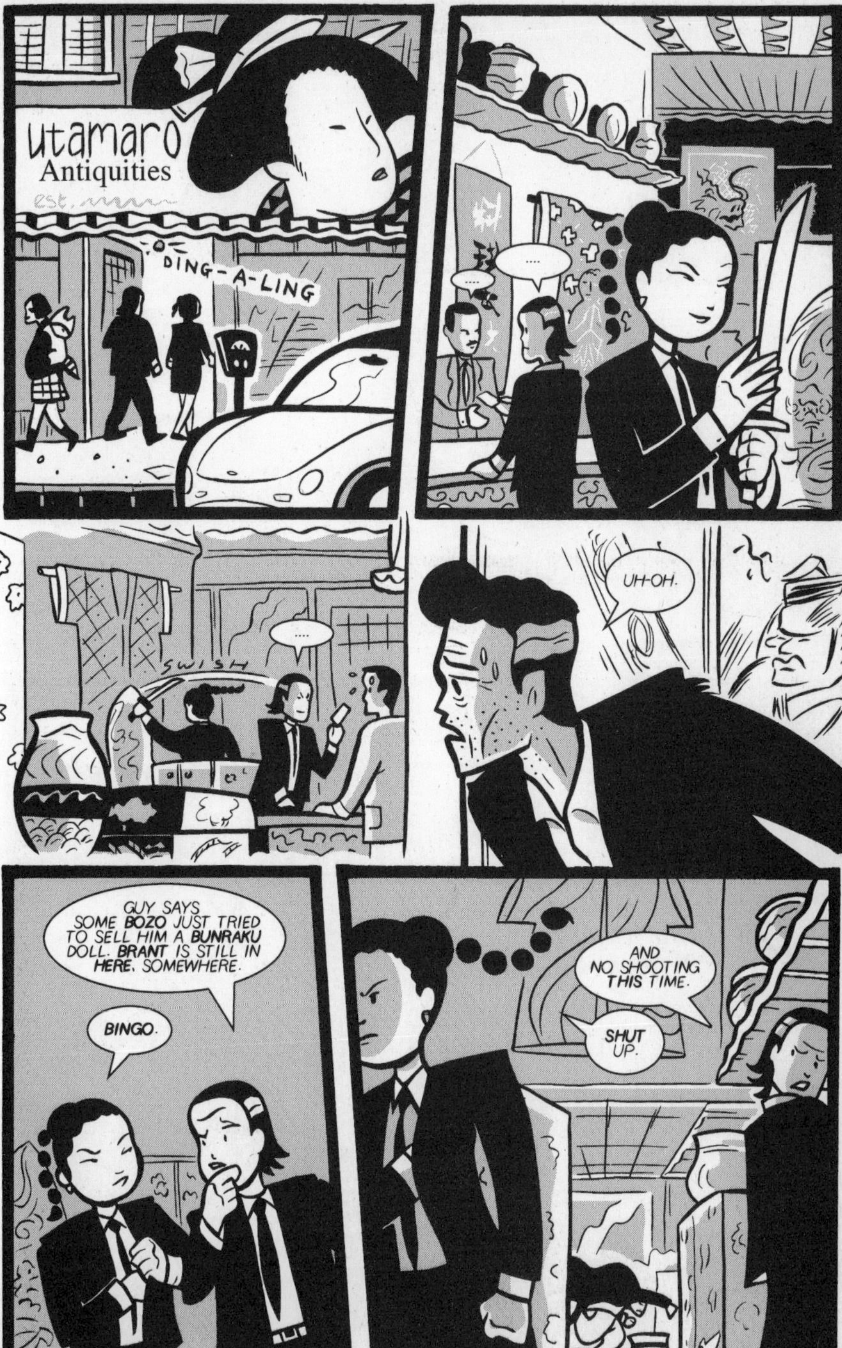
utamaro
Antiquities
DING-A-LING
....
....
....
SWISH
UH-OH.
GUY SAYS SOME BOZO JUST TRIED TO SELL HIM A BUNRAKU DOLL. BRANT IS STILL IN HERE, SOMEWHERE.
BINGO.
AND NO SHOOTING THIS TIME.
SHUT UP.

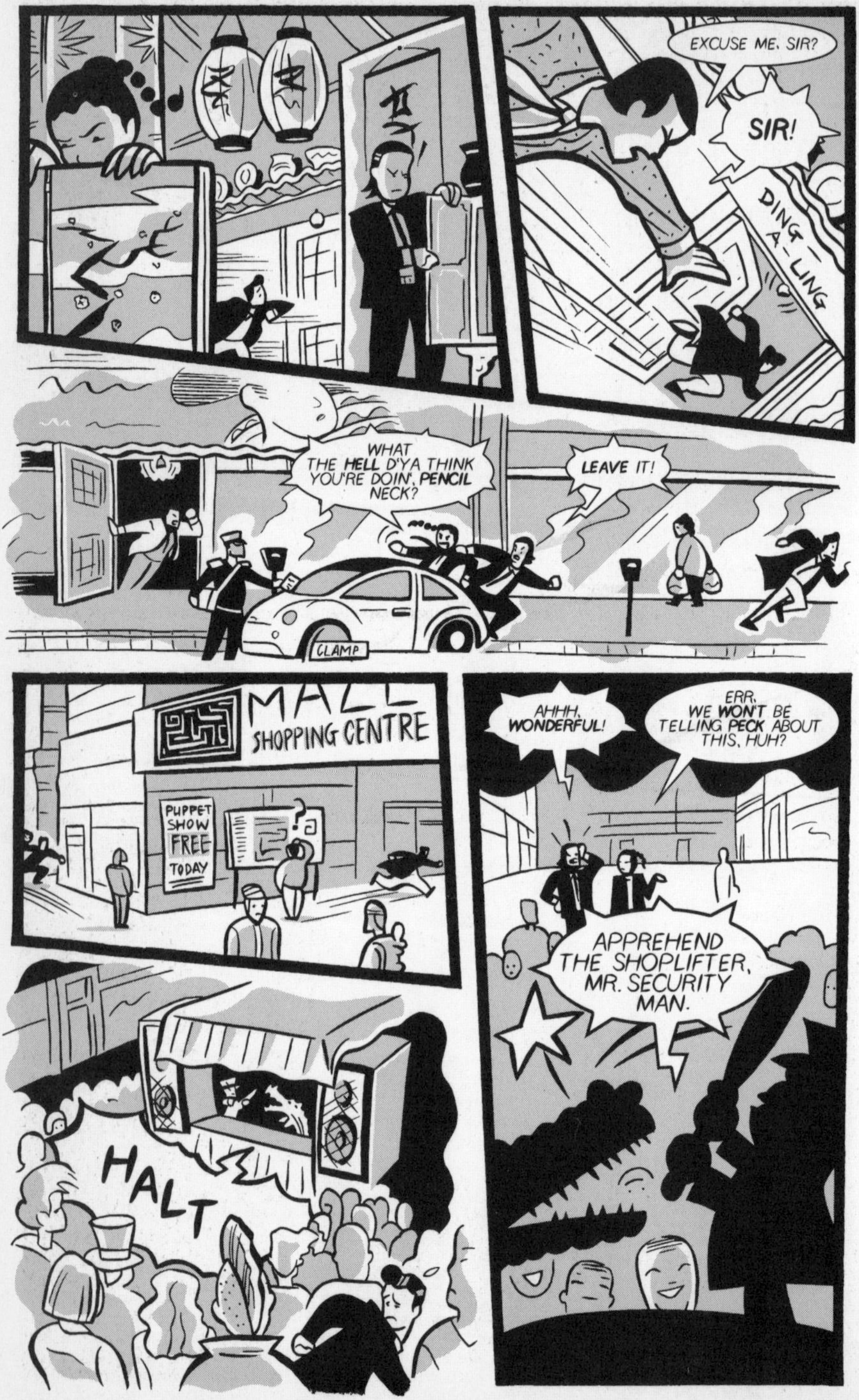
EXCUSE ME, SIR?
SIR!
DING A-LING
WHAT THE HELL D'YA THINK YOU'RE DOIN', PENCIL NECK?
LEAVE IT!
CLAMP
MALL
SHOPPING CENTRE
PUPPET SHOW FREE TODAY
AHHH, WONDERFUL!
ERR, WE WON'T BE TELLING PECK ABOUT THIS, HUH?
APPREHEND THE SHOPLIFTER, MR. SECURITY MAN.
HALT

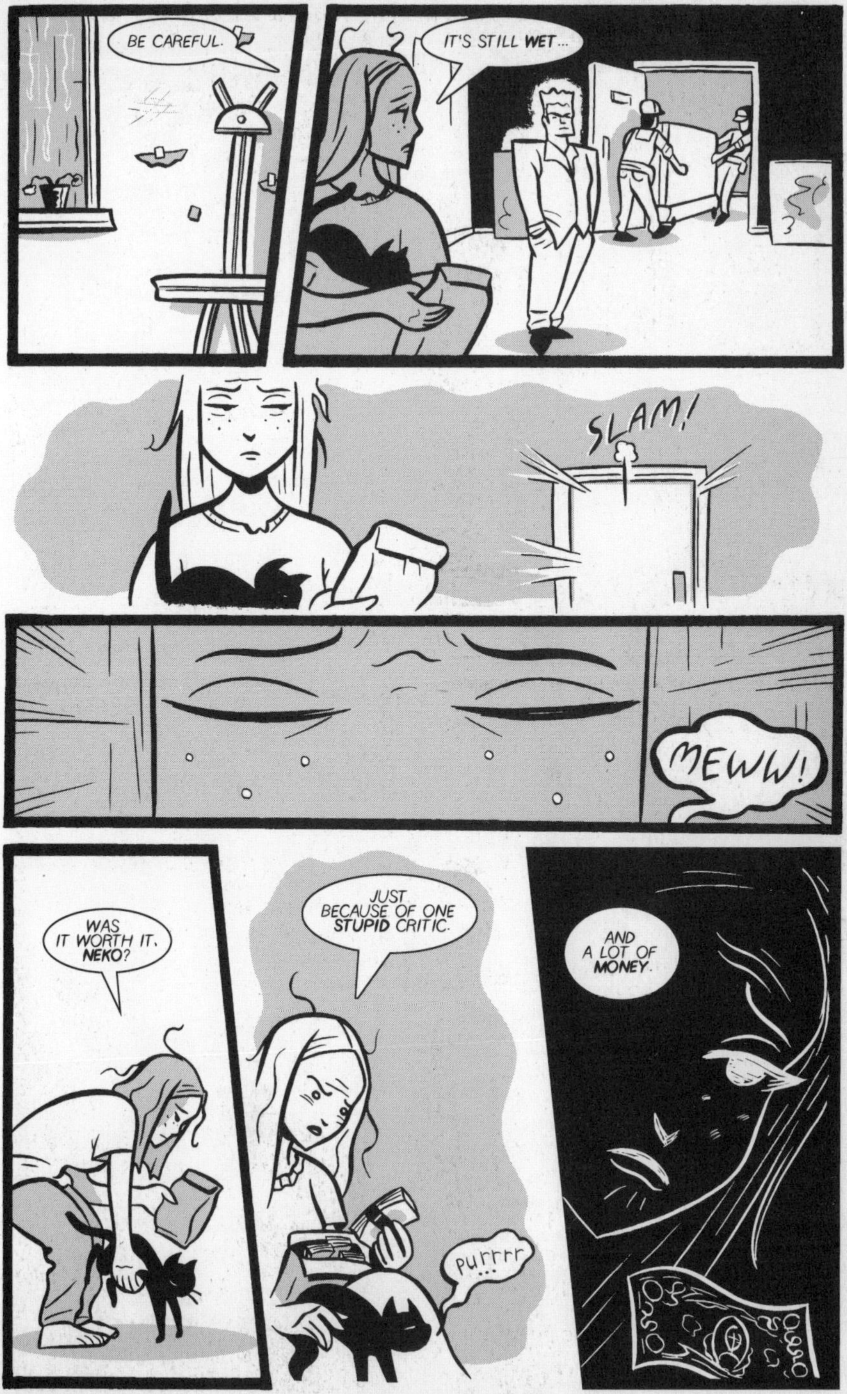

BE CAREFUL.
IT'S STILL WET...
SLAM!
MEWW!
WAS IT WORTH IT, NEKO?
JUST BECAUSE OF ONE STUPID CRITIC.
purrrr...
AND A LOT OF MONEY.

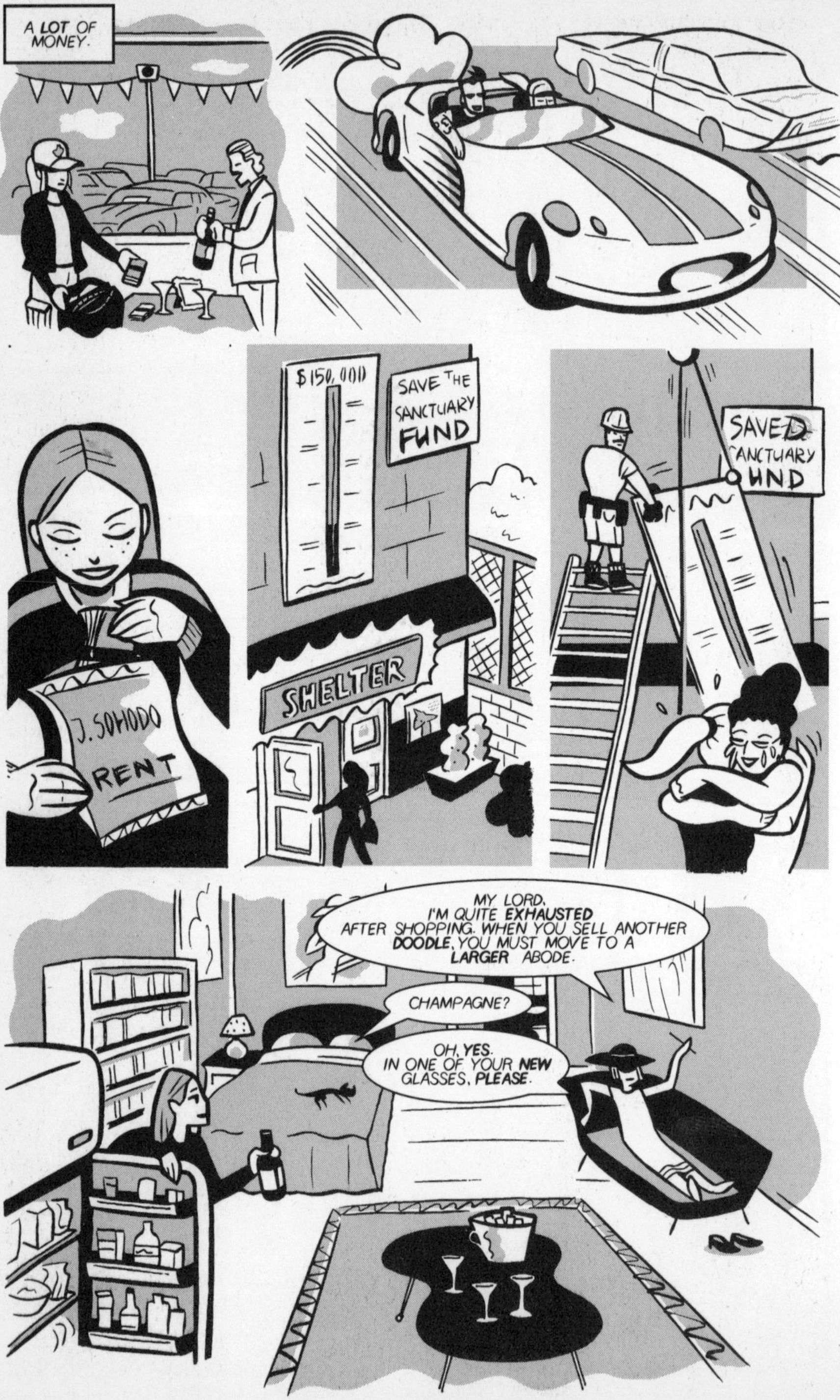
A LOT OF MONEY.
$150,000
SAVE THE SANCTUARY FUND
SHELTER
SAVED SANCTUARY UND
J. SOHODO
RENT
MY LORD, I'M QUITE EXHAUSTED AFTER SHOPPING. WHEN YOU SELL ANOTHER DOODLE, YOU MUST MOVE TO A LARGER ABODE.
CHAMPAGNE?
OH, YES. IN ONE OF YOUR NEW GLASSES, PLEASE.

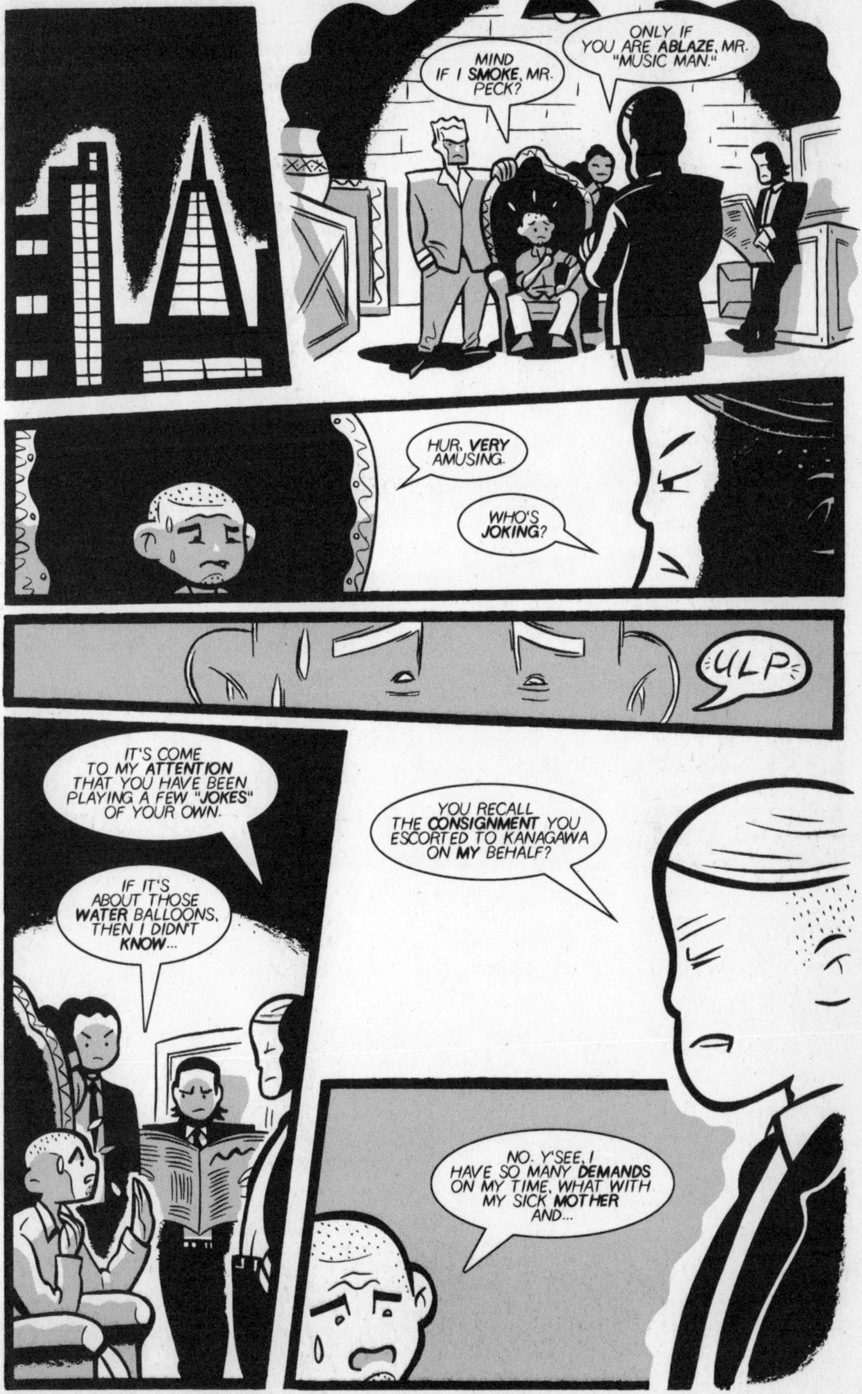
MIND IF I SMOKE, MR. PECK?
ONLY IF YOU ARE ABLAZE, MR. "MUSIC MAN."
HUR, VERY AMUSING.
WHO'S JOKING?
ULP
IT'S COME TO MY ATTENTION THAT YOU HAVE BEEN PLAYING A FEW "JOKES" OF YOUR OWN.
IF IT'S ABOUT THOSE WATER BALLOONS, THEN I DIDN'T KNOW...
YOU RECALL THE CONSIGNMENT YOU ESCORTED TO KANAGAWA ON MY BEHALF?
NO. Y'SEE, I HAVE SO MANY DEMANDS ON MY TIME, WHAT WITH MY SICK MOTHER AND...

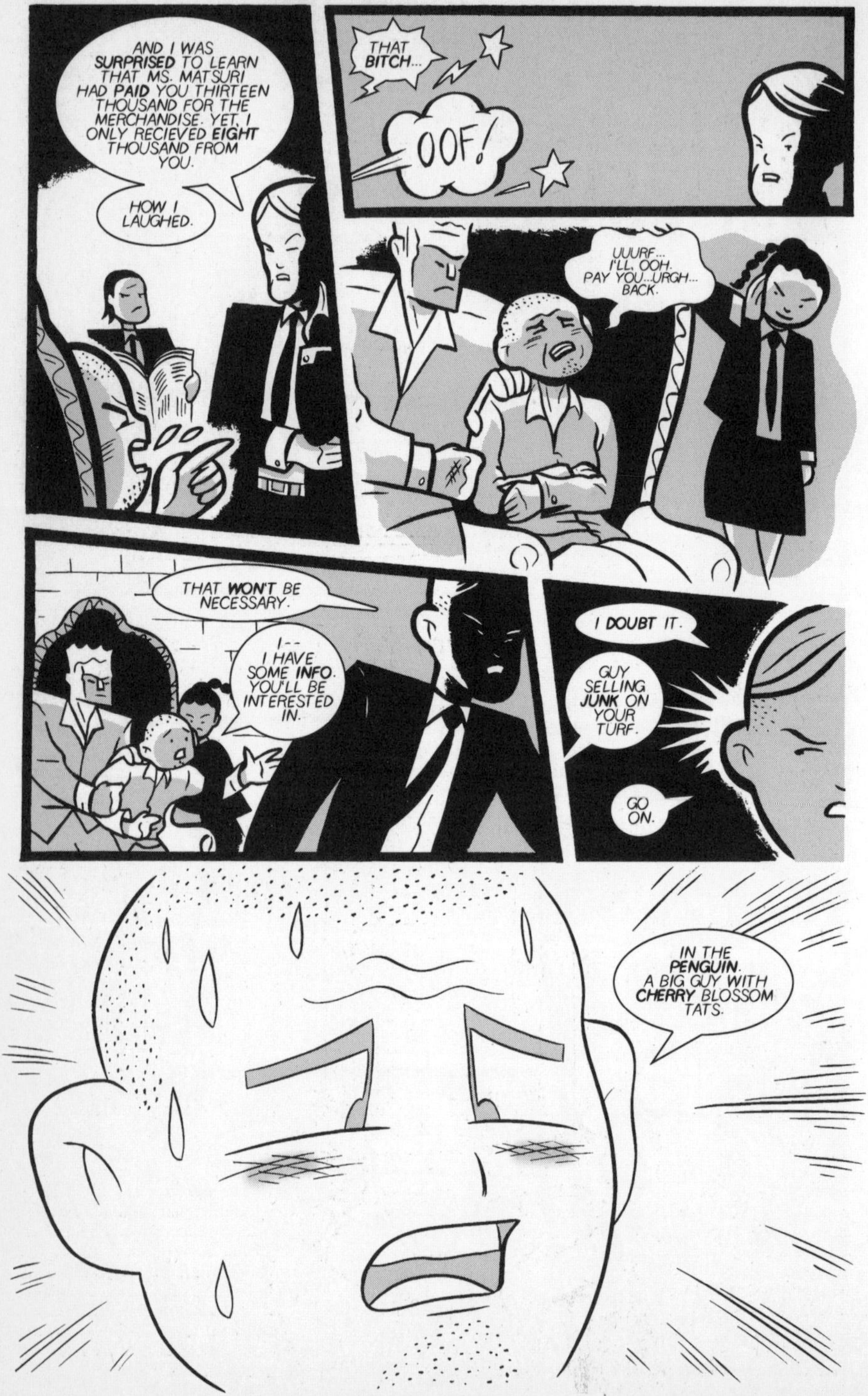
AND I WAS SURPRISED TO LEARN THAT MS. MATSURI HAD PAID YOU THIRTEEN THOUSAND FOR THE MERCHANDISE. YET, I ONLY RECIEVED EIGHT THOUSAND FROM YOU.
HOW I LAUGHED.
THAT BITCH...
OOF!
UUURF... I'LL, OOH. PAY YOU...URGH... BACK.
THAT WON'T BE NECESSARY.
I-- I HAVE SOME INFO. YOU'LL BE INTERESTED IN.
I DOUBT IT.
GUY SELLING JUNK ON YOUR TURF.
GO ON.
IN THE PENGUIN. A BIG GUY WITH CHERRY BLOSSOM TATS.

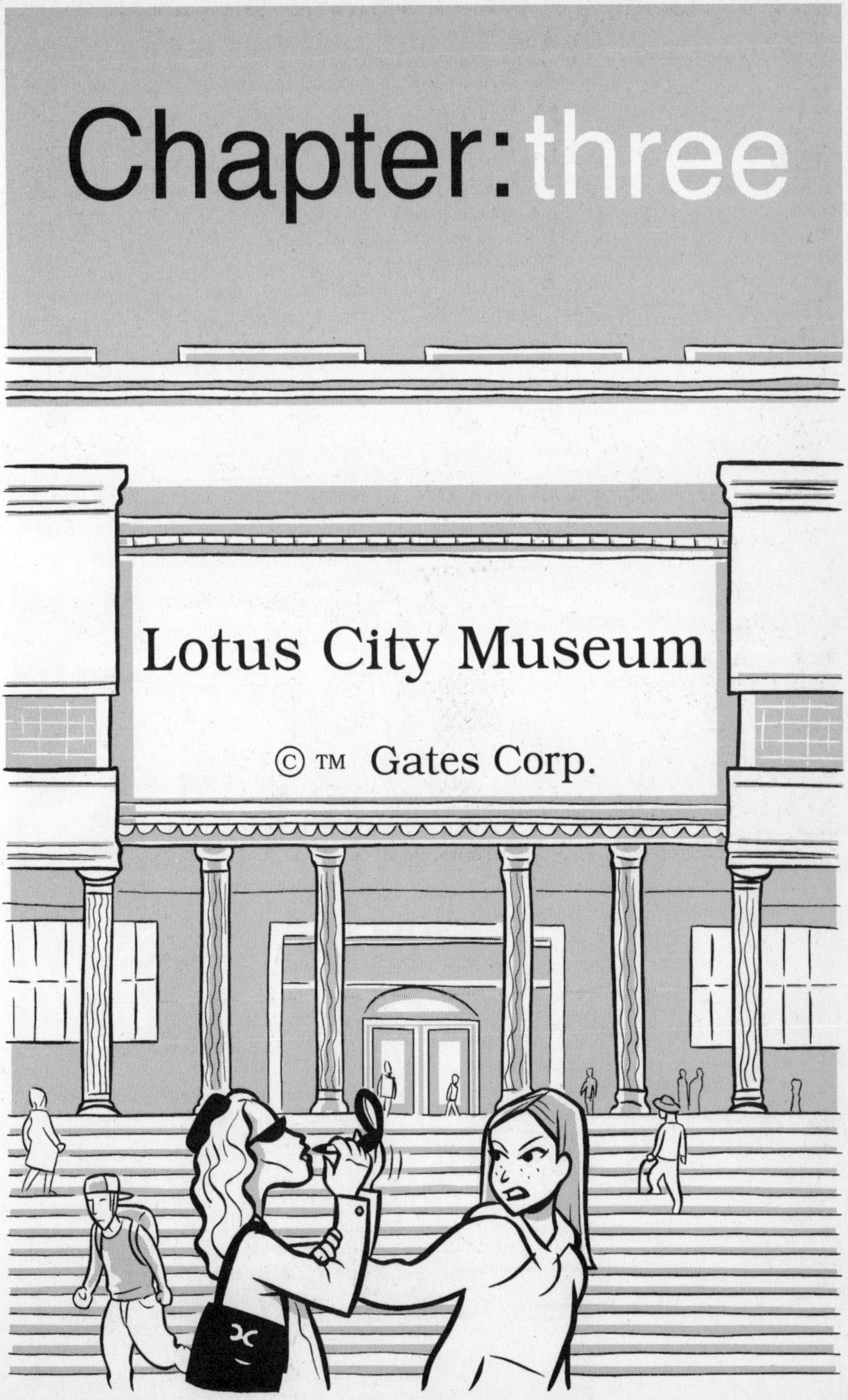
Chapter: three
Lotus City Museum
© ™ Gates Corp.

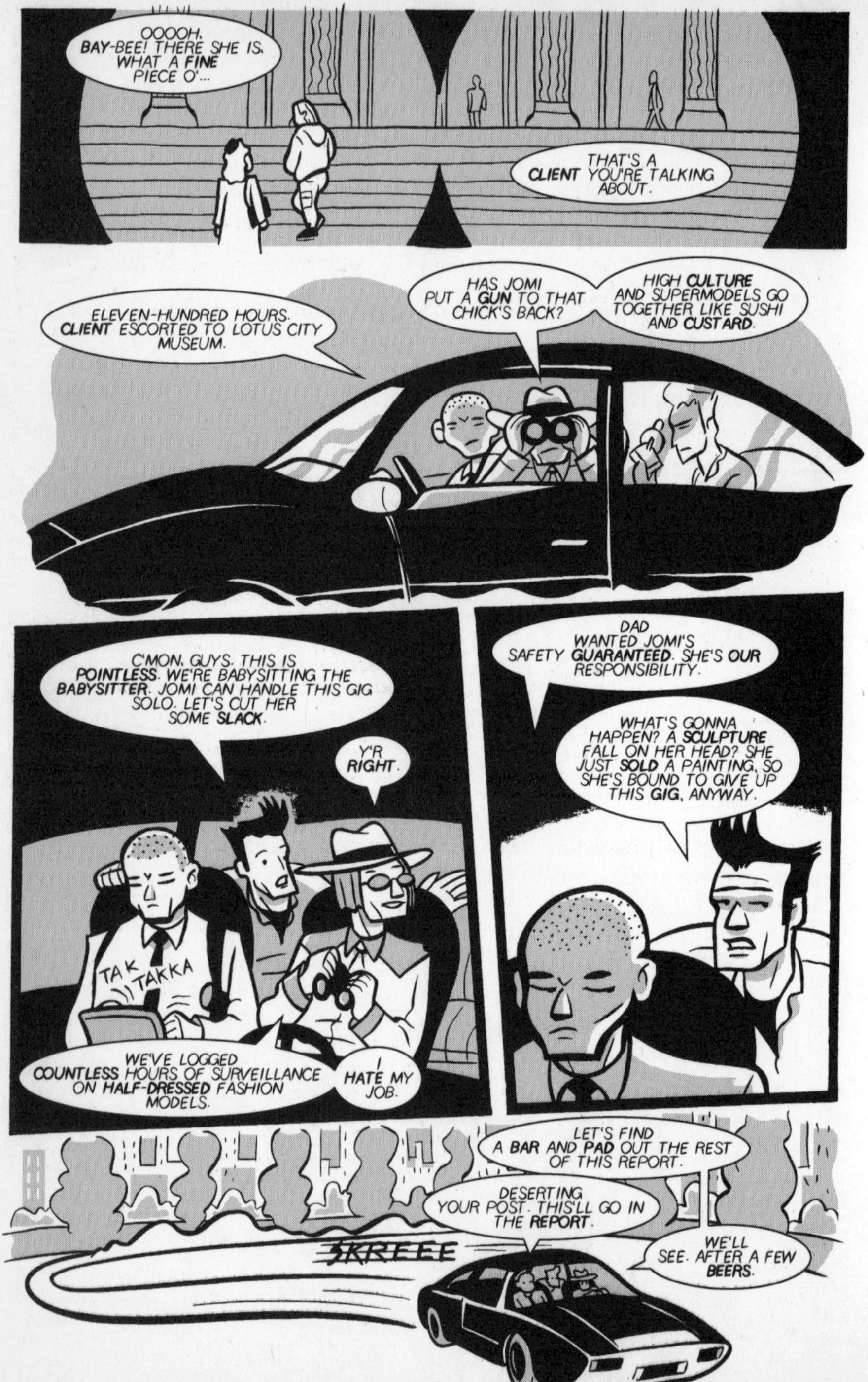
OOOOH, BAY-BEE! THERE SHE IS. WHAT A FINE PIECE O'...
THAT'S A CLIENT YOU'RE TALKING ABOUT.
ELEVEN-HUNDRED HOURS. CLIENT ESCORTED TO LOTUS CITY MUSEUM.
HAS JOMI PUT A GUN TO THAT CHICK'S BACK?
HIGH CULTURE AND SUPERMODELS GO TOGETHER LIKE SUSHI AND CUSTARD.
C'MON, GUYS. THIS IS POINTLESS. WE'RE BABYSITTING THE BABYSITTER. JOMI CAN HANDLE THIS GIG SOLO. LET'S CUT HER SOME SLACK.
Y'R RIGHT.
TAK TAKKA
WE'VE LOGGED COUNTLESS HOURS OF SURVEILLANCE ON HALF-DRESSED FASHION MODELS.
I HATE MY JOB.
DAD WANTED JOMI'S SAFETY GUARANTEED. SHE'S OUR RESPONSIBILITY.
WHAT'S GONNA HAPPEN? A SCULPTURE FALL ON HER HEAD? SHE JUST SOLD A PAINTING, SO SHE'S BOUND TO GIVE UP THIS GIG, ANYWAY.
LET'S FIND A BAR AND PAD OUT THE REST OF THIS REPORT.
DESERTING YOUR POST. THIS'LL GO IN THE REPORT.
SKREEEE
WE'LL SEE. AFTER A FEW BEERS.

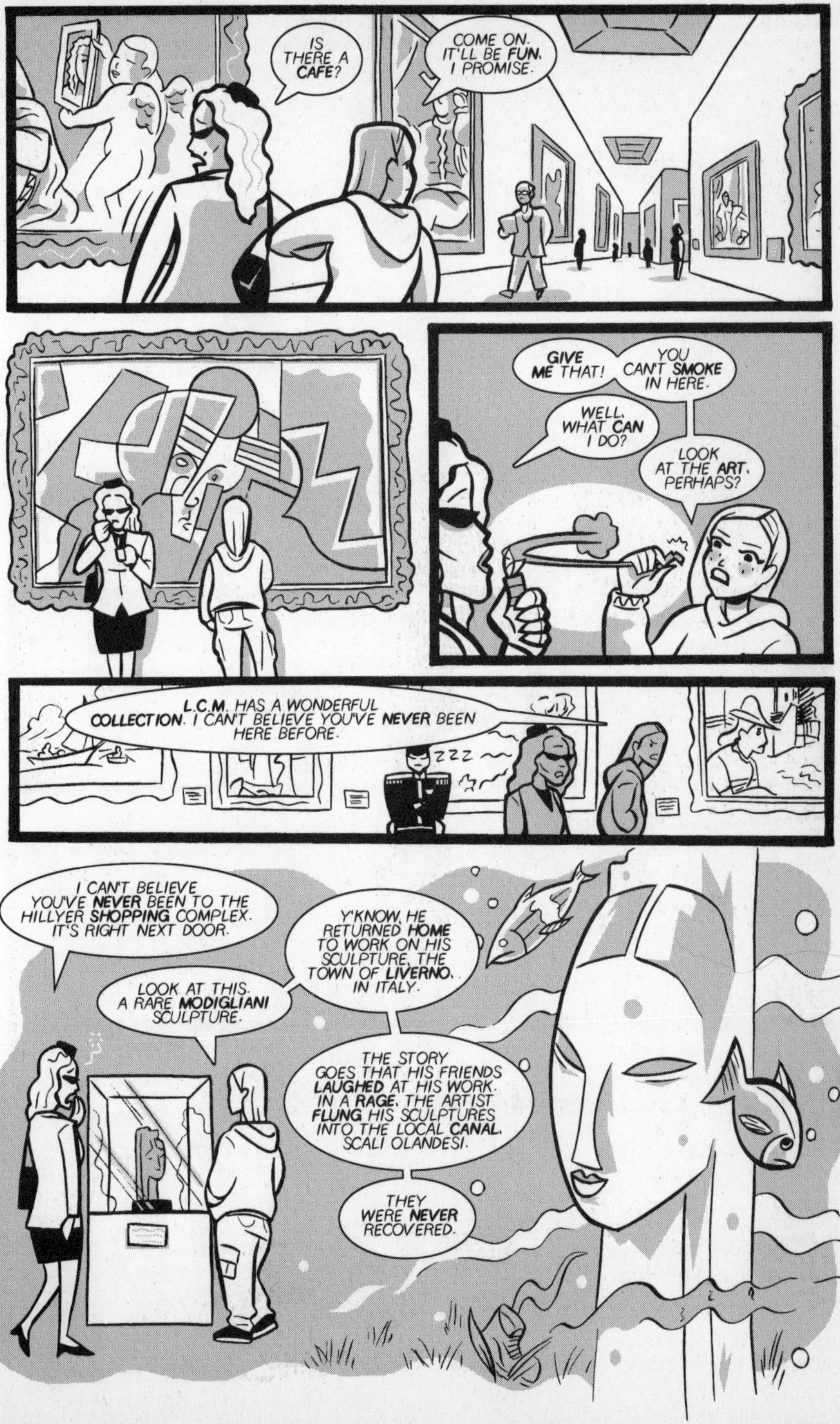
IS THERE A CAFE?
COME ON. IT'LL BE FUN. I PROMISE.
GIVE ME THAT!
YOU CAN'T SMOKE IN HERE.
WELL, WHAT CAN I DO?
LOOK AT THE ART, PERHAPS?
L.C.M. HAS A WONDERFUL COLLECTION. I CAN'T BELIEVE YOU'VE NEVER BEEN HERE BEFORE.
ZZZ
I CAN'T BELIEVE YOU'VE NEVER BEEN TO THE HILLYER SHOPPING COMPLEX. IT'S RIGHT NEXT DOOR.
LOOK AT THIS. A RARE MODIGLIANI SCULPTURE.
Y'KNOW, HE RETURNED HOME TO WORK ON HIS SCULPTURE, THE TOWN OF LIVERNO, IN ITALY.
THE STORY GOES THAT HIS FRIENDS LAUGHED AT HIS WORK. IN A RAGE, THE ARTIST FLUNG HIS SCULPTURES INTO THE LOCAL CANAL, SCALI OLANDESI.
THEY WERE NEVER RECOVERED.

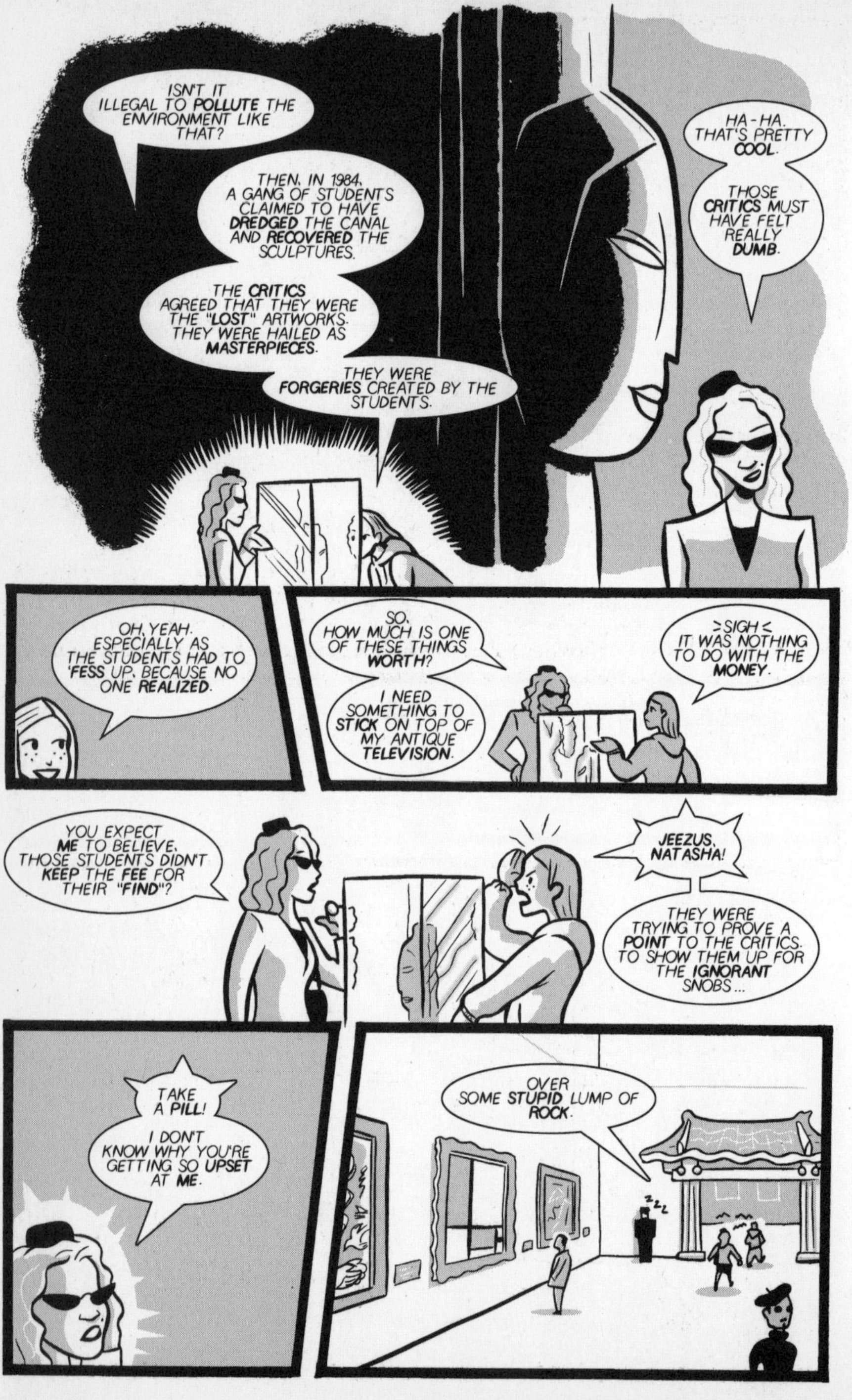

ISN'T IT ILLEGAL TO POLLUTE THE ENVIRONMENT LIKE THAT?
THEN, IN 1984, A GANG OF STUDENTS CLAIMED TO HAVE DREDGED THE CANAL AND RECOVERED THE SCULPTURES.
THE CRITICS AGREED THAT THEY WERE THE "LOST" ARTWORKS. THEY WERE HAILED AS MASTERPIECES.
THEY WERE FORGERIES CREATED BY THE STUDENTS.
HA-HA. THAT'S PRETTY COOL.
THOSE CRITICS MUST HAVE FELT REALLY DUMB.
OH, YEAH. ESPECIALLY AS THE STUDENTS HAD TO 'FESS UP, BECAUSE NO ONE REALIZED.
SO, HOW MUCH IS ONE OF THESE THINGS WORTH?
I NEED SOMETHING TO STICK ON TOP OF MY ANTIQUE TELEVISION.
>SIGH< IT WAS NOTHING TO DO WITH THE MONEY.
YOU EXPECT ME TO BELIEVE, THOSE STUDENTS DIDN'T KEEP THE FEE FOR THEIR "FIND"?
JEEZUS, NATASHA!
THEY WERE TRYING TO PROVE A POINT TO THE CRITICS. TO SHOW THEM UP FOR THE IGNORANT SNOBS...
TAKE A PILL!
I DON'T KNOW WHY YOU'RE GETTING SO UPSET AT ME.
OVER SOME STUPID LUMP OF ROCK.

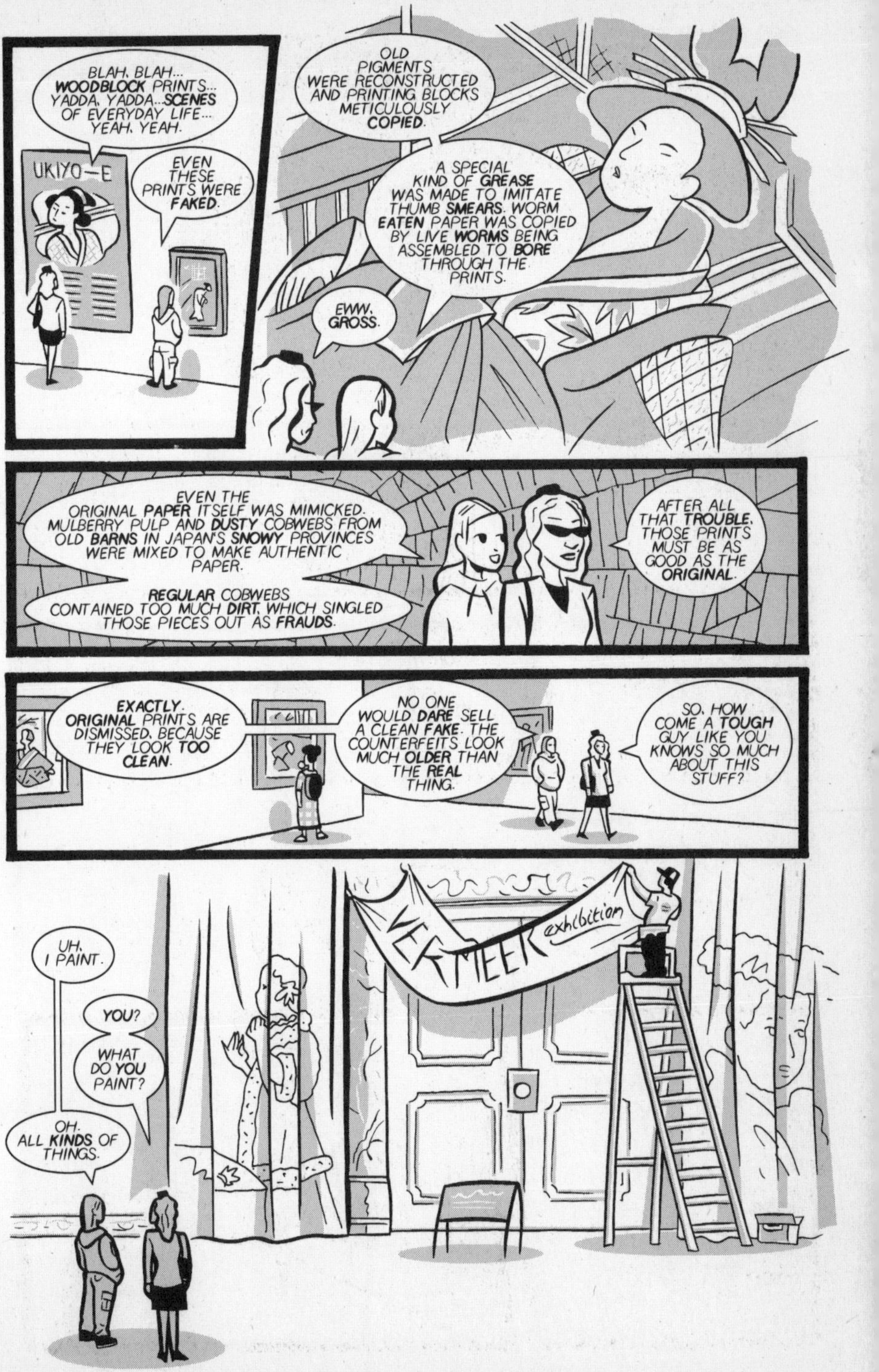

BLAH, BLAH... WOODBLOCK PRINTS... YADDA, YADDA...SCENES OF EVERYDAY LIFE... YEAH, YEAH.
UKIYO—E
EVEN THESE PRINTS WERE FAKED.
OLD PIGMENTS WERE RECONSTRUCTED AND PRINTING BLOCKS METICULOUSLY COPIED.
A SPECIAL KIND OF GREASE WAS MADE TO IMITATE THUMB SMEARS. WORM EATEN PAPER WAS COPIED BY LIVE WORMS BEING ASSEMBLED TO BORE THROUGH THE PRINTS.
EWW, GROSS.
EVEN THE ORIGINAL PAPER ITSELF WAS MIMICKED. MULBERRY PULP AND DUSTY COBWEBS FROM OLD BARNS IN JAPAN'S SNOWY PROVINCES WERE MIXED TO MAKE AUTHENTIC PAPER.
REGULAR COBWEBS CONTAINED TOO MUCH DIRT, WHICH SINGLED THOSE PIECES OUT AS FRAUDS.
AFTER ALL THAT TROUBLE, THOSE PRINTS MUST BE AS GOOD AS THE ORIGINAL.
EXACTLY. ORIGINAL PRINTS ARE DISMISSED, BECAUSE THEY LOOK TOO CLEAN.
NO ONE WOULD DARE SELL A CLEAN FAKE. THE COUNTERFEITS LOOK MUCH OLDER THAN THE REAL THING.
SO, HOW COME A TOUGH GUY LIKE YOU KNOWS SO MUCH ABOUT THIS STUFF?
VERMEER exhibition
UH, I PAINT.
YOU?
WHAT DO YOU PAINT?
OH. ALL KINDS OF THINGS.

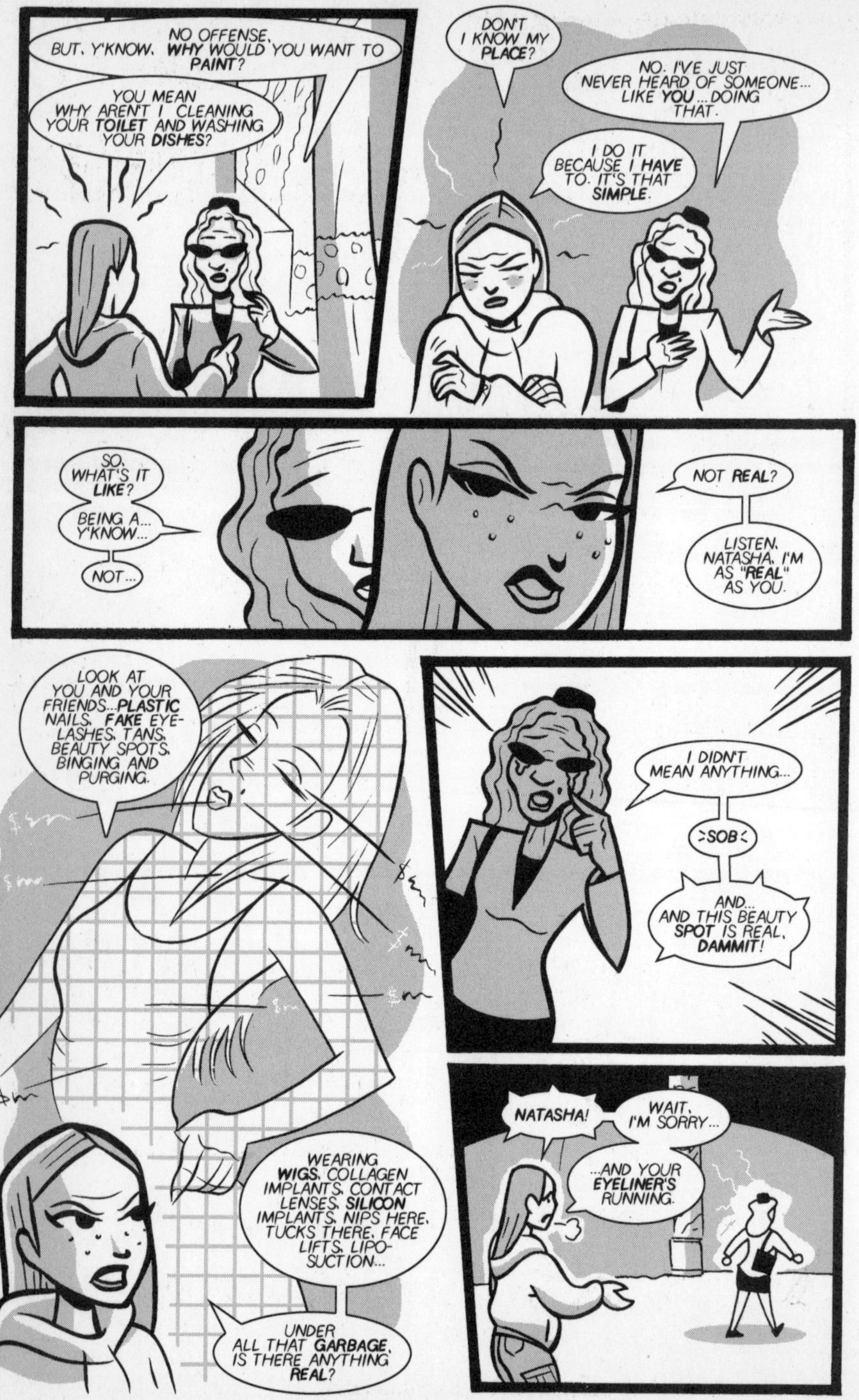
NO OFFENSE, BUT, Y'KNOW, WHY WOULD YOU WANT TO PAINT?
YOU MEAN WHY AREN'T I CLEANING YOUR TOILET AND WASHING YOUR DISHES?
DON'T I KNOW MY PLACE?
NO. I'VE JUST NEVER HEARD OF SOMEONE... LIKE YOU... DOING THAT.
I DO IT BECAUSE I HAVE TO. IT'S THAT SIMPLE.
SO, WHAT'S IT LIKE?
BEING A... Y'KNOW...
NOT...
NOT REAL?
LISTEN, NATASHA, I'M AS "REAL" AS YOU.
LOOK AT YOU AND YOUR FRIENDS...PLASTIC NAILS, FAKE EYE-LASHES, TANS, BEAUTY SPOTS, BINGING AND PURGING.
WEARING WIGS, COLLAGEN IMPLANTS, CONTACT LENSES, SILICON IMPLANTS, NIPS HERE, TUCKS THERE, FACE LIFTS, LIPO-SUCTION...
UNDER ALL THAT GARBAGE, IS THERE ANYTHING REAL?
I DIDN'T MEAN ANYTHING...
>SOB<
AND... AND THIS BEAUTY SPOT IS REAL, DAMMIT!
NATASHA!
WAIT, I'M SORRY...
...AND YOUR EYELINER'S RUNNING.

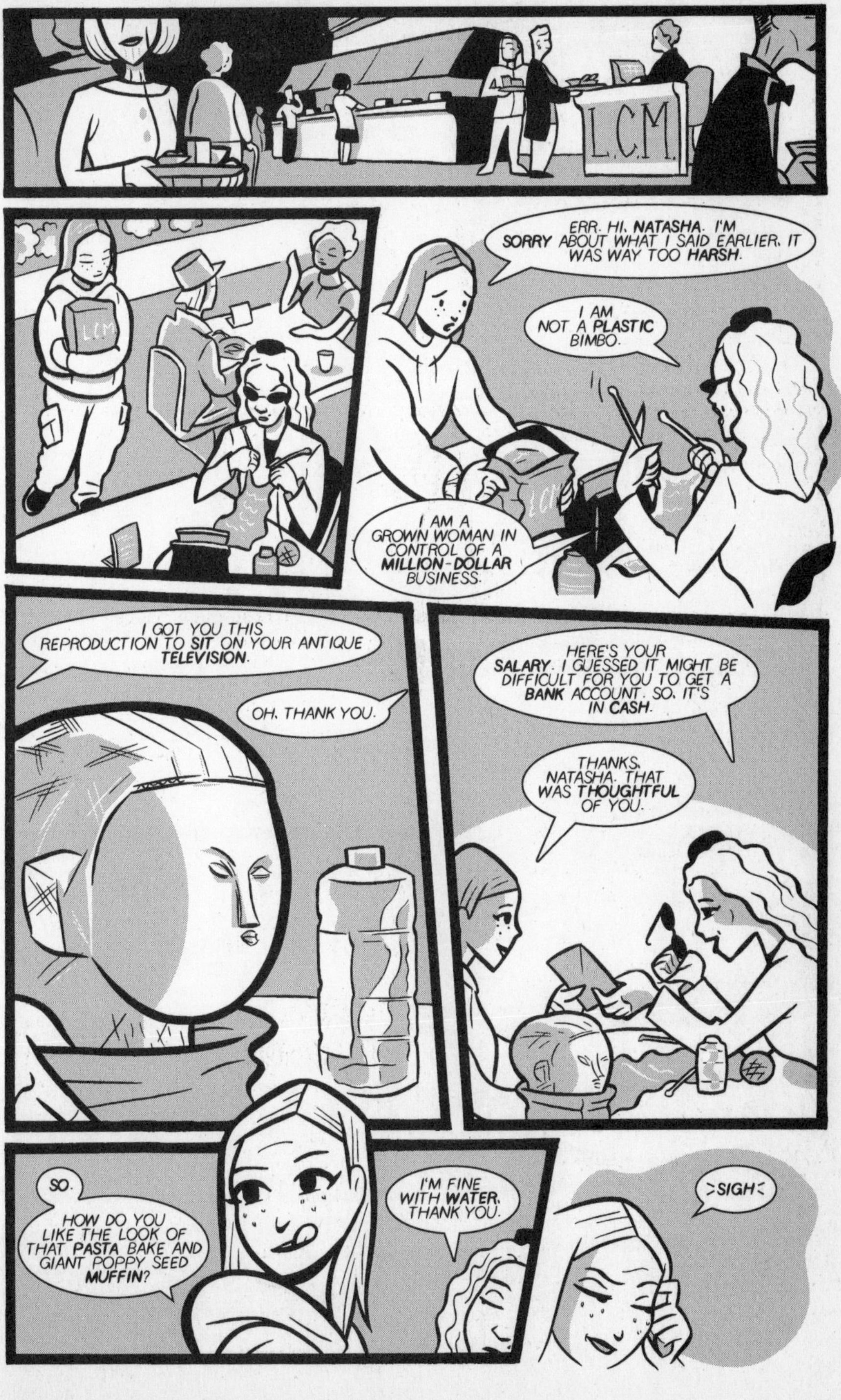
L.C.M.
ERR. HI. NATASHA. I'M SORRY ABOUT WHAT I SAID EARLIER. IT WAS WAY TOO HARSH.
I AM NOT A PLASTIC BIMBO.
I AM A GROWN WOMAN IN CONTROL OF A MILLION-DOLLAR BUSINESS.
I GOT YOU THIS REPRODUCTION TO SIT ON YOUR ANTIQUE TELEVISION.
OH. THANK YOU.
HERE'S YOUR SALARY. I GUESSED IT MIGHT BE DIFFICULT FOR YOU TO GET A BANK ACCOUNT. SO, IT'S IN CASH.
THANKS, NATASHA. THAT WAS THOUGHTFUL OF YOU.
SO.
HOW DO YOU LIKE THE LOOK OF THAT PASTA BAKE AND GIANT POPPY SEED MUFFIN?
I'M FINE WITH WATER. THANK YOU.
>SIGH<

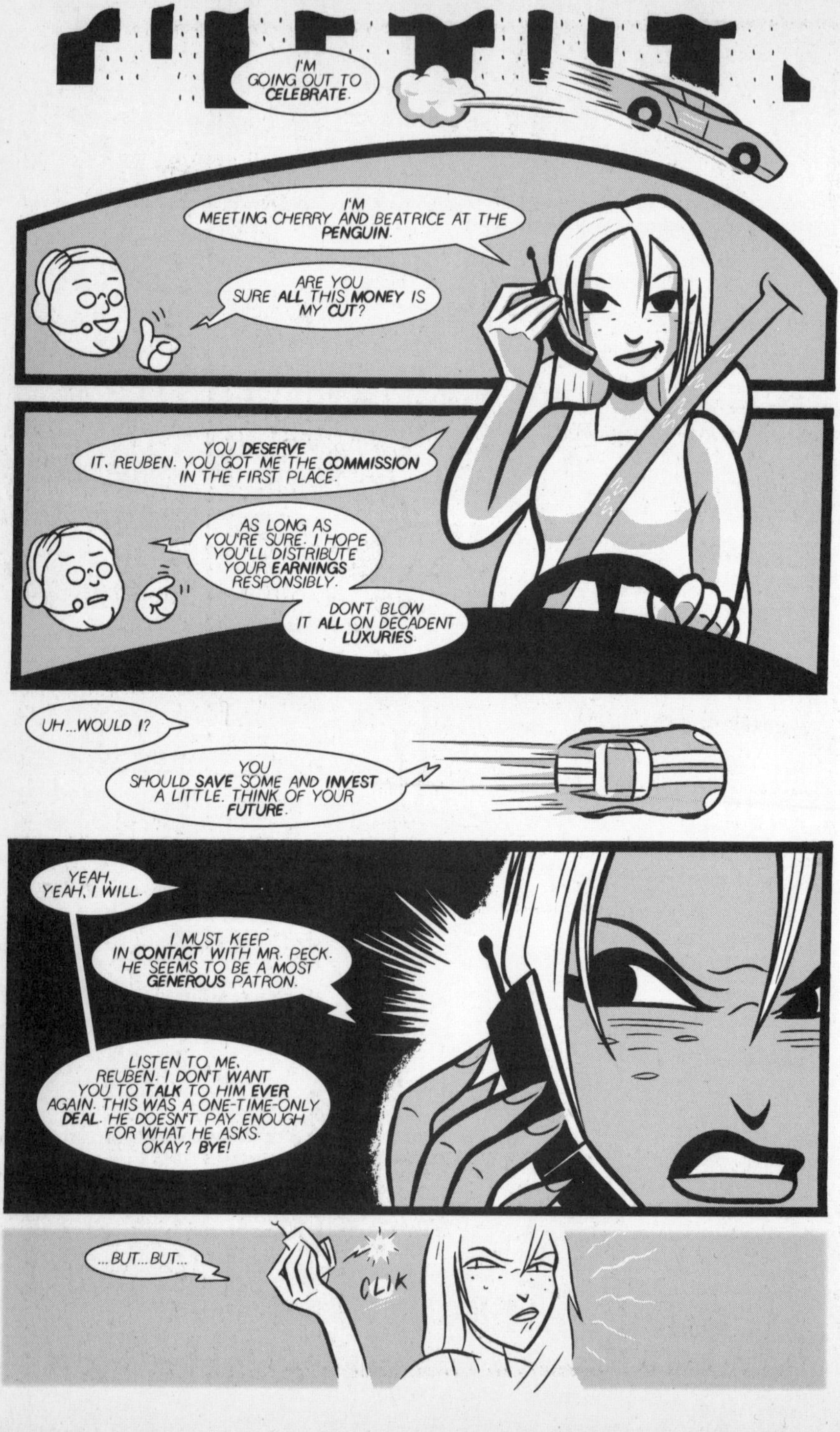
I'M GOING OUT TO CELEBRATE.
I'M MEETING CHERRY AND BEATRICE AT THE PENGUIN.
ARE YOU SURE ALL THIS MONEY IS MY CUT?
YOU DESERVE IT, REUBEN. YOU GOT ME THE COMMISSION IN THE FIRST PLACE.
AS LONG AS YOU'RE SURE. I HOPE YOU'LL DISTRIBUTE YOUR EARNINGS RESPONSIBLY.
DON'T BLOW IT ALL ON DECADENT LUXURIES.
UH...WOULD I?
YOU SHOULD SAVE SOME AND INVEST A LITTLE. THINK OF YOUR FUTURE.
YEAH, YEAH, I WILL.
I MUST KEEP IN CONTACT WITH MR. PECK. HE SEEMS TO BE A MOST GENEROUS PATRON.
LISTEN TO ME, REUBEN. I DON'T WANT YOU TO TALK TO HIM EVER AGAIN. THIS WAS A ONE-TIME-ONLY DEAL. HE DOESN'T PAY ENOUGH FOR WHAT HE ASKS. OKAY? BYE!
...BUT...BUT...
CLIK

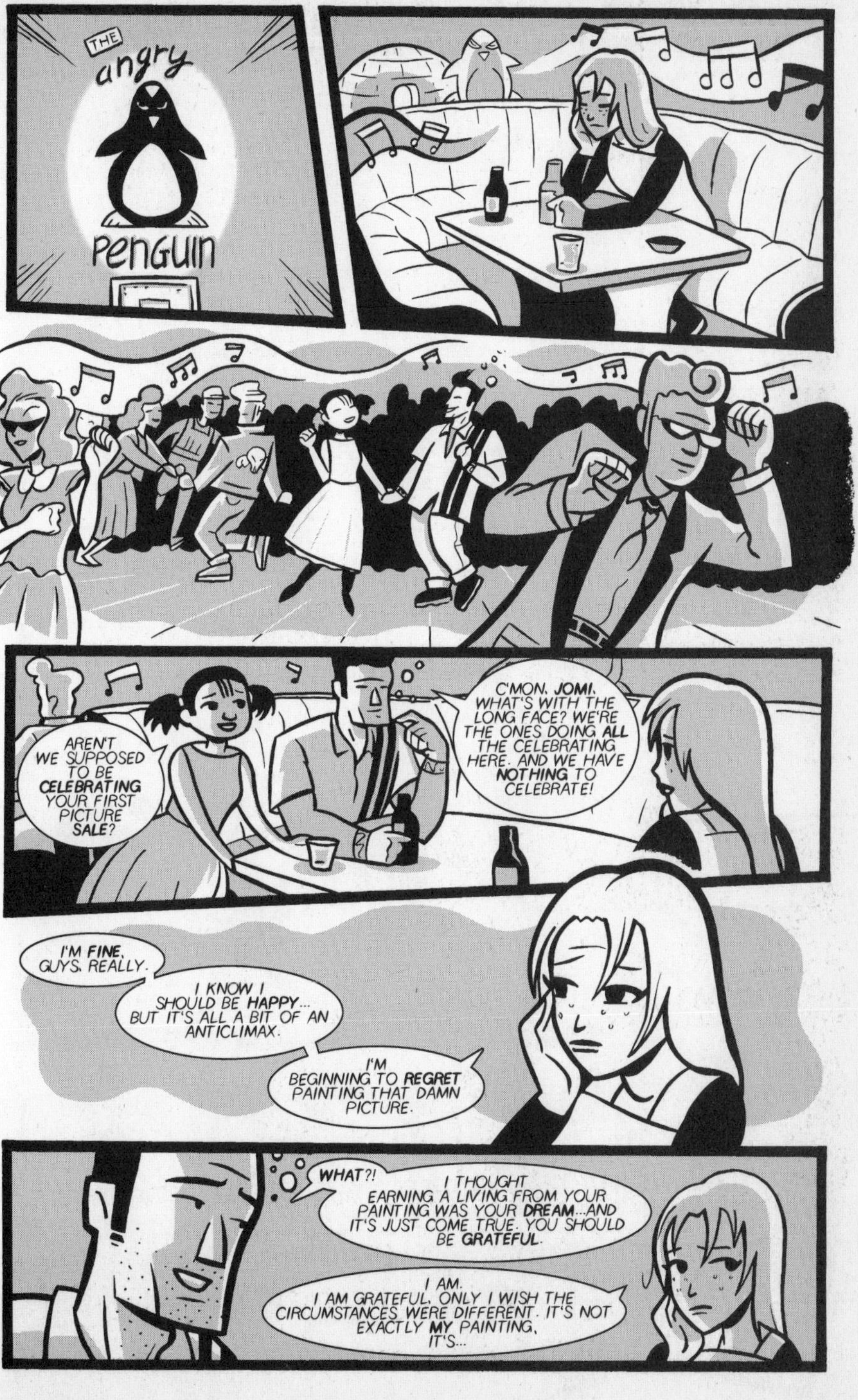
THE angry Penguin
AREN'T WE SUPPOSED TO BE CELEBRATING YOUR FIRST PICTURE SALE?
C'MON, JOMI, WHAT'S WITH THE LONG FACE? WE'RE THE ONES DOING ALL THE CELEBRATING HERE. AND WE HAVE NOTHING TO CELEBRATE!
I'M FINE, GUYS, REALLY.
I KNOW I SHOULD BE HAPPY... BUT IT'S ALL A BIT OF AN ANTICLIMAX.
I'M BEGINNING TO REGRET PAINTING THAT DAMN PICTURE.
WHAT?!
I THOUGHT EARNING A LIVING FROM YOUR PAINTING WAS YOUR DREAM...AND IT'S JUST COME TRUE. YOU SHOULD BE GRATEFUL.
I AM. I AM GRATEFUL, ONLY I WISH THE CIRCUMSTANCES WERE DIFFERENT. IT'S NOT EXACTLY MY PAINTING, IT'S...

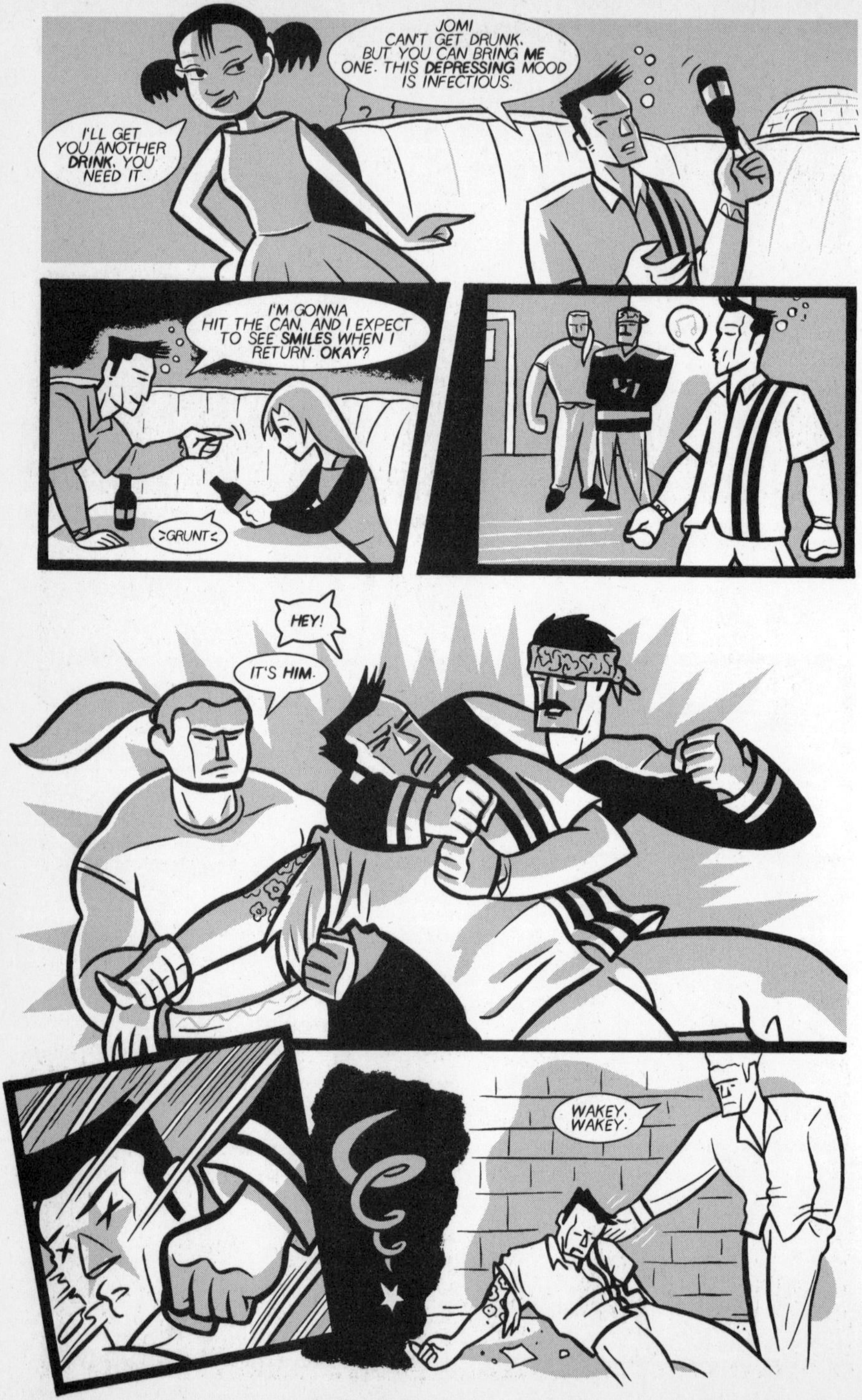
I'LL GET YOU ANOTHER DRINK. YOU NEED IT.
JOMI CAN'T GET DRUNK, BUT YOU CAN BRING ME ONE. THIS DEPRESSING MOOD IS INFECTIOUS.
I'M GONNA HIT THE CAN, AND I EXPECT TO SEE SMILES WHEN I RETURN. OKAY?
GRUNT
HEY!
IT'S HIM.
WAKEY, WAKEY.

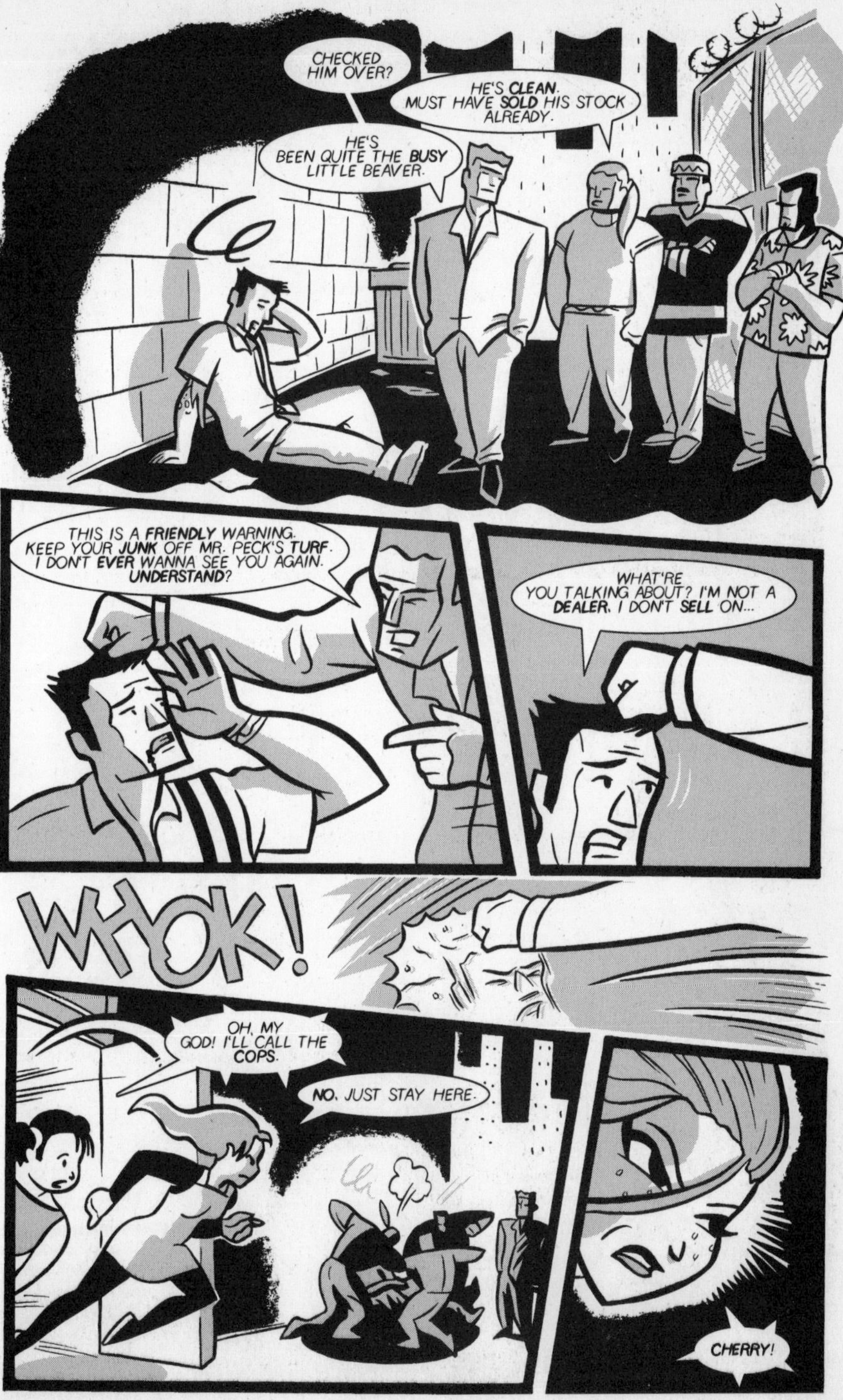
CHECKED HIM OVER?
HE'S CLEAN. MUST HAVE SOLD HIS STOCK ALREADY.
HE'S BEEN QUITE THE BUSY LITTLE BEAVER.
THIS IS A FRIENDLY WARNING. KEEP YOUR JUNK OFF MR. PECK'S TURF. I DON'T EVER WANNA SEE YOU AGAIN. UNDERSTAND?
WHAT'RE YOU TALKING ABOUT? I'M NOT A DEALER. I DON'T SELL ON...
WHOK!
OH, MY GOD! I'LL CALL THE COPS.
NO. JUST STAY HERE.
CHERRY!

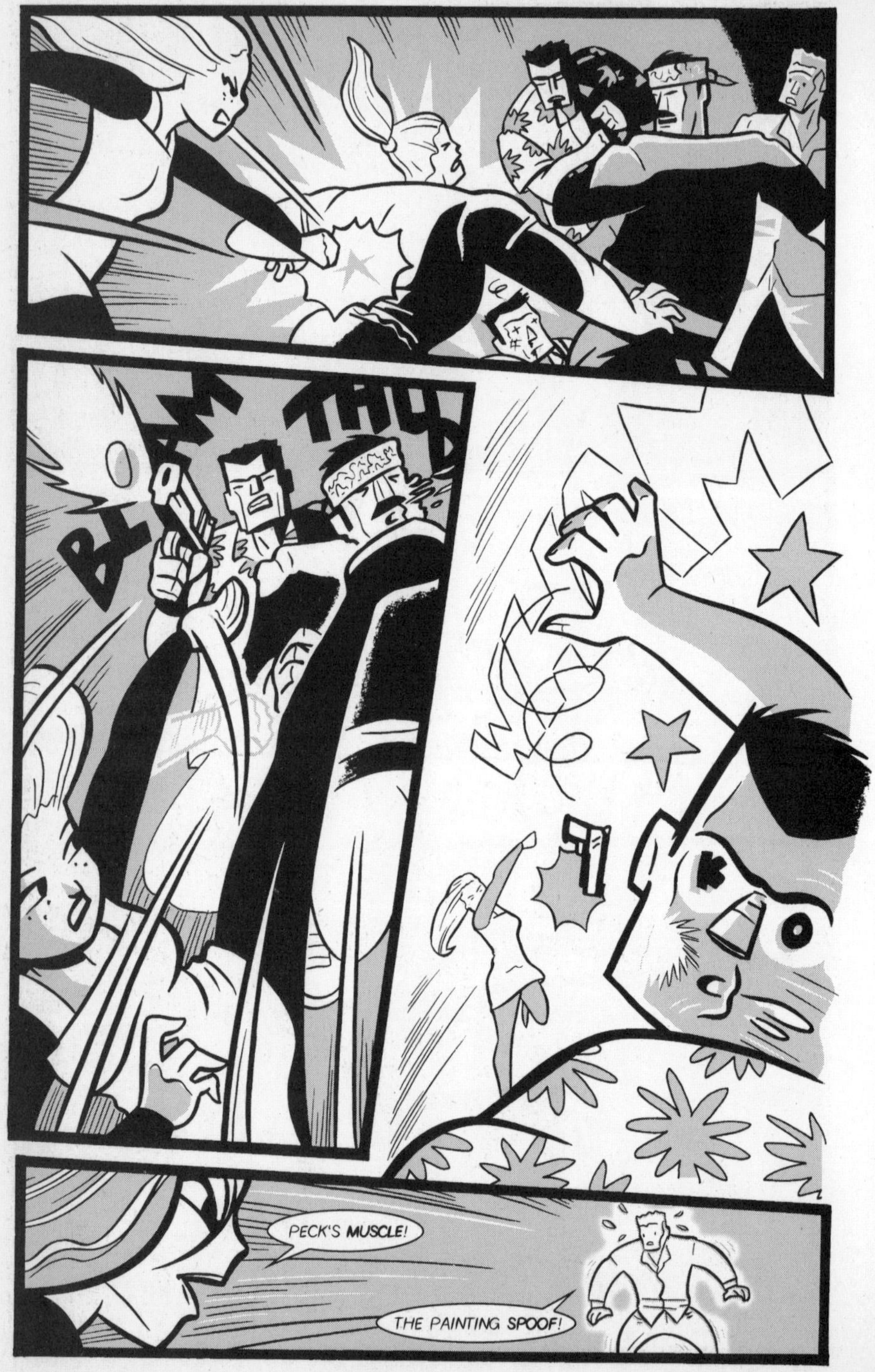
BLAM
THUD
PECK'S MUSCLE!
THE PAINTING SPOOF!

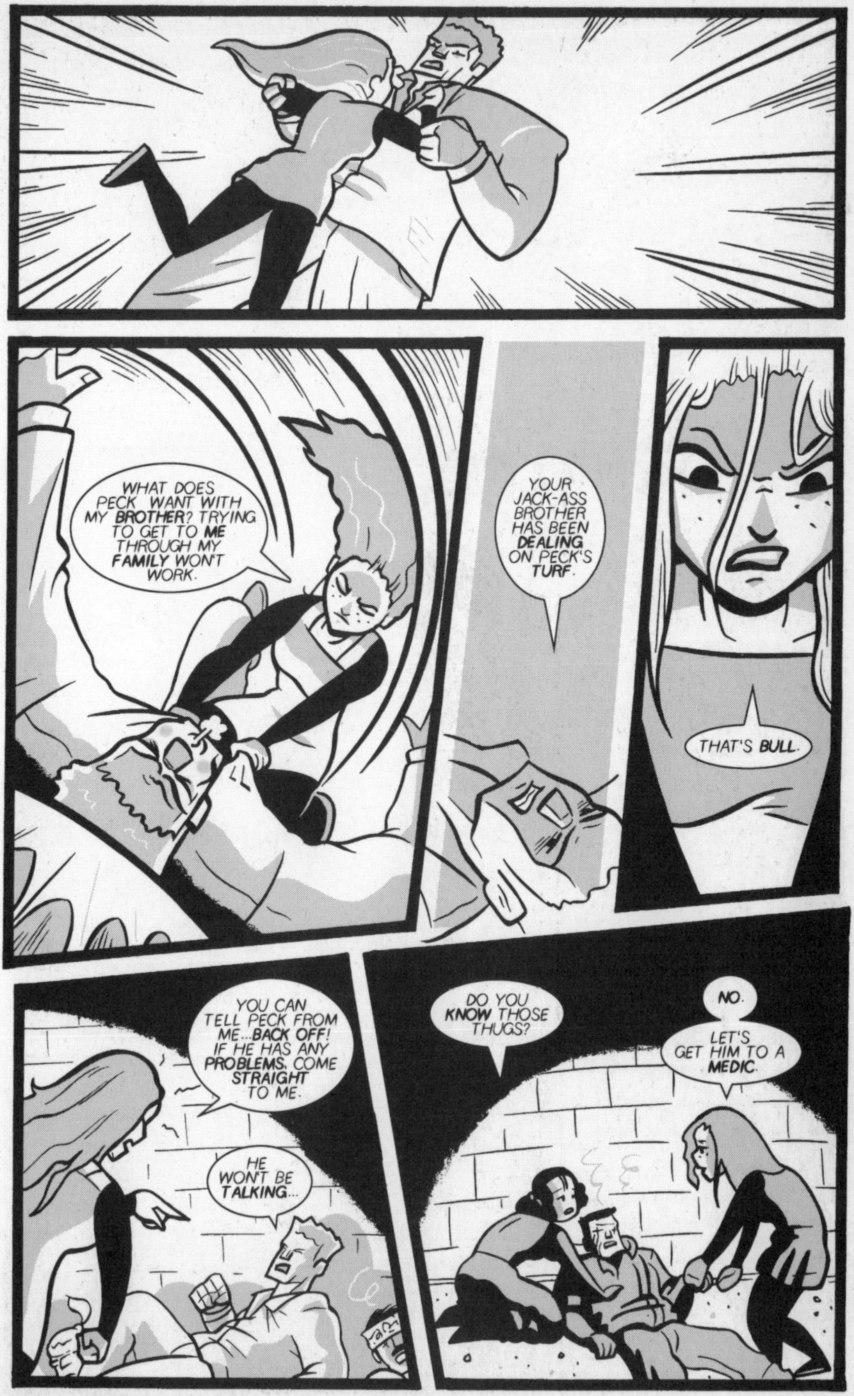
WHAT DOES PECK WANT WITH MY BROTHER? TRYING TO GET TO ME THROUGH MY FAMILY WON'T WORK.
YOUR JACK-ASS BROTHER HAS BEEN DEALING ON PECK'S TURF.
THAT'S BULL.
YOU CAN TELL PECK FROM ME...BACK OFF! IF HE HAS ANY PROBLEMS, COME STRAIGHT TO ME.
HE WON'T BE TALKING...
DO YOU KNOW THOSE THUGS?
NO.
LET'S GET HIM TO A MEDIC.

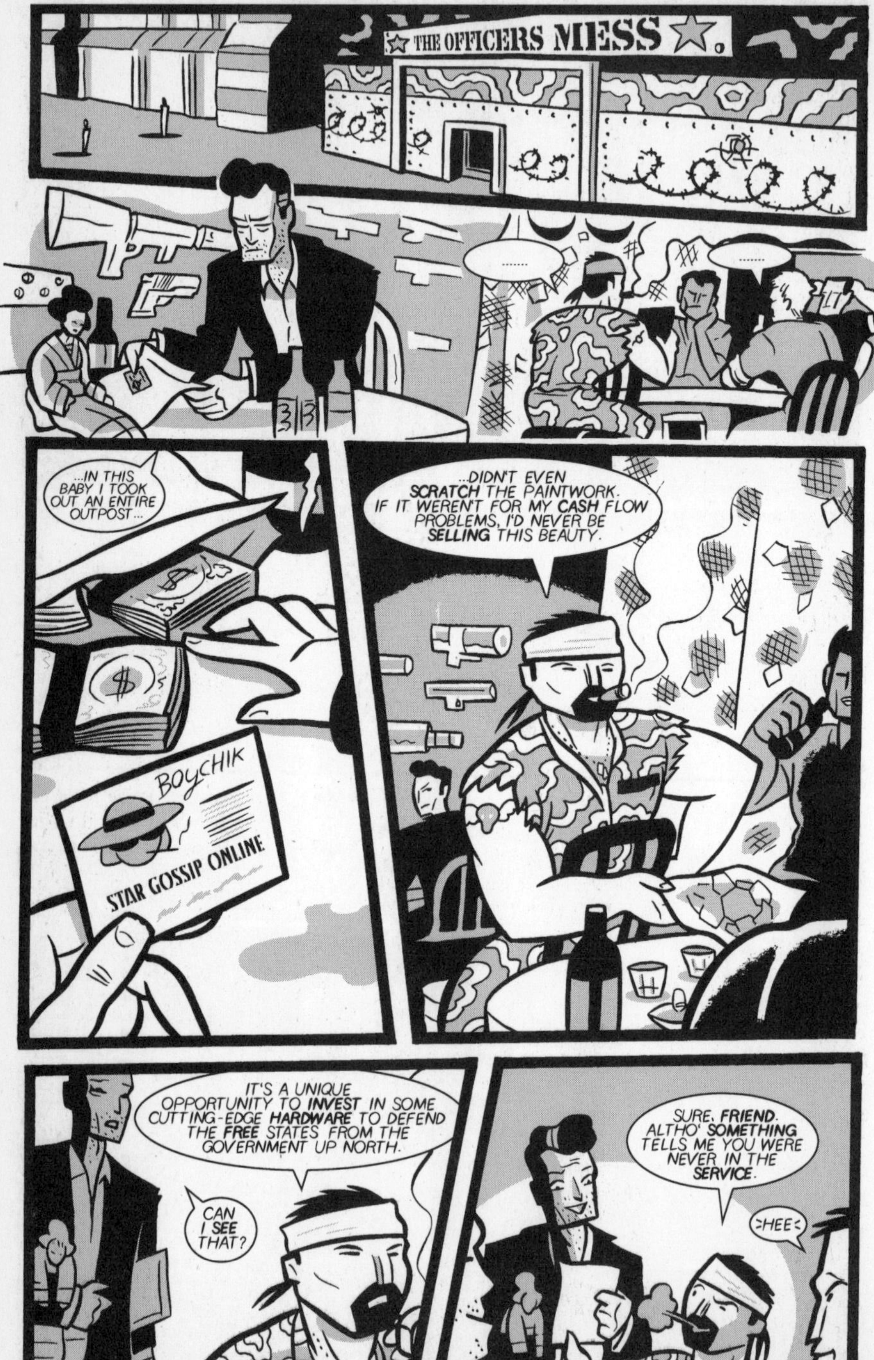
THE OFFICERS MESS
......
......
...IN THIS BABY I TOOK OUT AN ENTIRE OUTPOST...
...DIDN'T EVEN SCRATCH THE PAINTWORK. IF IT WEREN'T FOR MY CASH FLOW PROBLEMS, I'D NEVER BE SELLING THIS BEAUTY.
BOYCHIK
STAR GOSSIP ONLINE
IT'S A UNIQUE OPPORTUNITY TO INVEST IN SOME CUTTING-EDGE HARDWARE TO DEFEND THE FREE STATES FROM THE GOVERNMENT UP NORTH.
CAN I SEE THAT?
SURE, FRIEND. ALTHO' SOMETHING TELLS ME YOU WERE NEVER IN THE SERVICE.
HEE

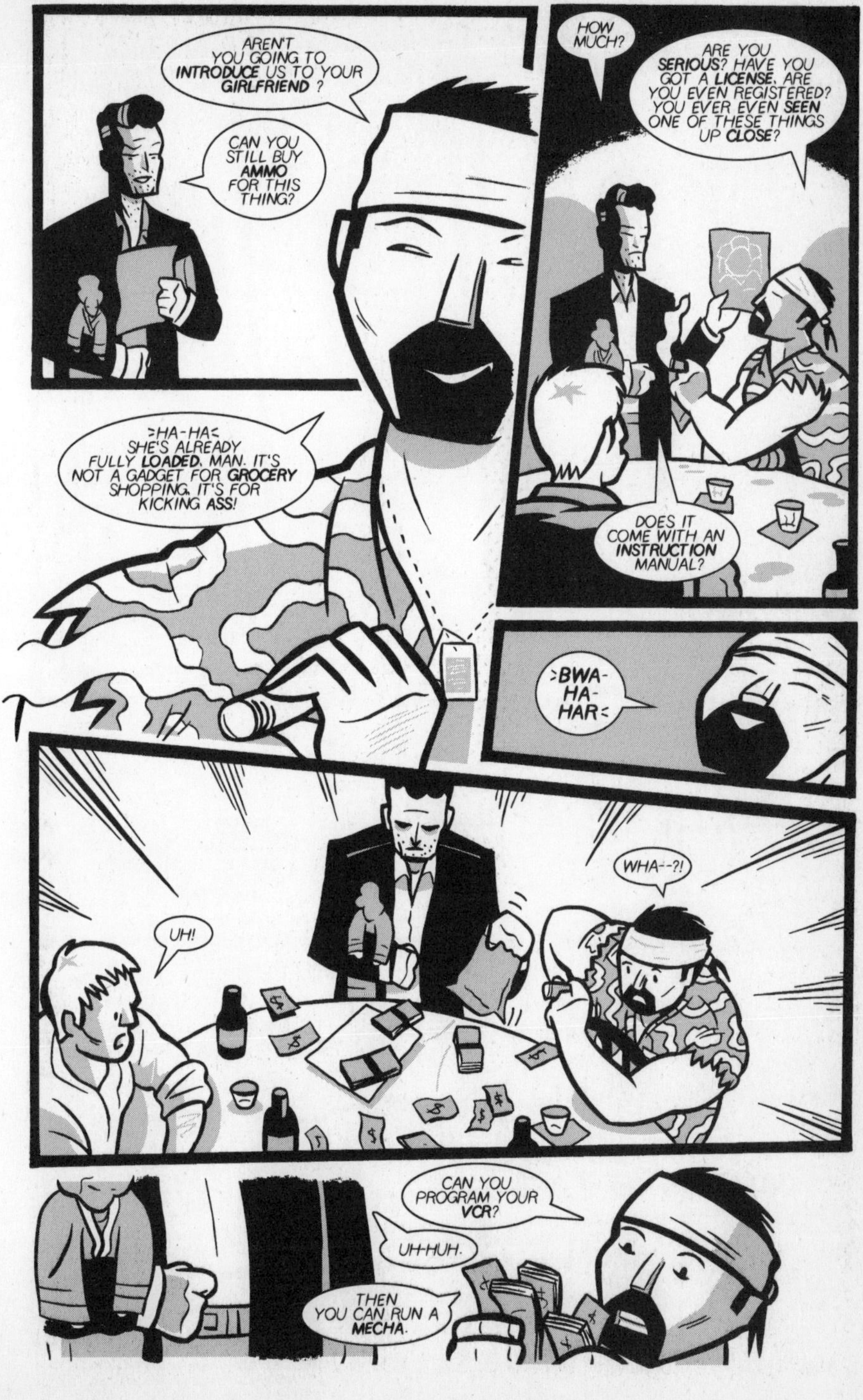

AREN'T YOU GOING TO INTRODUCE US TO YOUR GIRLFRIEND ?
CAN YOU STILL BUY AMMO FOR THIS THING?
HOW MUCH?
ARE YOU SERIOUS? HAVE YOU GOT A LICENSE, ARE YOU EVEN REGISTERED? YOU EVER EVEN SEEN ONE OF THESE THINGS UP CLOSE?
>HA-HA< SHE'S ALREADY FULLY LOADED, MAN. IT'S NOT A GADGET FOR GROCERY SHOPPING, IT'S FOR KICKING ASS!
DOES IT COME WITH AN INSTRUCTION MANUAL?
>BWA-HA-HAR<
WHA--?!
UH!
CAN YOU PROGRAM YOUR VCR?
UH-HUH.
THEN YOU CAN RUN A MECHA.

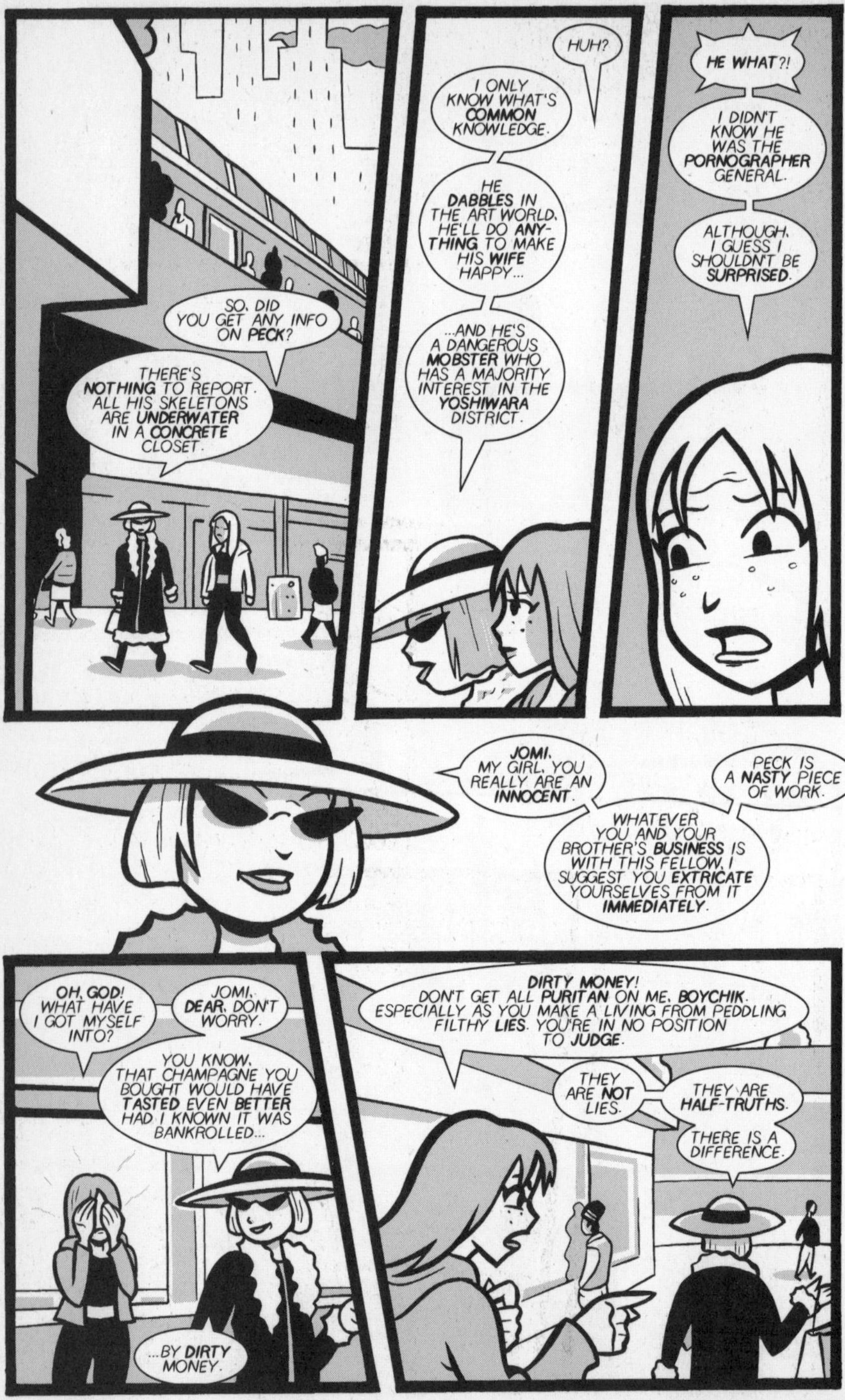
SO, DID YOU GET ANY INFO ON PECK?
THERE'S NOTHING TO REPORT. ALL HIS SKELETONS ARE UNDERWATER IN A CONCRETE CLOSET.
HUH?
I ONLY KNOW WHAT'S COMMON KNOWLEDGE.
HE DABBLES IN THE ART WORLD. HE'LL DO ANY-THING TO MAKE HIS WIFE HAPPY...
...AND HE'S A DANGEROUS MOBSTER WHO HAS A MAJORITY INTEREST IN THE YOSHIWARA DISTRICT.
HE WHAT?!
I DIDN'T KNOW HE WAS THE PORNOGRAPHER GENERAL.
ALTHOUGH, I GUESS I SHOULDN'T BE SURPRISED.
JOMI, MY GIRL, YOU REALLY ARE AN INNOCENT.
PECK IS A NASTY PIECE OF WORK.
WHATEVER YOU AND YOUR BROTHER'S BUSINESS IS WITH THIS FELLOW, I SUGGEST YOU EXTRICATE YOURSELVES FROM IT IMMEDIATELY.
OH, GOD! WHAT HAVE I GOT MYSELF INTO?
JOMI, DEAR, DON'T WORRY.
YOU KNOW, THAT CHAMPAGNE YOU BOUGHT WOULD HAVE TASTED EVEN BETTER HAD I KNOWN IT WAS BANKROLLED...
...BY DIRTY MONEY.
DIRTY MONEY! DON'T GET ALL PURITAN ON ME, BOYCHIK. ESPECIALLY AS YOU MAKE A LIVING FROM PEDDLING FILTHY LIES. YOU'RE IN NO POSITION TO JUDGE.
THEY ARE NOT LIES.
THEY ARE HALF-TRUTHS.
THERE IS A DIFFERENCE.

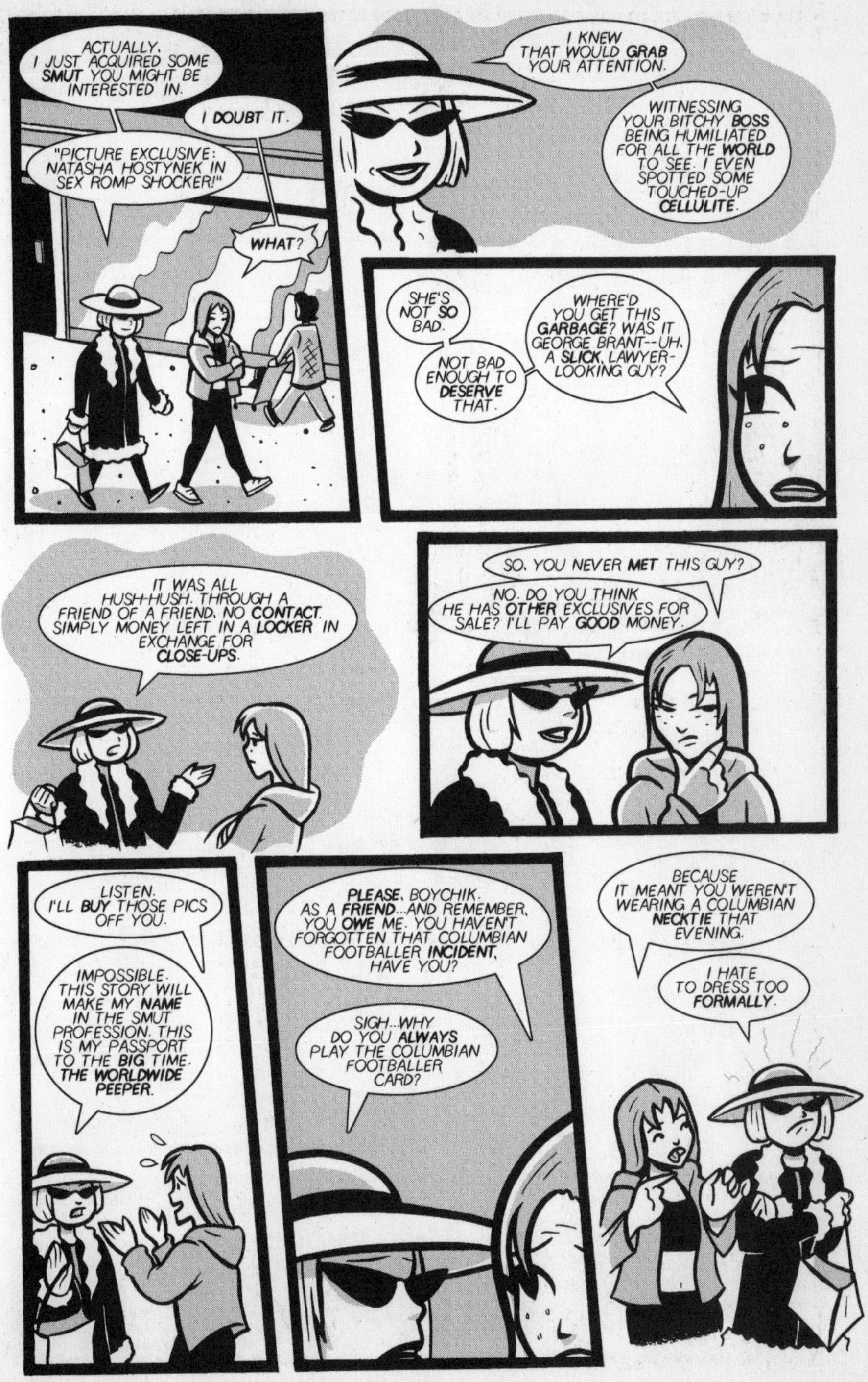
ACTUALLY. I JUST ACQUIRED SOME SMUT YOU MIGHT BE INTERESTED IN.
I DOUBT IT.
"PICTURE EXCLUSIVE: NATASHA HOSTYNEK IN SEX ROMP SHOCKER!"
WHAT?
I KNEW THAT WOULD GRAB YOUR ATTENTION.
WITNESSING YOUR BITCHY BOSS BEING HUMILIATED FOR ALL THE WORLD TO SEE. I EVEN SPOTTED SOME TOUCHED-UP CELLULITE.
SHE'S NOT SO BAD.
NOT BAD ENOUGH TO DESERVE THAT.
WHERE'D YOU GET THIS GARBAGE? WAS IT GEORGE BRANT--UH, A SLICK, LAWYER-LOOKING GUY?
IT WAS ALL HUSH-HUSH. THROUGH A FRIEND OF A FRIEND, NO CONTACT. SIMPLY MONEY LEFT IN A LOCKER IN EXCHANGE FOR CLOSE-UPS.
SO, YOU NEVER MET THIS GUY?
NO. DO YOU THINK HE HAS OTHER EXCLUSIVES FOR SALE? I'LL PAY GOOD MONEY.
LISTEN. I'LL BUY THOSE PICS OFF YOU.
IMPOSSIBLE. THIS STORY WILL MAKE MY NAME IN THE SMUT PROFESSION. THIS IS MY PASSPORT TO THE BIG TIME. THE WORLDWIDE PEEPER.
PLEASE, BOYCHIK. AS A FRIEND...AND REMEMBER, YOU OWE ME. YOU HAVEN'T FORGOTTEN THAT COLUMBIAN FOOTBALLER INCIDENT, HAVE YOU?
SIGH...WHY DO YOU ALWAYS PLAY THE COLUMBIAN FOOTBALLER CARD?
BECAUSE IT MEANT YOU WEREN'T WEARING A COLUMBIAN NECKTIE THAT EVENING.
I HATE TO DRESS TOO FORMALLY.

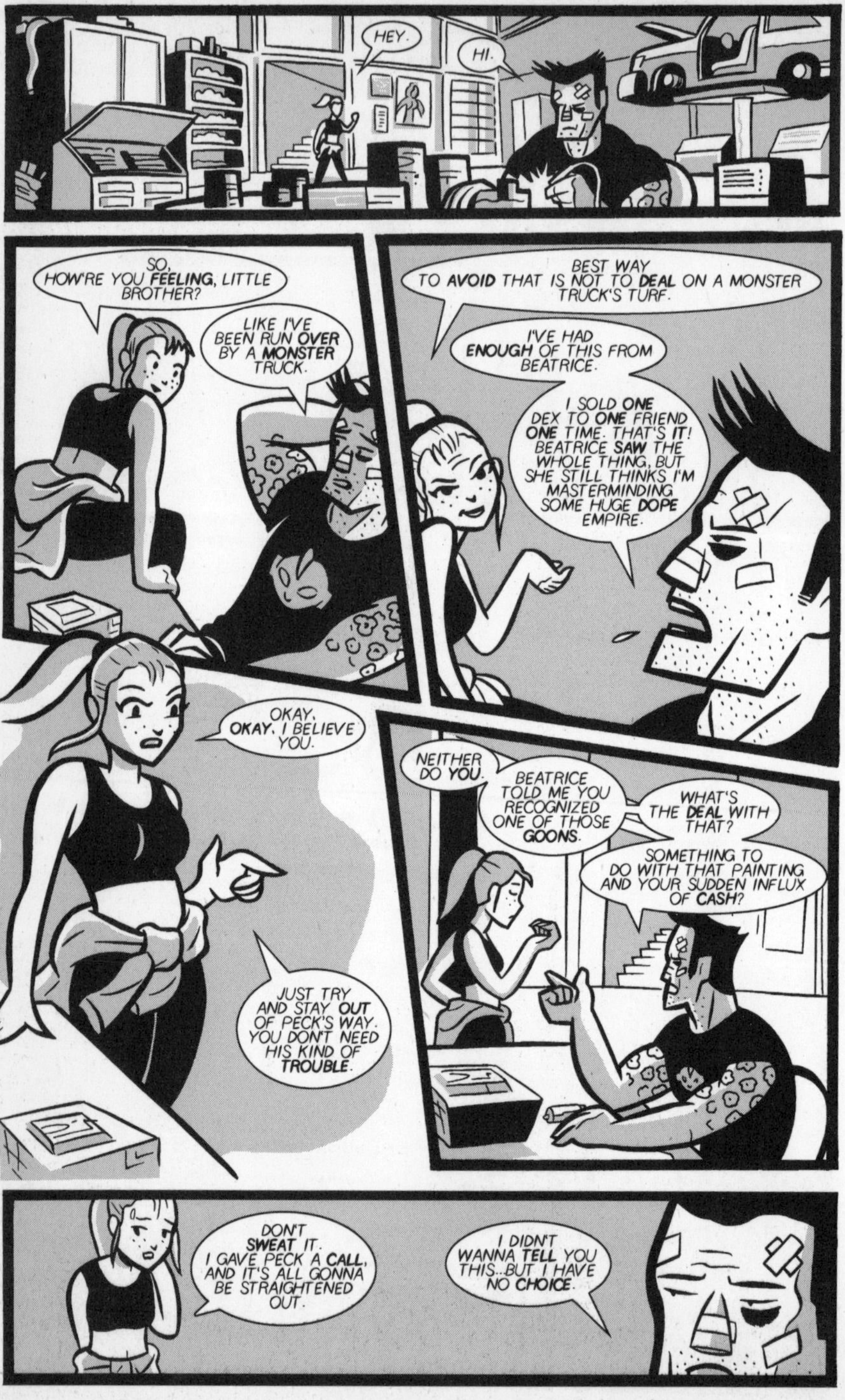
HEY.
HI.
SO, HOW'RE YOU FEELING, LITTLE BROTHER?
LIKE I'VE BEEN RUN OVER BY A MONSTER TRUCK.
BEST WAY TO AVOID THAT IS NOT TO DEAL ON A MONSTER TRUCK'S TURF.
I'VE HAD ENOUGH OF THIS FROM BEATRICE.
I SOLD ONE DEX TO ONE FRIEND ONE TIME. THAT'S IT! BEATRICE SAW THE WHOLE THING, BUT SHE STILL THINKS I'M MASTERMINDING SOME HUGE DOPE EMPIRE.
OKAY, OKAY, I BELIEVE YOU.
JUST TRY AND STAY OUT OF PECK'S WAY. YOU DON'T NEED HIS KIND OF TROUBLE.
NEITHER DO YOU.
BEATRICE TOLD ME YOU RECOGNIZED ONE OF THOSE GOONS.
WHAT'S THE DEAL WITH THAT?
SOMETHING TO DO WITH THAT PAINTING AND YOUR SUDDEN INFLUX OF CASH?
DON'T SWEAT IT. I GAVE PECK A CALL, AND IT'S ALL GONNA BE STRAIGHTENED OUT.
I DIDN'T WANNA TELL YOU THIS...BUT I HAVE NO CHOICE.

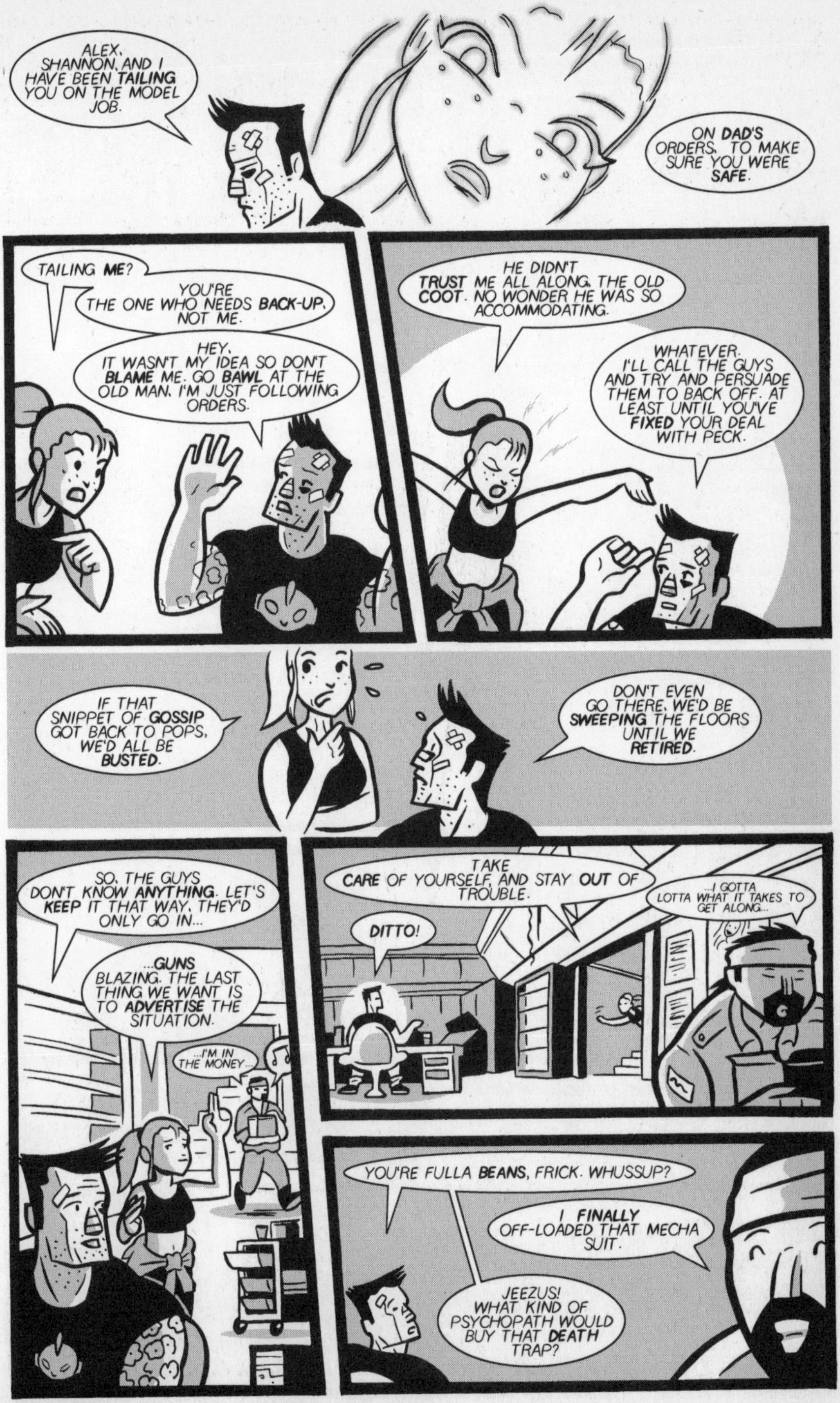
ALEX, SHANNON, AND I HAVE BEEN TAILING YOU ON THE MODEL JOB.
ON DAD'S ORDERS, TO MAKE SURE YOU WERE SAFE.
TAILING ME?
YOU'RE THE ONE WHO NEEDS BACK-UP, NOT ME.
HEY, IT WASN'T MY IDEA SO DON'T BLAME ME. GO BAWL AT THE OLD MAN. I'M JUST FOLLOWING ORDERS.
HE DIDN'T TRUST ME ALL ALONG, THE OLD COOT. NO WONDER HE WAS SO ACCOMMODATING.
WHATEVER. I'LL CALL THE GUYS AND TRY AND PERSUADE THEM TO BACK OFF. AT LEAST UNTIL YOU'VE FIXED YOUR DEAL WITH PECK.
IF THAT SNIPPET OF GOSSIP GOT BACK TO POPS, WE'D ALL BE BUSTED.
DON'T EVEN GO THERE. WE'D BE SWEEPING THE FLOORS UNTIL WE RETIRED.
SO, THE GUYS DON'T KNOW ANYTHING. LET'S KEEP IT THAT WAY. THEY'D ONLY GO IN...
...GUNS BLAZING. THE LAST THING WE WANT IS TO ADVERTISE THE SITUATION.
...I'M IN THE MONEY...
TAKE CARE OF YOURSELF, AND STAY OUT OF TROUBLE.
DITTO!
...I GOTTA LOTTA WHAT IT TAKES TO GET ALONG...
YOU'RE FULLA BEANS, FRICK. WHUSSUP?
I FINALLY OFF-LOADED THAT MECHA SUIT.
JEEZUS! WHAT KIND OF PSYCHOPATH WOULD BUY THAT DEATH TRAP?

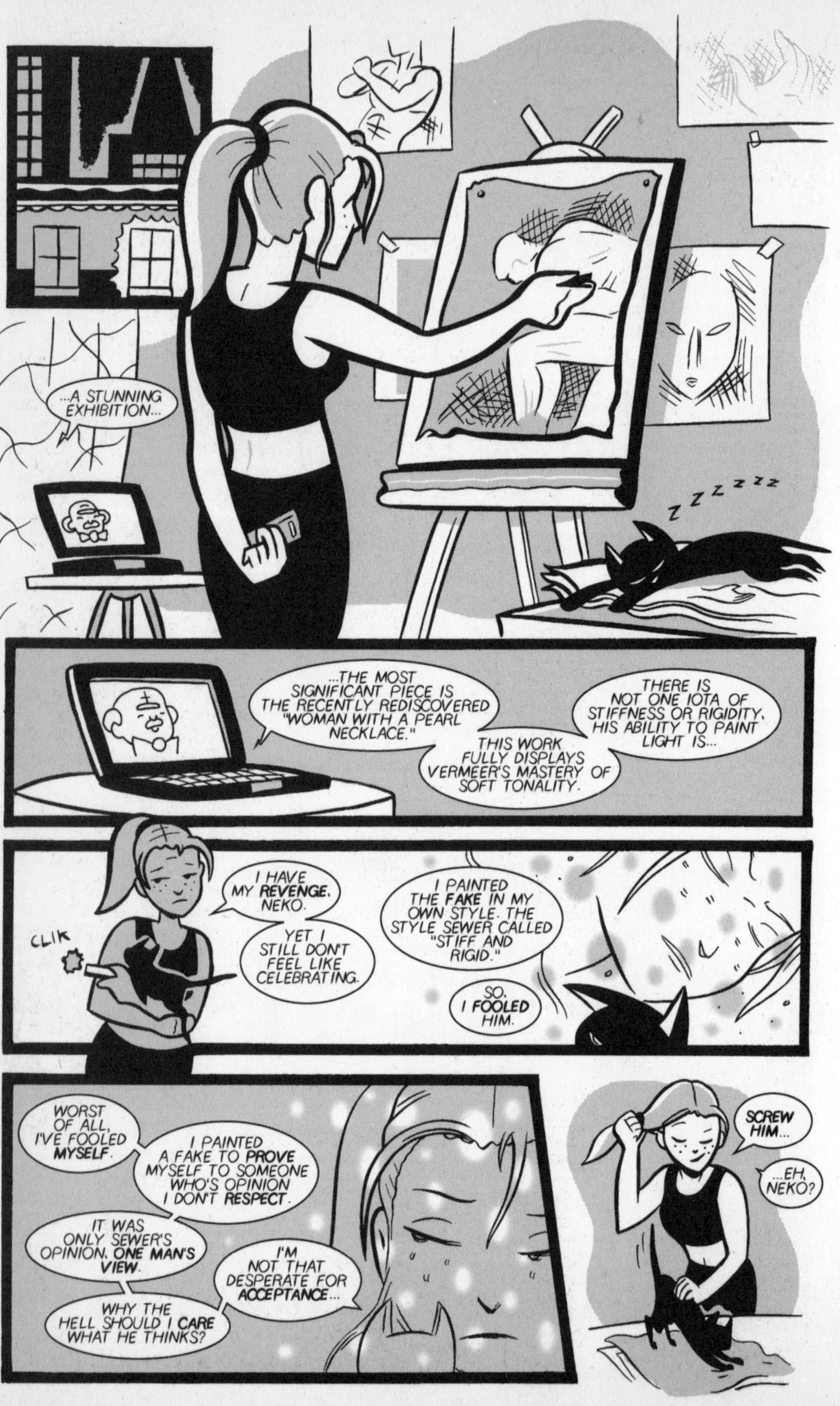
...A STUNNING EXHIBITION...
Z Z Z Z Z Z Z
...THE MOST SIGNIFICANT PIECE IS THE RECENTLY REDISCOVERED "WOMAN WITH A PEARL NECKLACE."
THIS WORK FULLY DISPLAYS VERMEER'S MASTERY OF SOFT TONALITY.
THERE IS NOT ONE IOTA OF STIFFNESS OR RIGIDITY. HIS ABILITY TO PAINT LIGHT IS...
CLIK
I HAVE MY REVENGE, NEKO.
YET I STILL DON'T FEEL LIKE CELEBRATING.
I PAINTED THE FAKE IN MY OWN STYLE. THE STYLE SEWER CALLED "STIFF AND RIGID."
SO, I FOOLED HIM.
WORST OF ALL, I'VE FOOLED MYSELF.
I PAINTED A FAKE TO PROVE MYSELF TO SOMEONE WHO'S OPINION I DON'T RESPECT.
IT WAS ONLY SEWER'S OPINION. ONE MAN'S VIEW.
I'M NOT THAT DESPERATE FOR ACCEPTANCE...
WHY THE HELL SHOULD I CARE WHAT HE THINKS?
SCREW HIM...
...EH, NEKO?

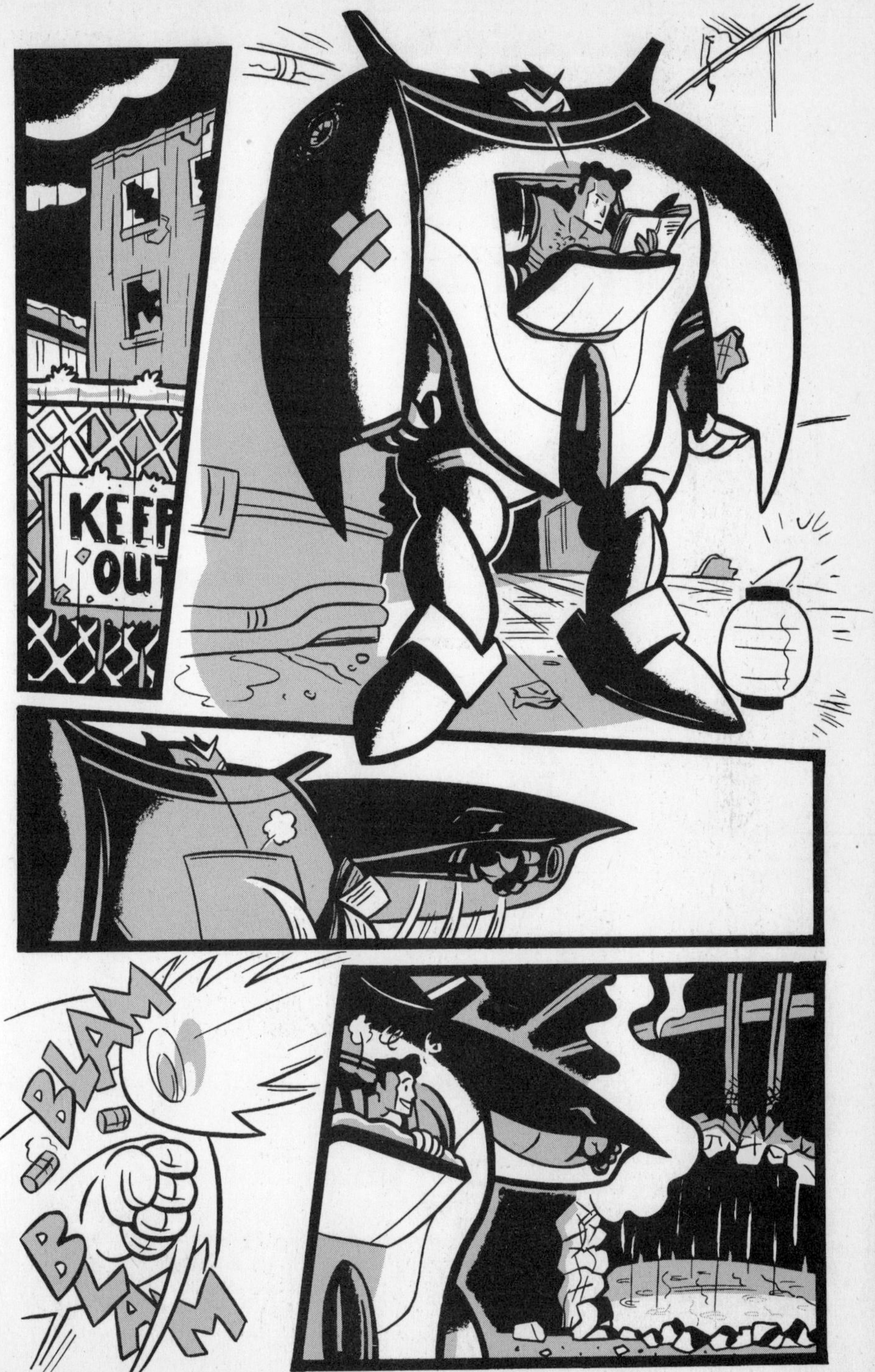
KEEP OUT
BLAM
BLAM

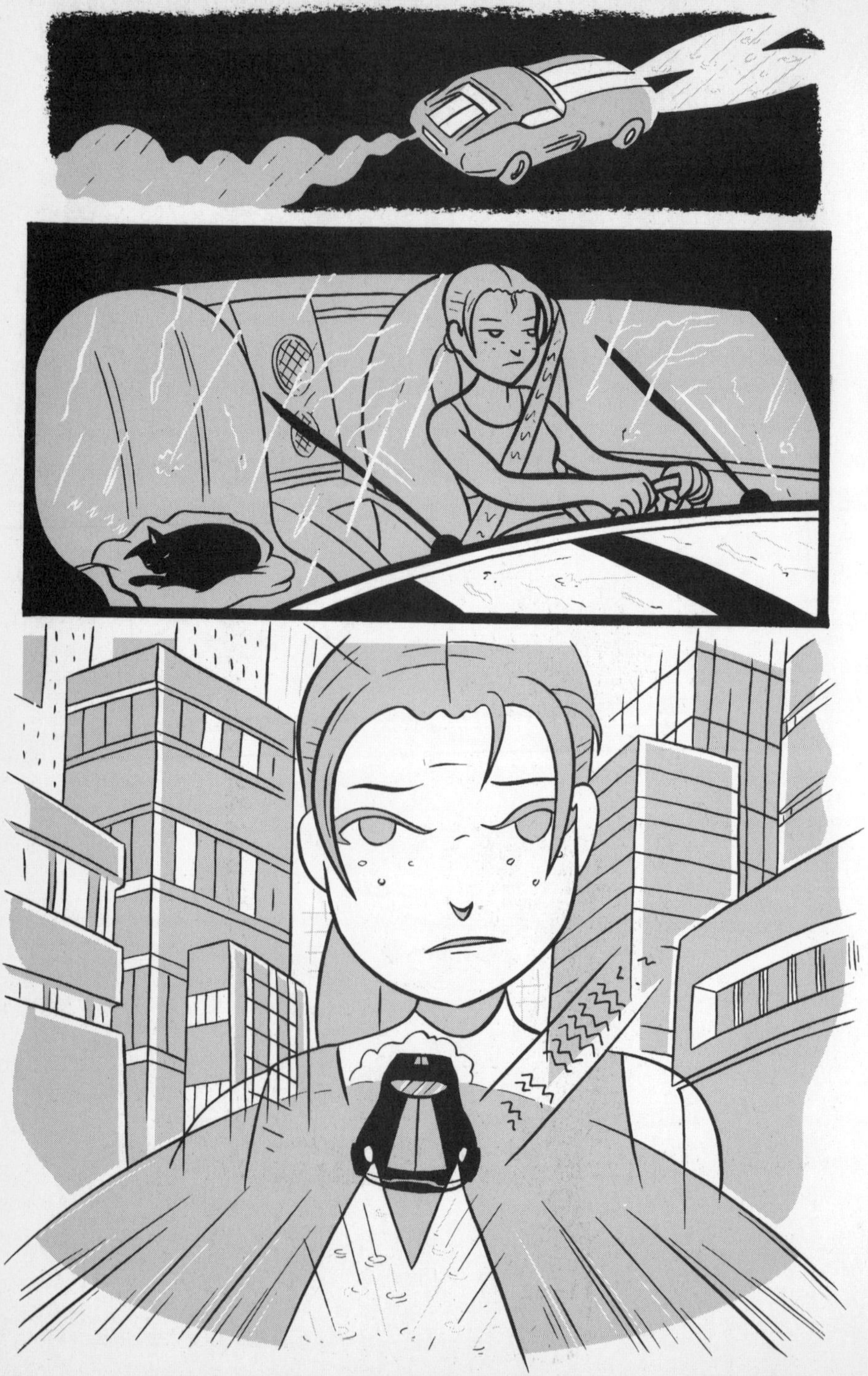

Chapter: four

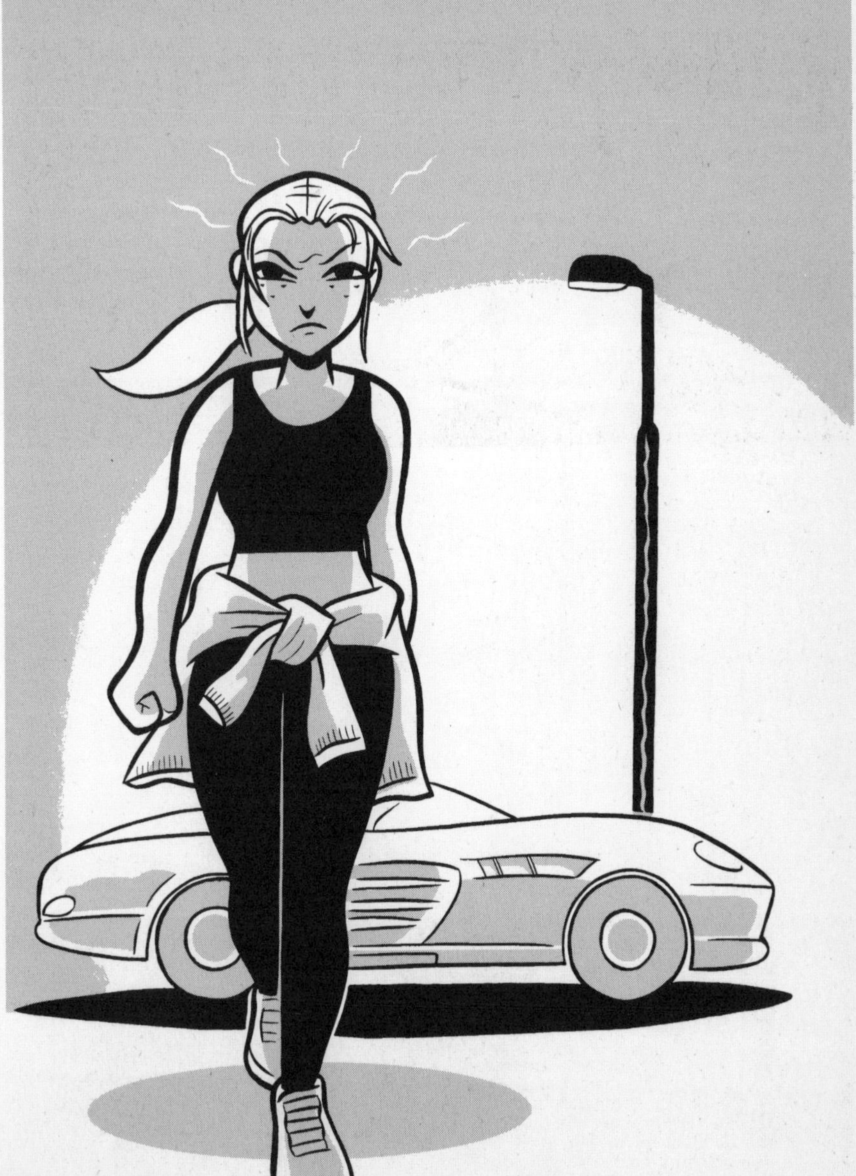

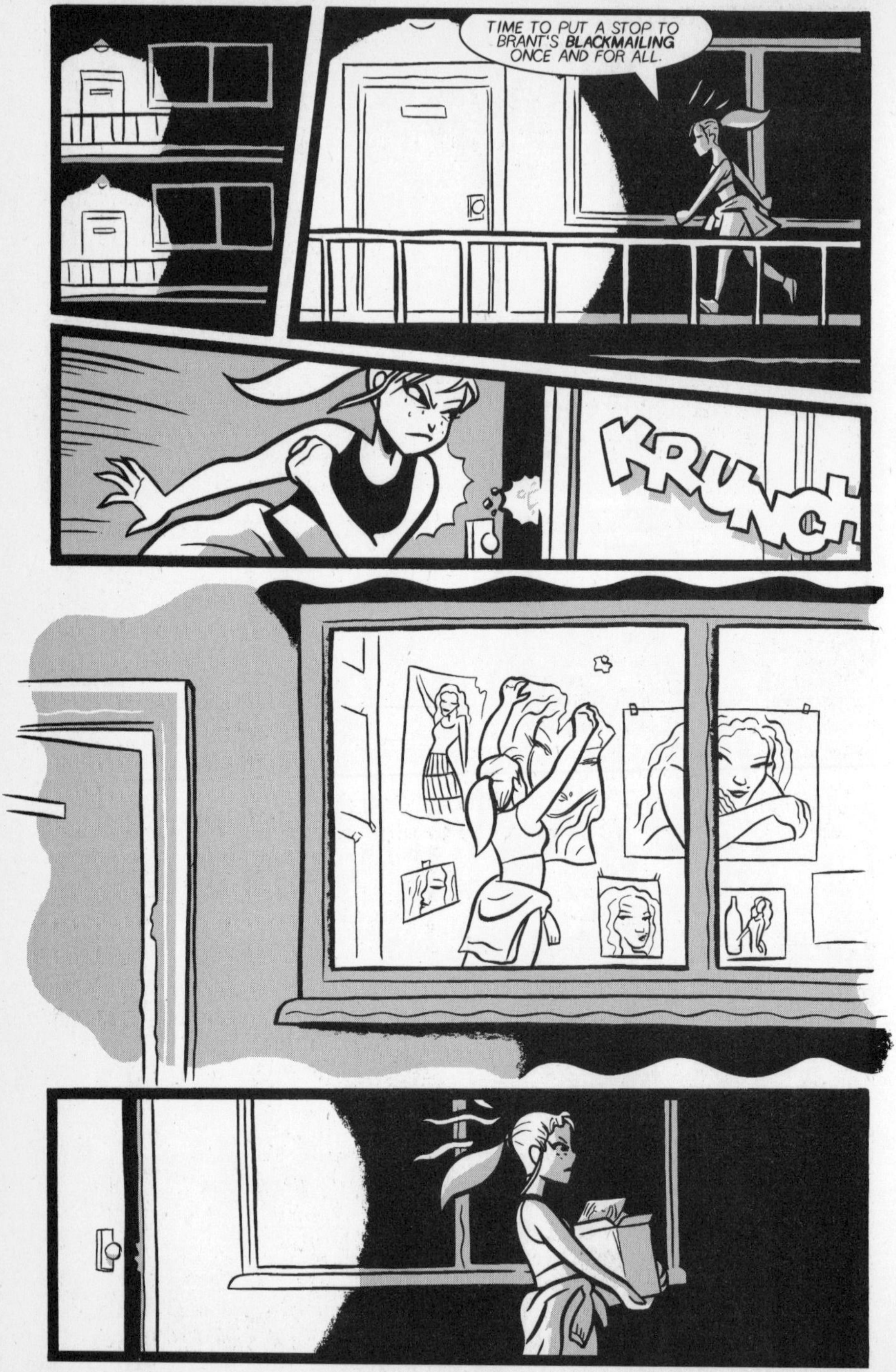
TIME TO PUT A STOP TO BRANT'S **BLACKMAILING** ONCE AND FOR ALL.
KRUNCH

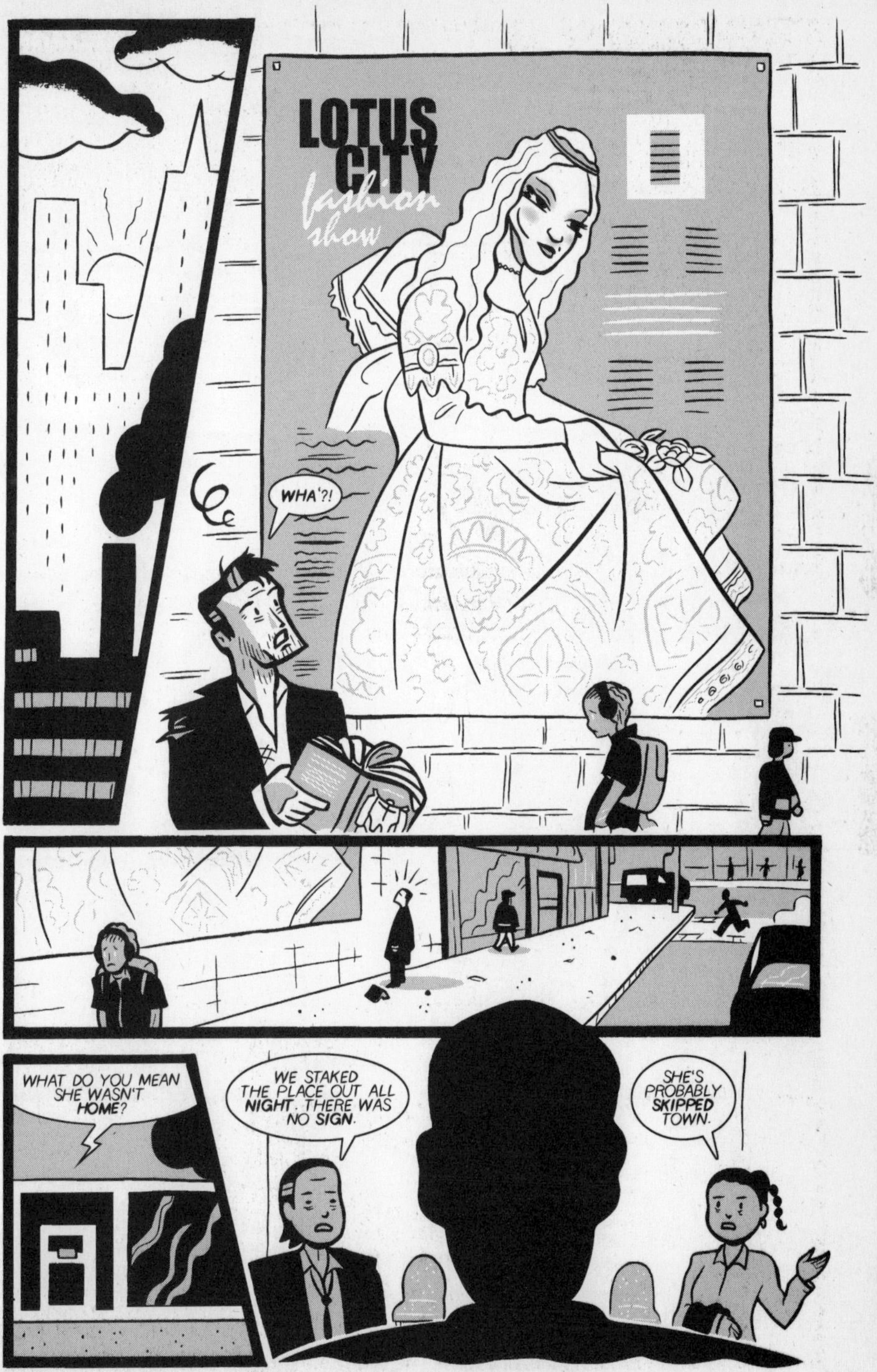
LOTUS CITY
fashion show
WHA'?!
WHAT DO YOU MEAN SHE WASN'T HOME?
WE STAKED THE PLACE OUT ALL NIGHT. THERE WAS NO SIGN.
SHE'S PROBABLY SKIPPED TOWN.

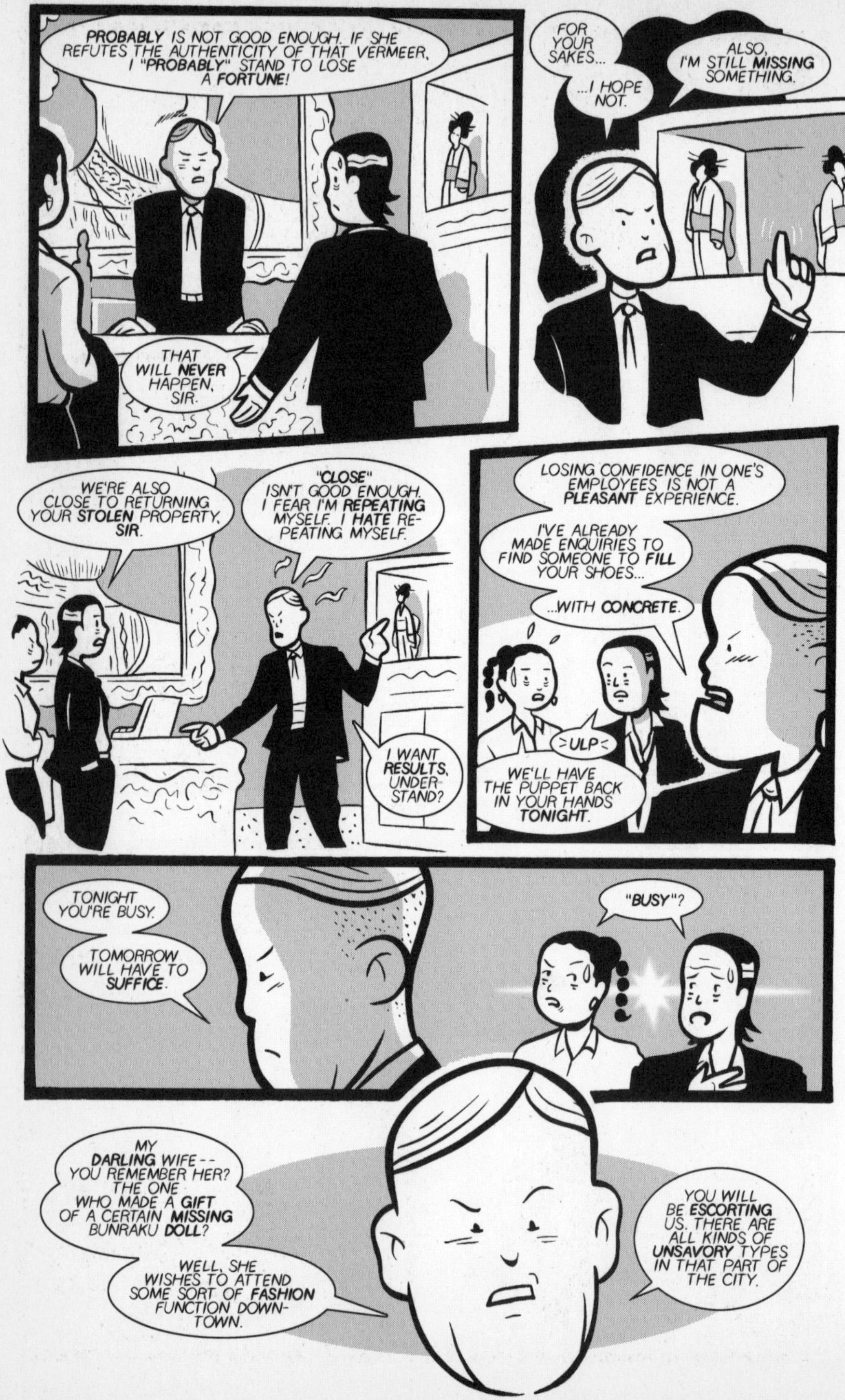
PROBABLY IS NOT GOOD ENOUGH. IF SHE REFUTES THE AUTHENTICITY OF THAT VERMEER, I "PROBABLY" STAND TO LOSE A FORTUNE!
THAT WILL NEVER HAPPEN, SIR.
FOR YOUR SAKES...
...I HOPE NOT.
ALSO, I'M STILL MISSING SOMETHING.
WE'RE ALSO CLOSE TO RETURNING YOUR STOLEN PROPERTY, SIR.
"CLOSE" ISN'T GOOD ENOUGH. I FEAR I'M REPEATING MYSELF. I HATE RE-PEATING MYSELF.
I WANT RESULTS, UNDER-STAND?
LOSING CONFIDENCE IN ONE'S EMPLOYEES IS NOT A PLEASANT EXPERIENCE.
I'VE ALREADY MADE ENQUIRIES TO FIND SOMEONE TO FILL YOUR SHOES...
...WITH CONCRETE.
>ULP<
WE'LL HAVE THE PUPPET BACK IN YOUR HANDS TONIGHT.
TONIGHT YOU'RE BUSY.
TOMORROW WILL HAVE TO SUFFICE.
"BUSY"?
MY DARLING WIFE-- YOU REMEMBER HER? THE ONE WHO MADE A GIFT OF A CERTAIN MISSING BUNRAKU DOLL?
WELL, SHE WISHES TO ATTEND SOME SORT OF FASHION FUNCTION DOWN-TOWN.
YOU WILL BE ESCORTING US. THERE ARE ALL KINDS OF UNSAVORY TYPES IN THAT PART OF THE CITY.

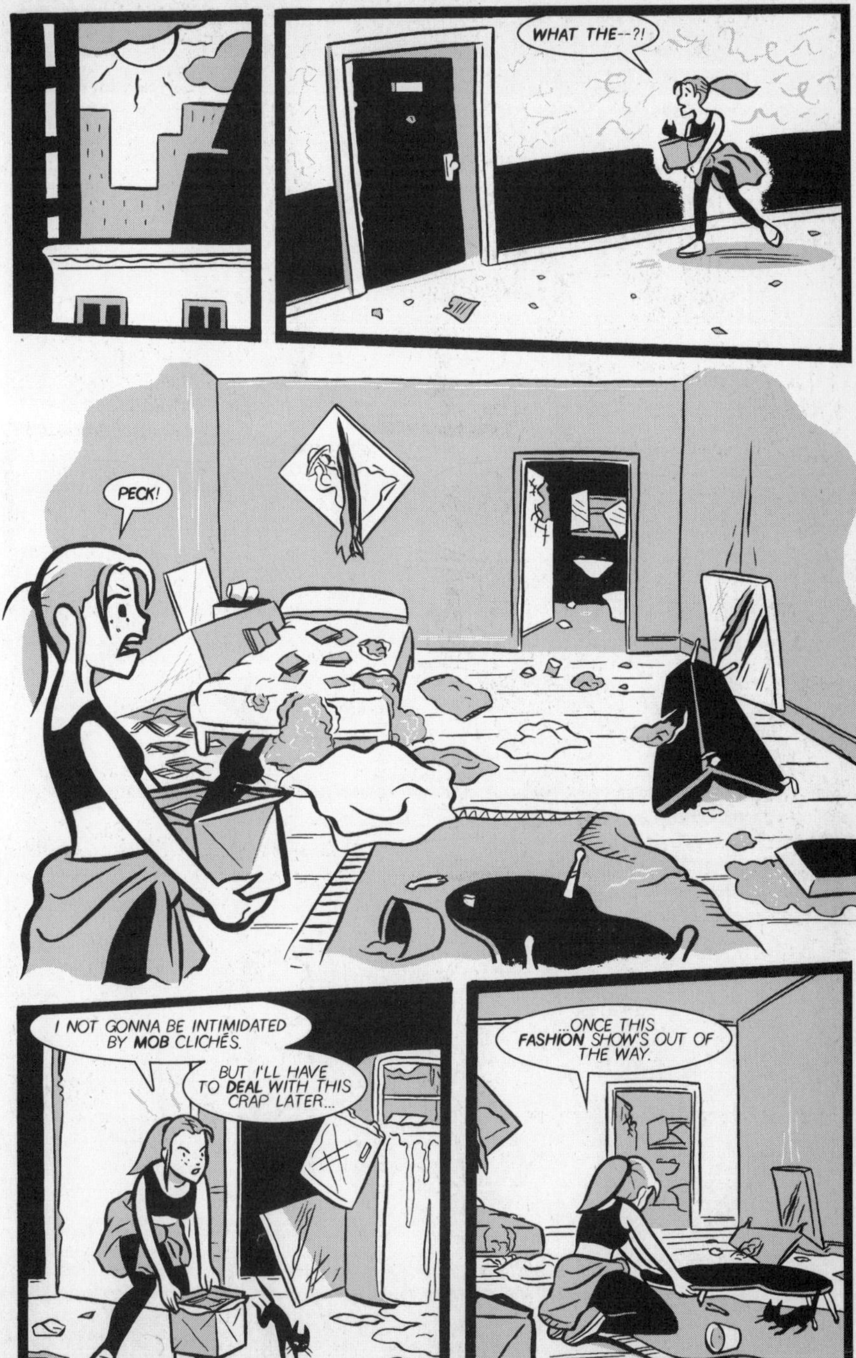
WHAT THE--?!
PECK!
I NOT GONNA BE INTIMIDATED BY MOB CLICHÉS.
BUT I'LL HAVE TO DEAL WITH THIS CRAP LATER...
...ONCE THIS FASHION SHOW'S OUT OF THE WAY.

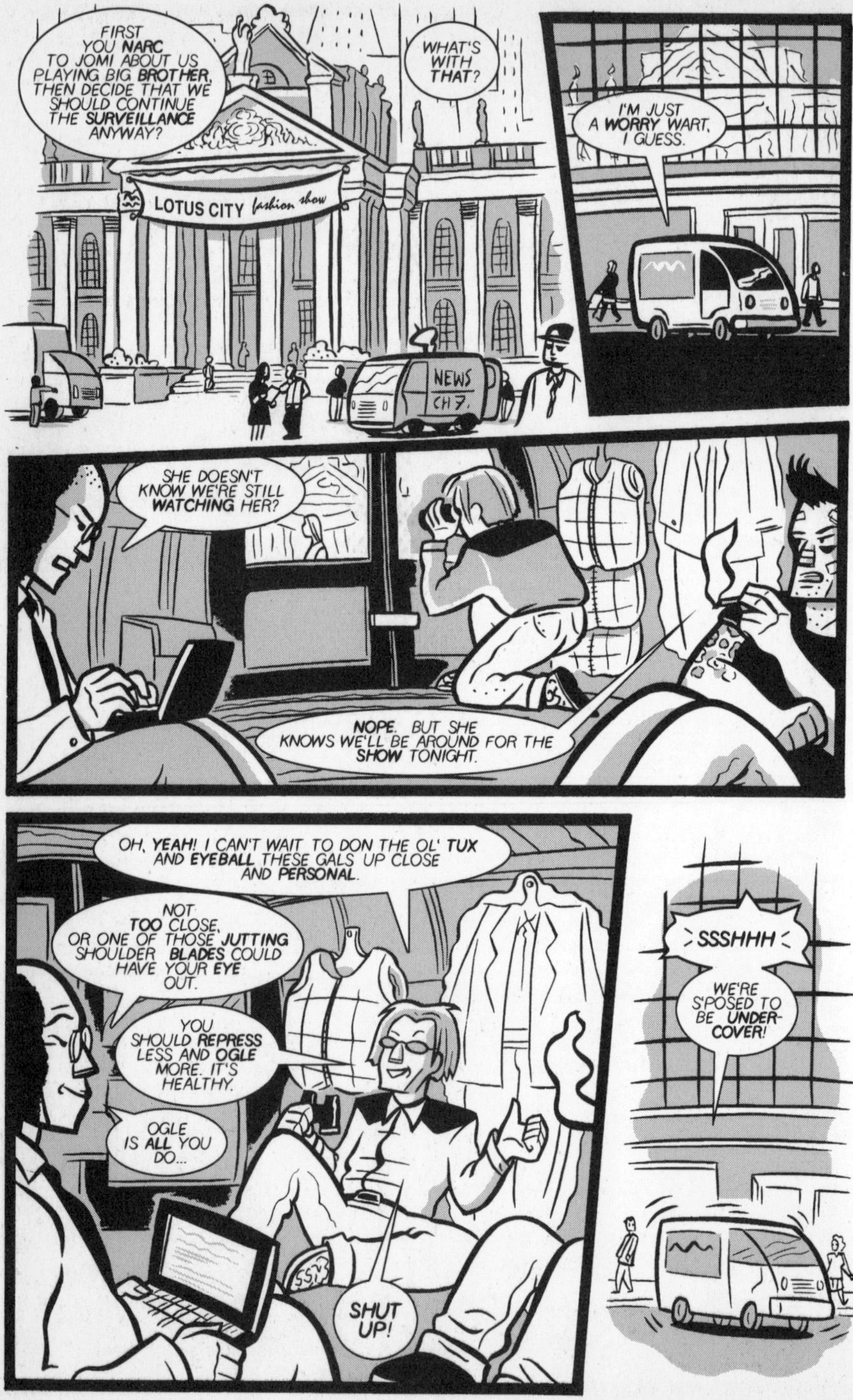
FIRST YOU NARC TO JOMI ABOUT US PLAYING BIG BROTHER, THEN DECIDE THAT WE SHOULD CONTINUE THE SURVEILLANCE ANYWAY?
WHAT'S WITH THAT?
LOTUS CITY fashion show
NEWS CH 7
I'M JUST A WORRY WART, I GUESS.
SHE DOESN'T KNOW WE'RE STILL WATCHING HER?
NOPE. BUT SHE KNOWS WE'LL BE AROUND FOR THE SHOW TONIGHT.
OH, YEAH! I CAN'T WAIT TO DON THE OL' TUX AND EYEBALL THESE GALS UP CLOSE AND PERSONAL.
NOT TOO CLOSE, OR ONE OF THOSE JUTTING SHOULDER BLADES COULD HAVE YOUR EYE OUT.
YOU SHOULD REPRESS LESS AND OGLE MORE. IT'S HEALTHY.
OGLE IS ALL YOU DO...
SHUT UP!
SSSHHH
WE'RE S'POSED TO BE UNDER-COVER!

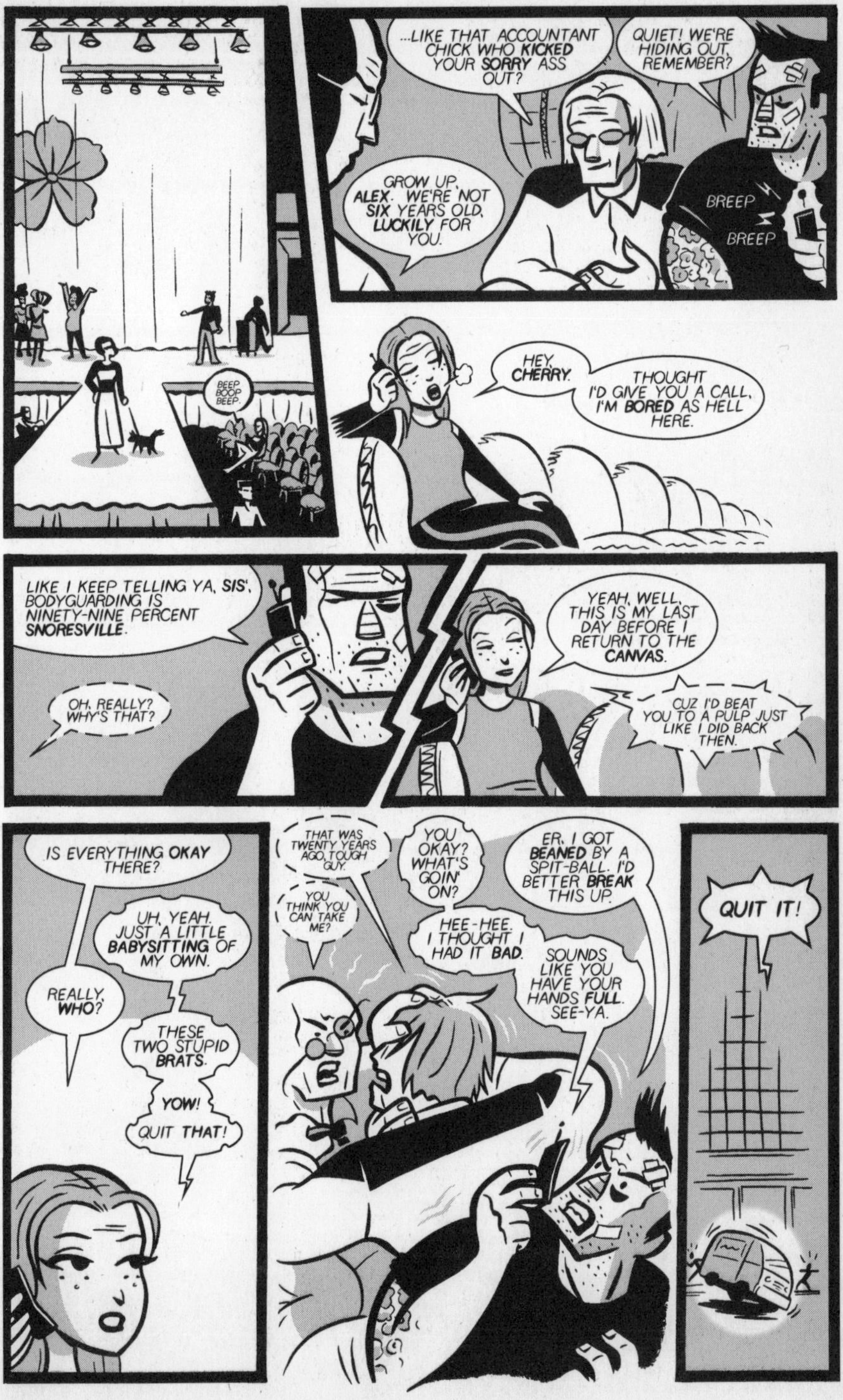
BEEP BOOP BEEP.
...LIKE THAT ACCOUNTANT CHICK WHO KICKED YOUR SORRY ASS OUT?
QUIET! WE'RE HIDING OUT, REMEMBER?
GROW UP, ALEX. WE'RE NOT SIX YEARS OLD, LUCKILY FOR YOU.
BREEP
BREEP
HEY, CHERRY.
THOUGHT I'D GIVE YOU A CALL, I'M BORED AS HELL HERE.
LIKE I KEEP TELLING YA, SIS', BODYGUARDING IS NINETY-NINE PERCENT SNORESVILLE.
OH, REALLY? WHY'S THAT?
YEAH, WELL, THIS IS MY LAST DAY BEFORE I RETURN TO THE CANVAS.
CUZ I'D BEAT YOU TO A PULP JUST LIKE I DID BACK THEN.
IS EVERYTHING OKAY THERE?
UH, YEAH. JUST A LITTLE BABYSITTING OF MY OWN.
REALLY, WHO?
THESE TWO STUPID BRATS.
YOW!
QUIT THAT!
THAT WAS TWENTY YEARS AGO, TOUGH GUY.
YOU THINK YOU CAN TAKE ME?
YOU OKAY? WHAT'S GOIN' ON?
ER, I GOT BEANED BY A SPIT-BALL. I'D BETTER BREAK THIS UP.
HEE-HEE. I THOUGHT I HAD IT BAD.
SOUNDS LIKE YOU HAVE YOUR HANDS FULL. SEE-YA.
QUIT IT!

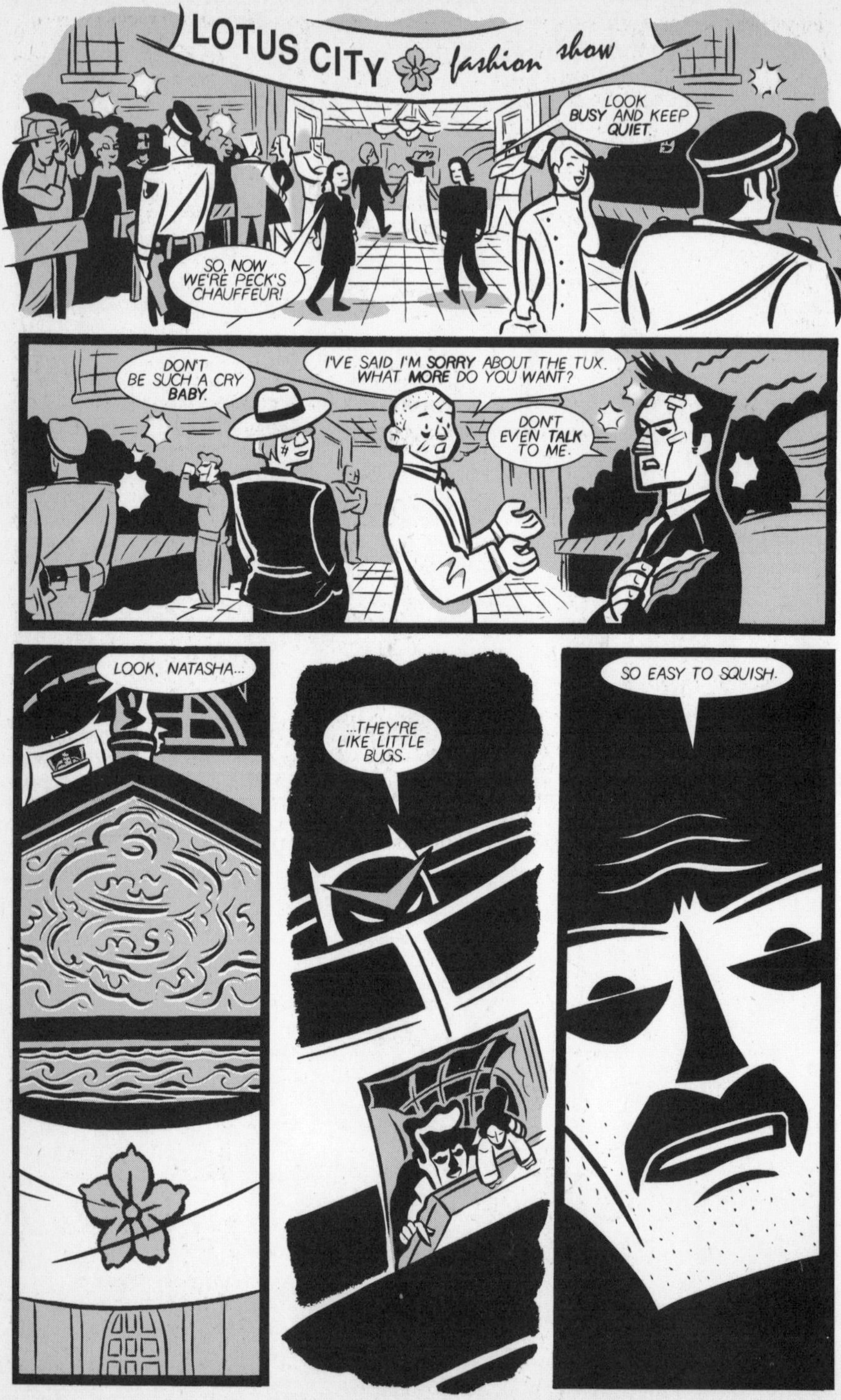

LOTUS CITY fashion show
LOOK BUSY AND KEEP QUIET.
SO, NOW WE'RE PECK'S CHAUFFEUR!
DON'T BE SUCH A CRY BABY.
I'VE SAID I'M SORRY ABOUT THE TUX. WHAT MORE DO YOU WANT?
DON'T EVEN TALK TO ME.
LOOK, NATASHA...
...THEY'RE LIKE LITTLE BUGS.
SO EASY TO SQUISH.

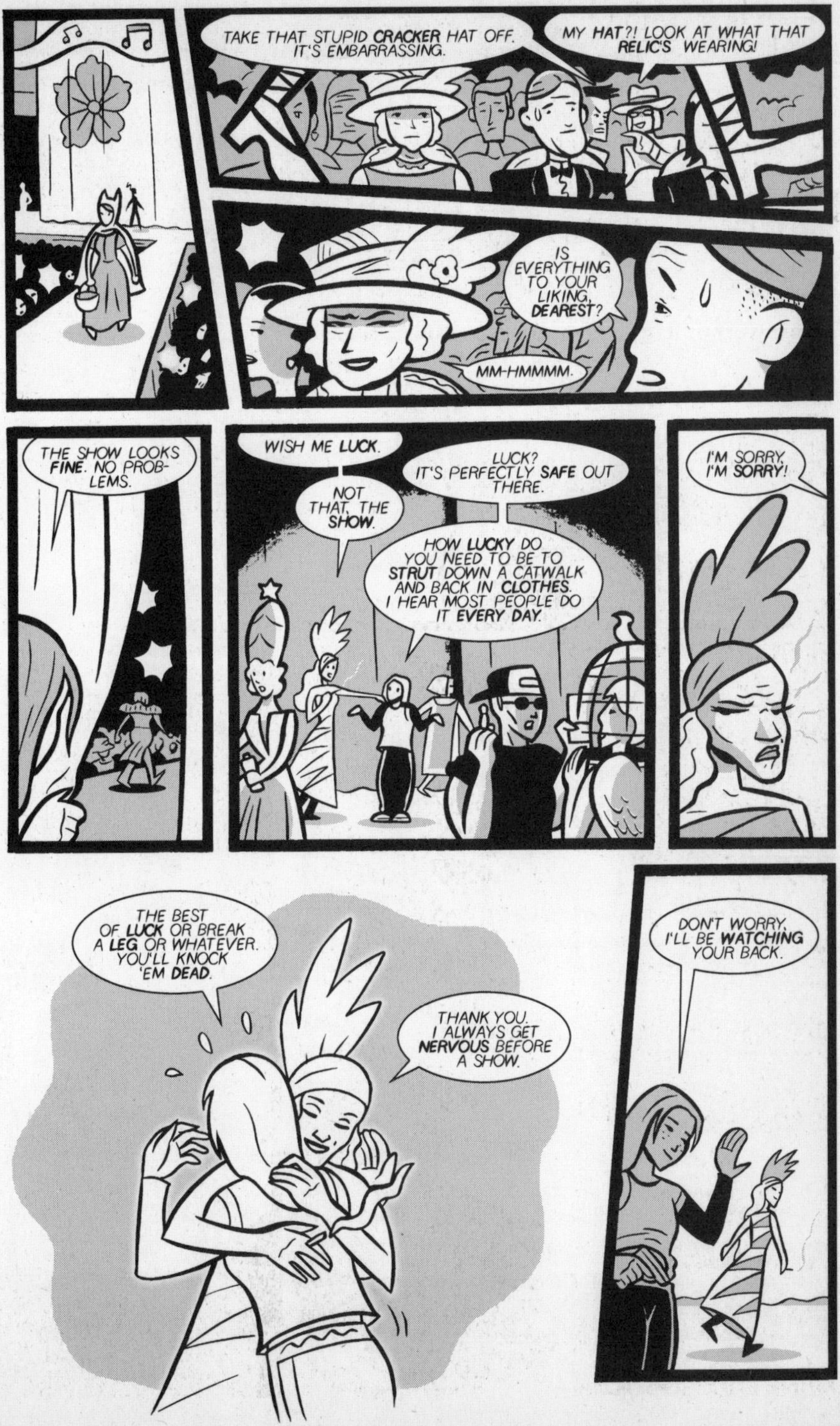
TAKE THAT STUPID CRACKER HAT OFF. IT'S EMBARRASSING.
MY HAT?! LOOK AT WHAT THAT RELIC'S WEARING!
IS EVERYTHING TO YOUR LIKING, DEAREST?
MM-HMMMM.
THE SHOW LOOKS FINE. NO PROBLEMS.
WISH ME LUCK.
LUCK? IT'S PERFECTLY SAFE OUT THERE.
NOT THAT, THE SHOW.
HOW LUCKY DO YOU NEED TO BE TO STRUT DOWN A CATWALK AND BACK IN CLOTHES. I HEAR MOST PEOPLE DO IT EVERY DAY.
I'M SORRY, I'M SORRY!
THE BEST OF LUCK OR BREAK A LEG OR WHATEVER. YOU'LL KNOCK 'EM DEAD.
THANK YOU. I ALWAYS GET NERVOUS BEFORE A SHOW.
DON'T WORRY. I'LL BE WATCHING YOUR BACK.

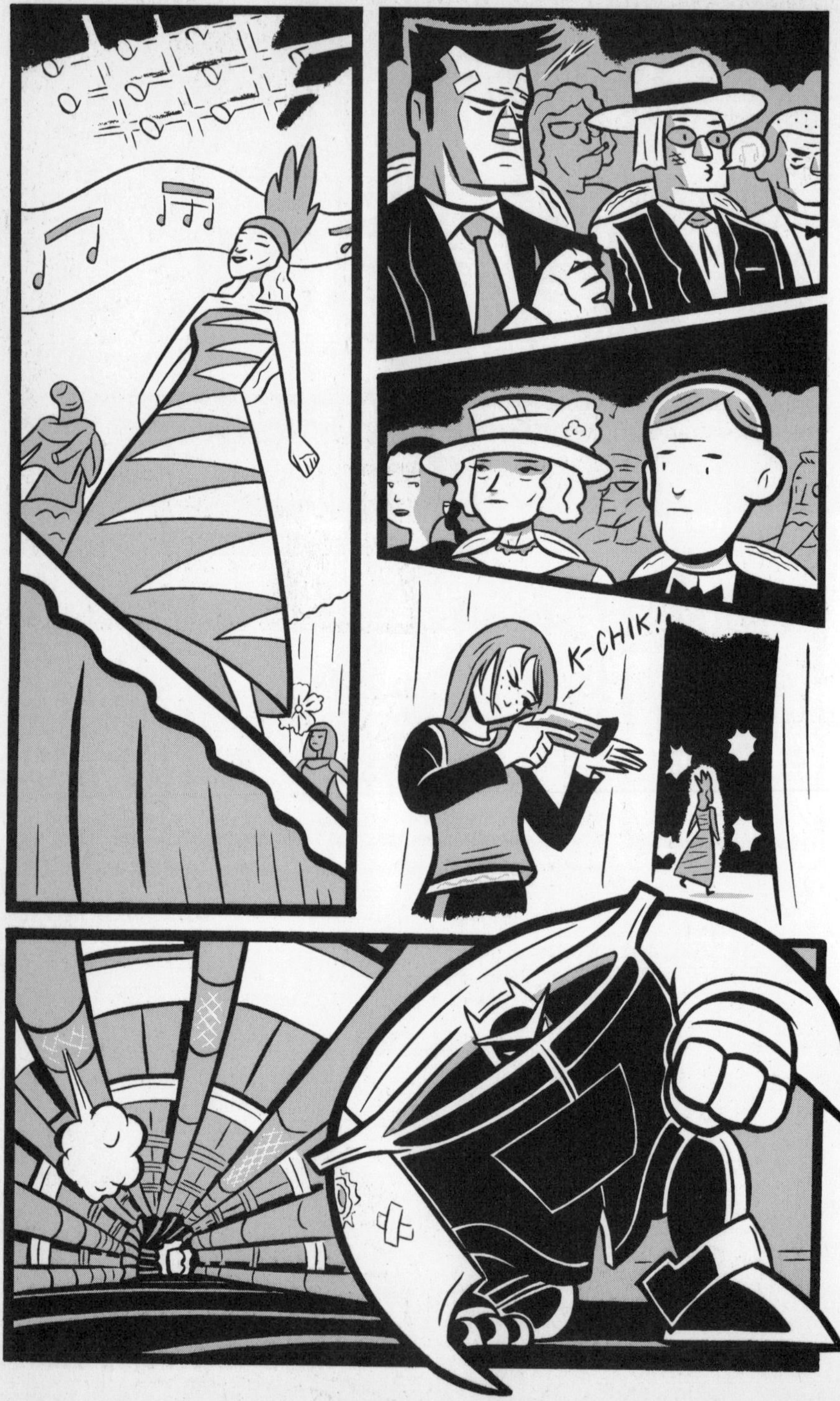
K-CHIK!

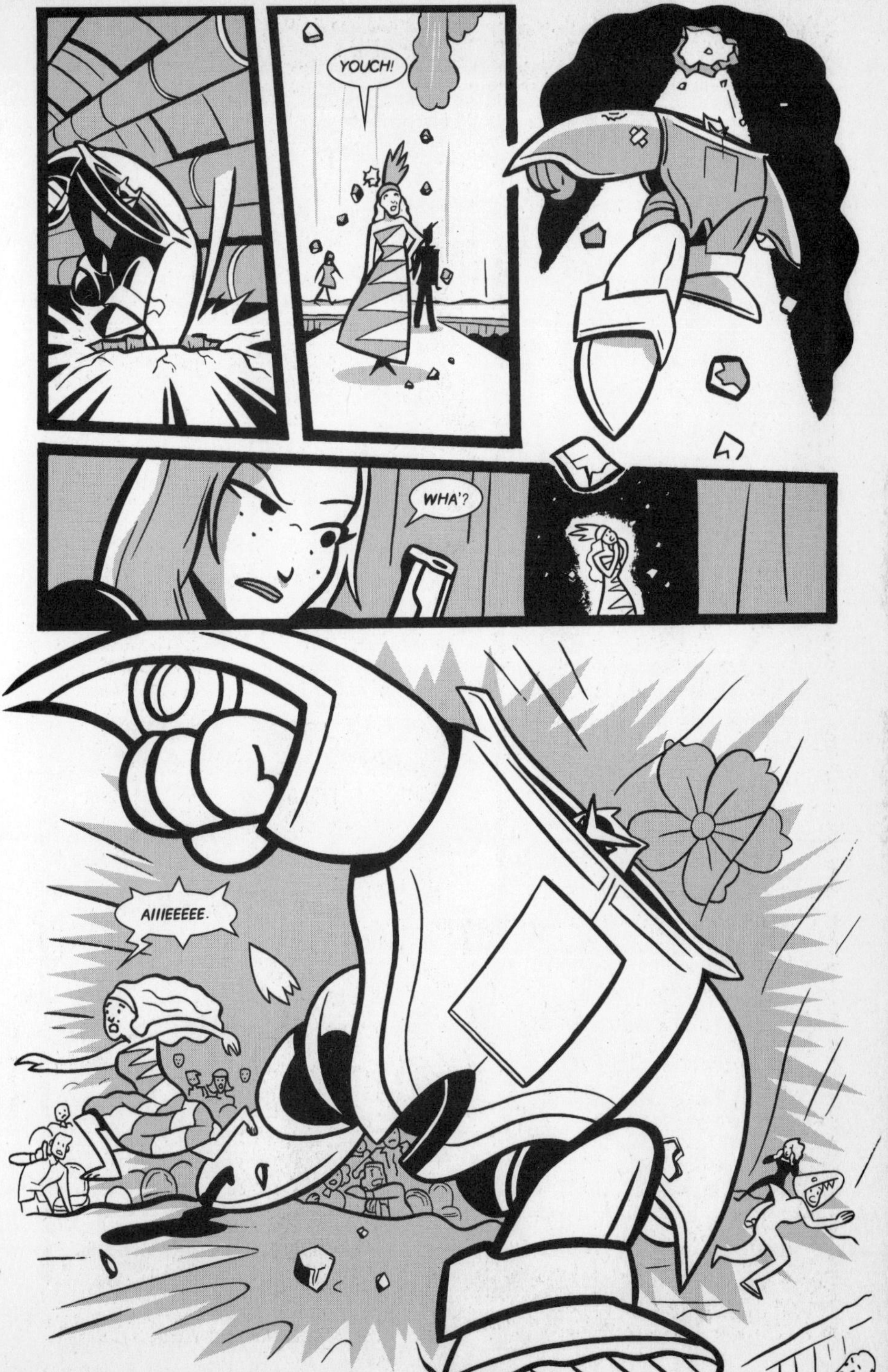
YOUCH!
WHA'?
AIIIEEEEE.

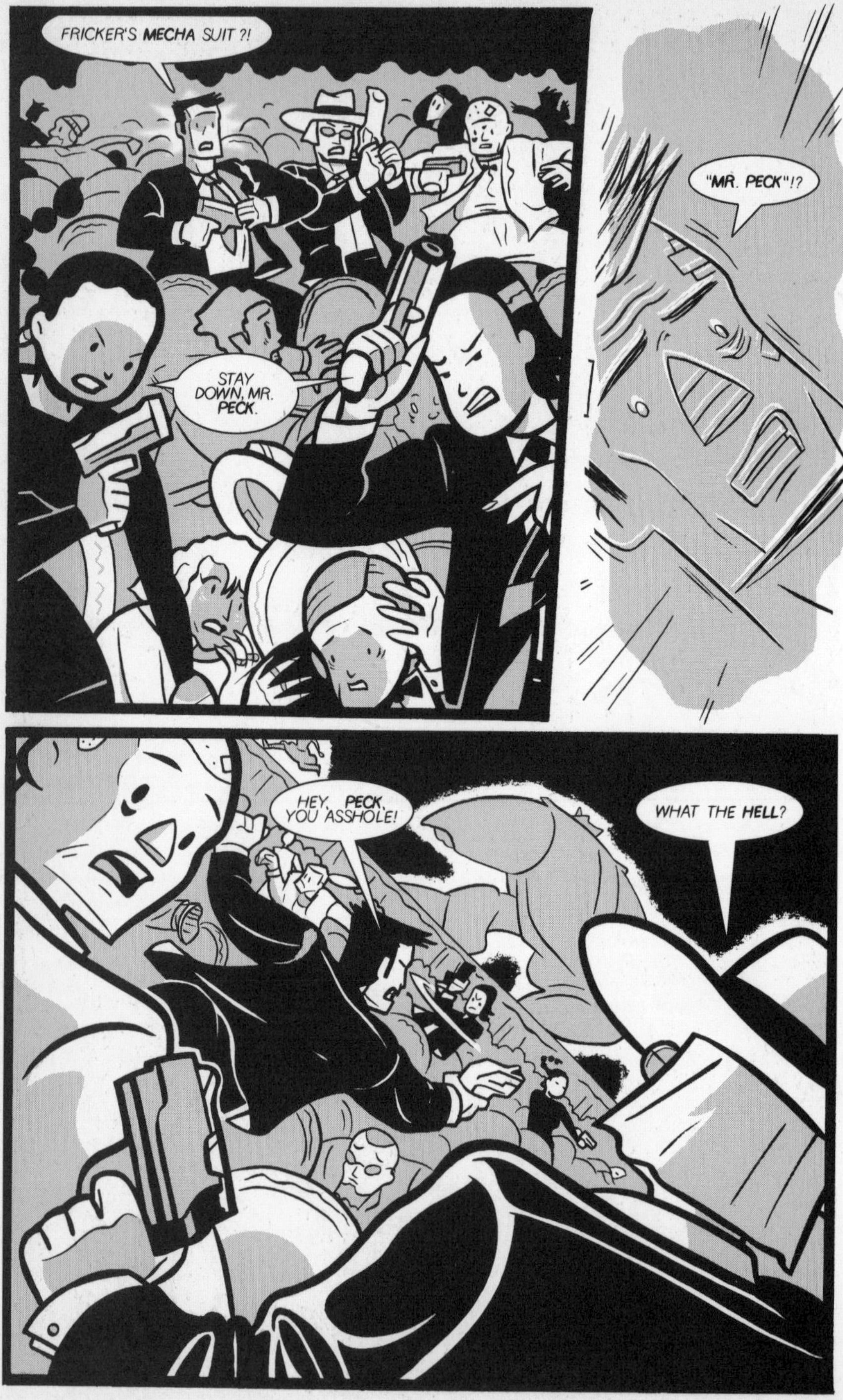
FRICKER'S MECHA SUIT?!
STAY DOWN, MR. PECK.
"MR. PECK"!?
HEY, PECK, YOU ASSHOLE!
WHAT THE HELL?

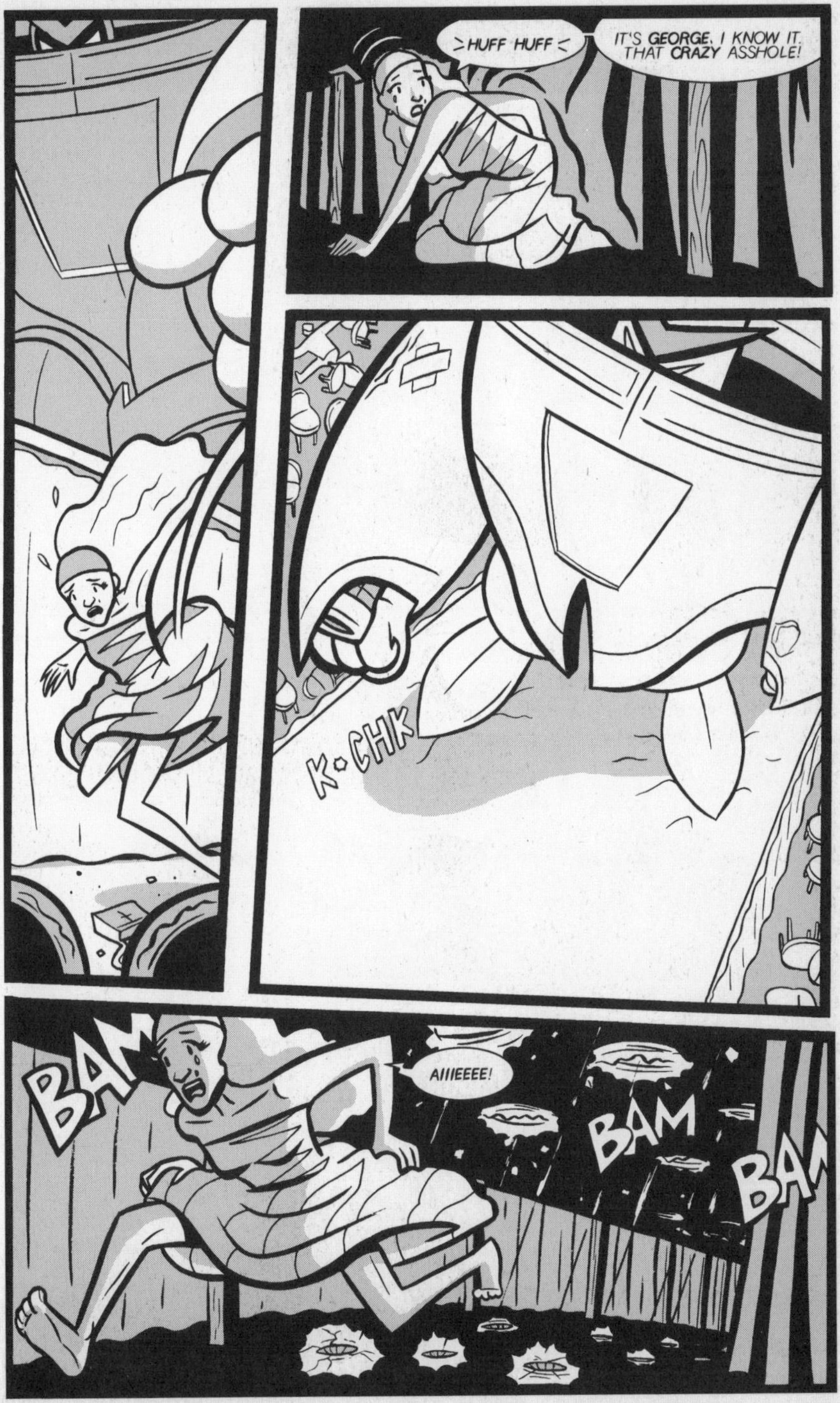
HUFF HUFF
IT'S GEORGE, I KNOW IT. THAT CRAZY ASSHOLE!
K•CHK
BAM
AIIIEEEE!
BAM
BAM

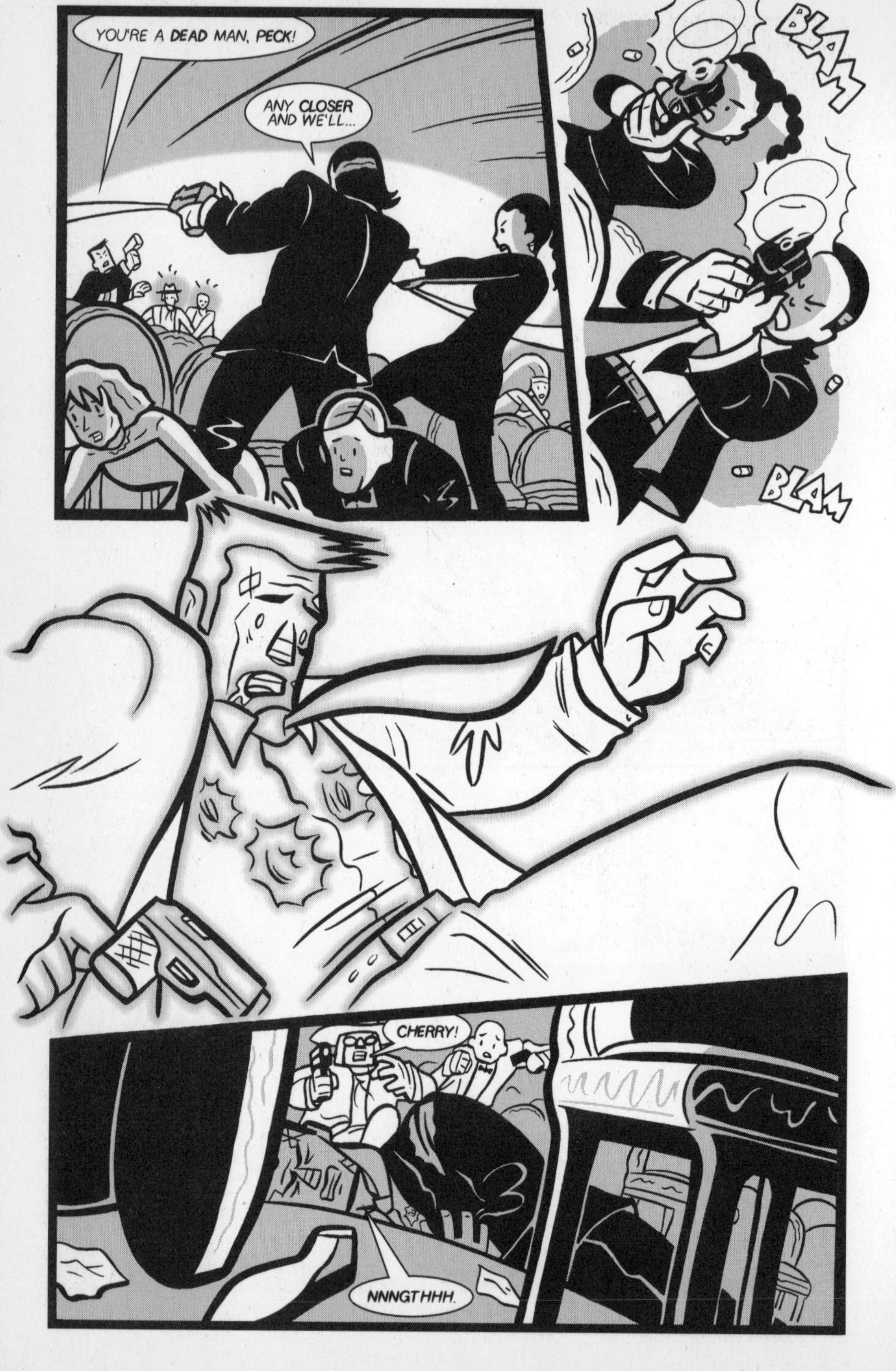
YOU'RE A DEAD MAN, PECK!
ANY CLOSER AND WE'LL...
BLAM
BLAM
CHERRY!
NNNGTHHH.

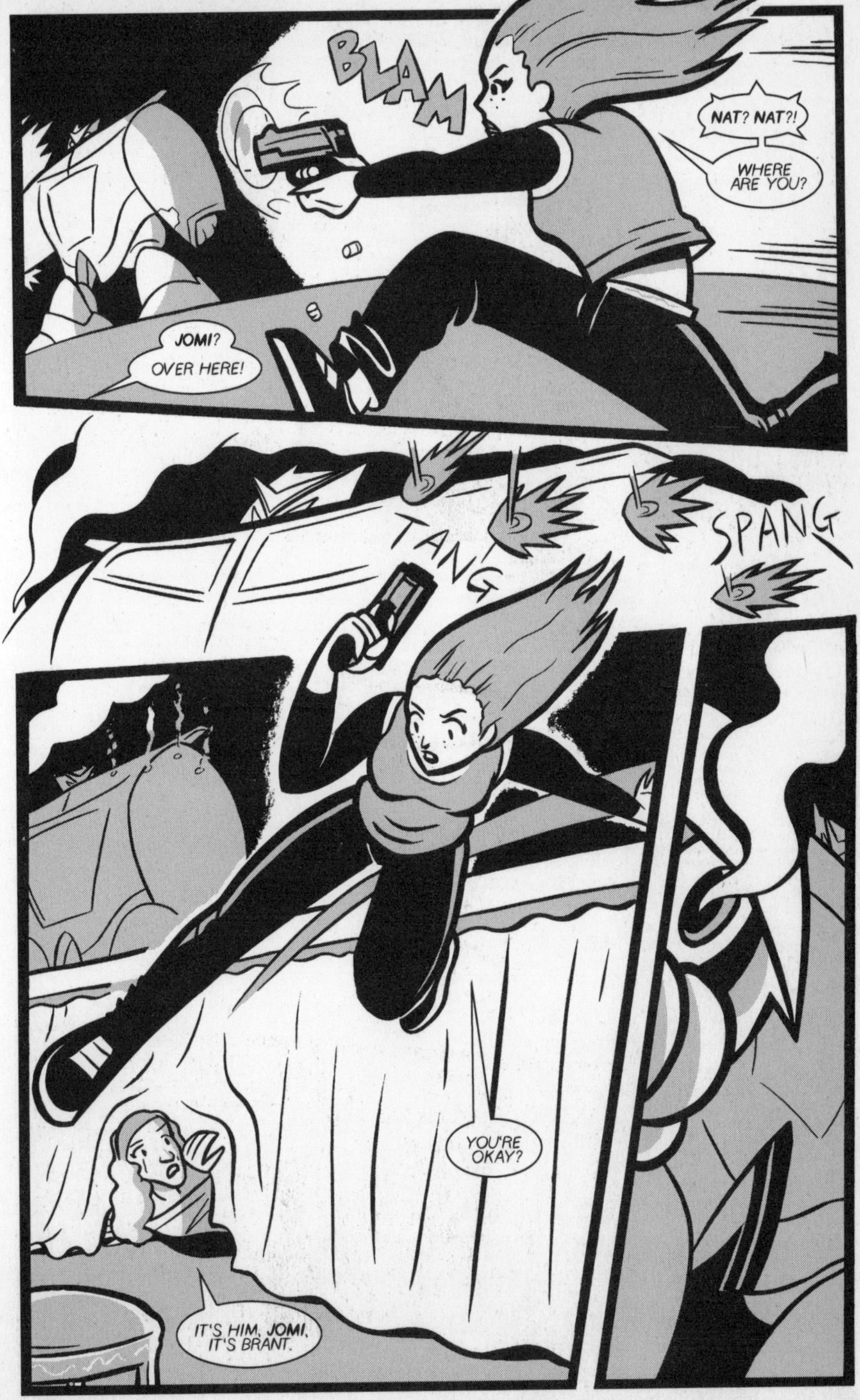
BLAM
NAT? NAT?!
WHERE ARE YOU?
JOMI? OVER HERE!
TANG
SPANG
YOU'RE OKAY?
IT'S HIM, JOMI, IT'S BRANT.

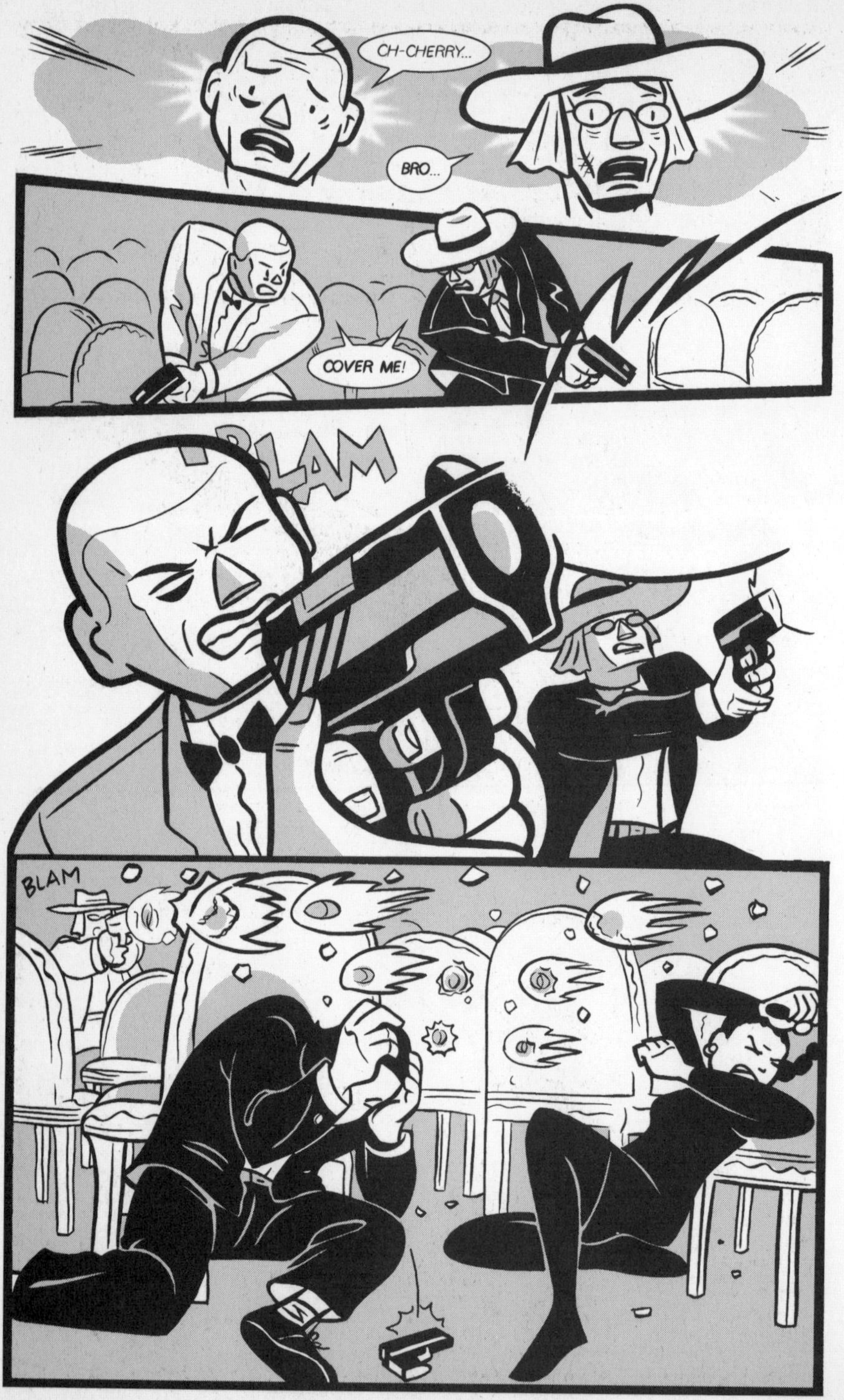
CH-CHERRY...
BRO...
COVER ME!
BLAM
BLAM

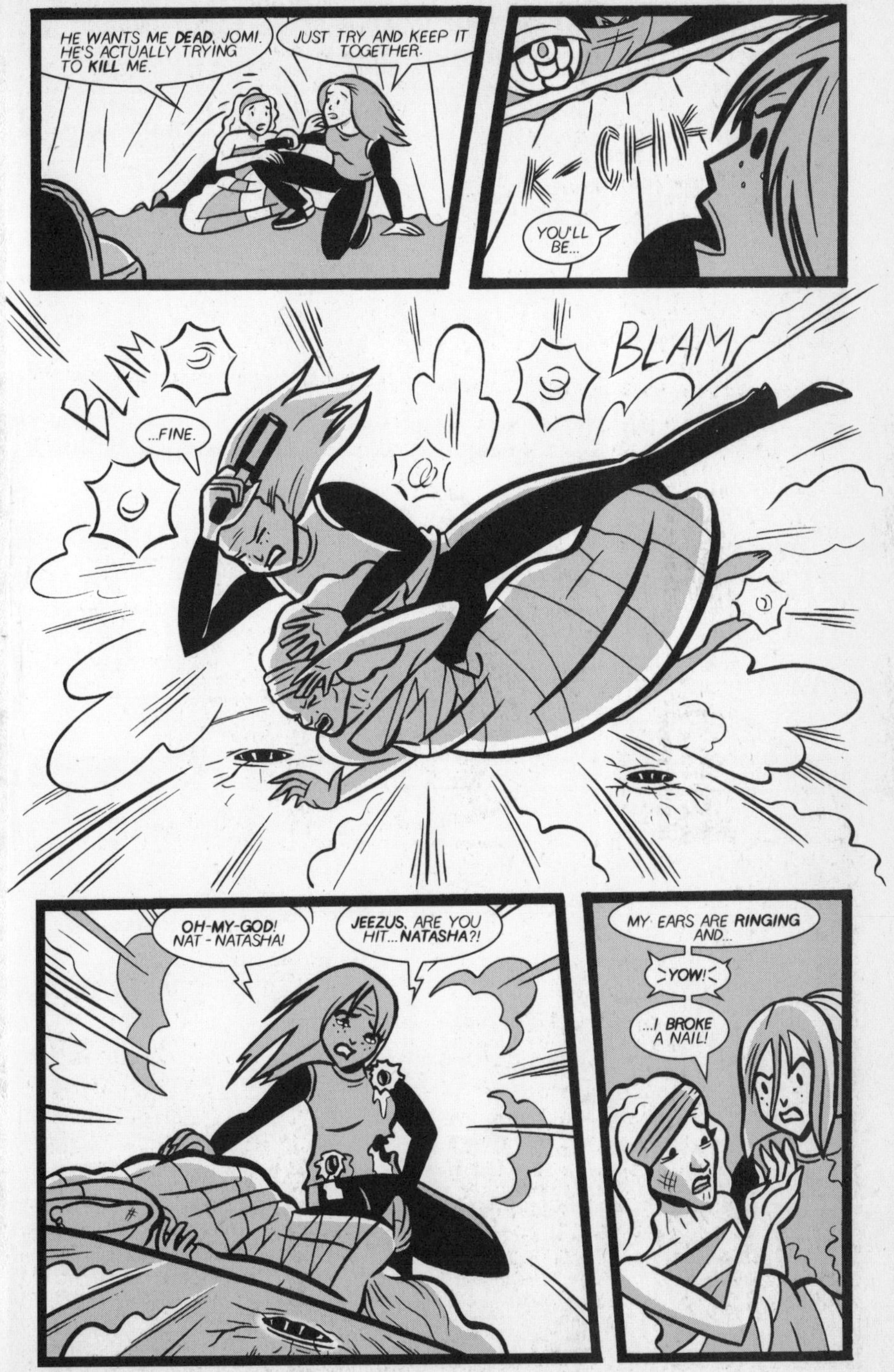

HE WANTS ME DEAD, JOMI. HE'S ACTUALLY TRYING TO KILL ME.
JUST TRY AND KEEP IT TOGETHER.
K-CHK
YOU'LL BE...
BLAM
...FINE.
BLAM
OH-MY-GOD! NAT-NATASHA!
JEEZUS, ARE YOU HIT...NATASHA?!
MY EARS ARE RINGING AND...
YOW!
...I BROKE A NAIL!

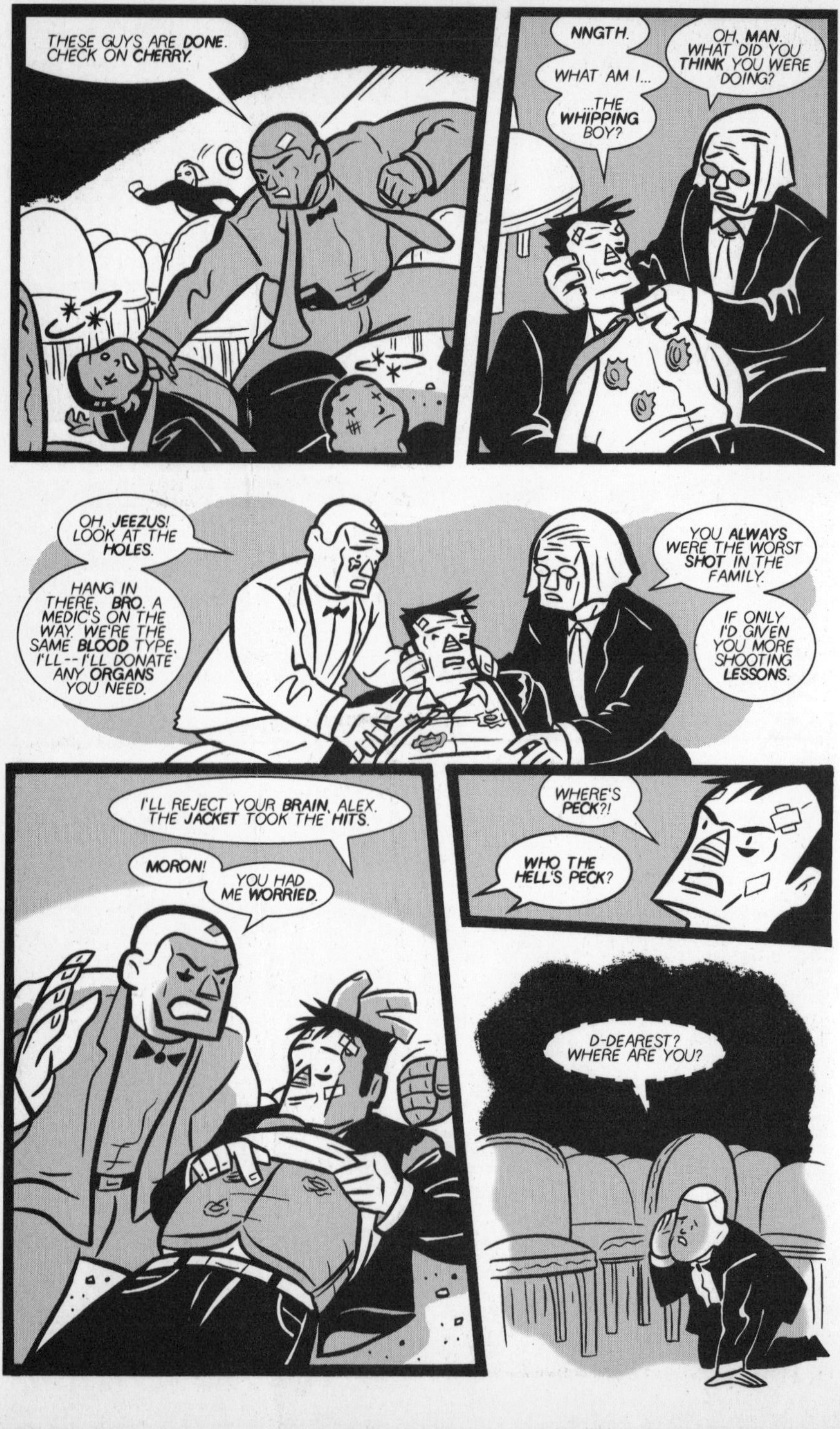
THESE GUYS ARE DONE. CHECK ON CHERRY.
NNGTH.
WHAT AM I...
...THE WHIPPING BOY?
OH, MAN. WHAT DID YOU THINK YOU WERE DOING?
OH, JEEZUS! LOOK AT THE HOLES.
HANG IN THERE, BRO. A MEDIC'S ON THE WAY. WE'RE THE SAME BLOOD TYPE. I'LL--I'LL DONATE ANY ORGANS YOU NEED.
YOU ALWAYS WERE THE WORST SHOT IN THE FAMILY.
IF ONLY I'D GIVEN YOU MORE SHOOTING LESSONS.
I'LL REJECT YOUR BRAIN, ALEX. THE JACKET TOOK THE HITS.
MORON!
YOU HAD ME WORRIED.
WHERE'S PECK?!
WHO THE HELL'S PECK?
D-DEAREST? WHERE ARE YOU?

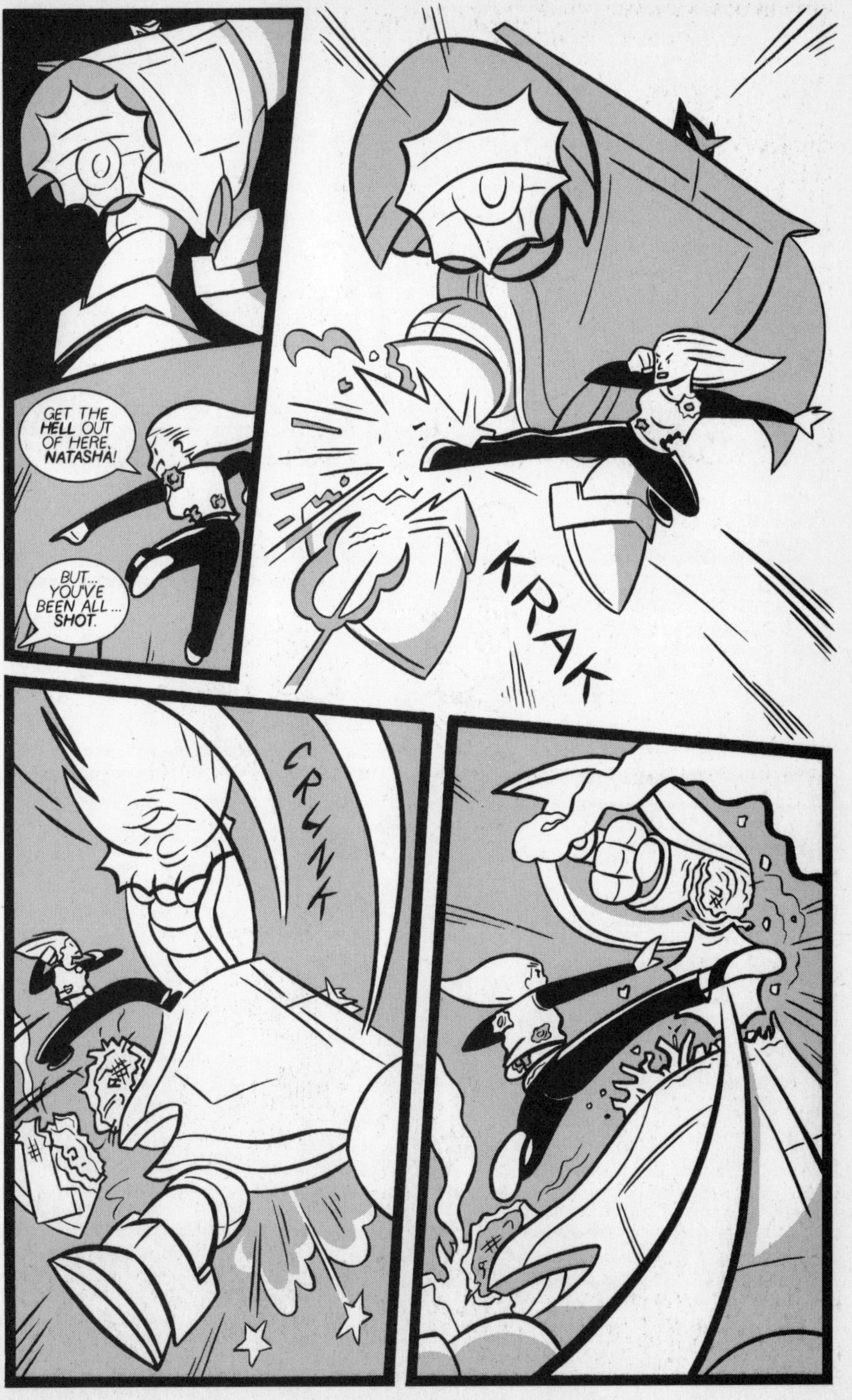
GET THE **HELL** OUT OF HERE, **NATASHA**!
BUT... YOU'VE BEEN ALL... **SHOT**.
KRAK
CRUNK

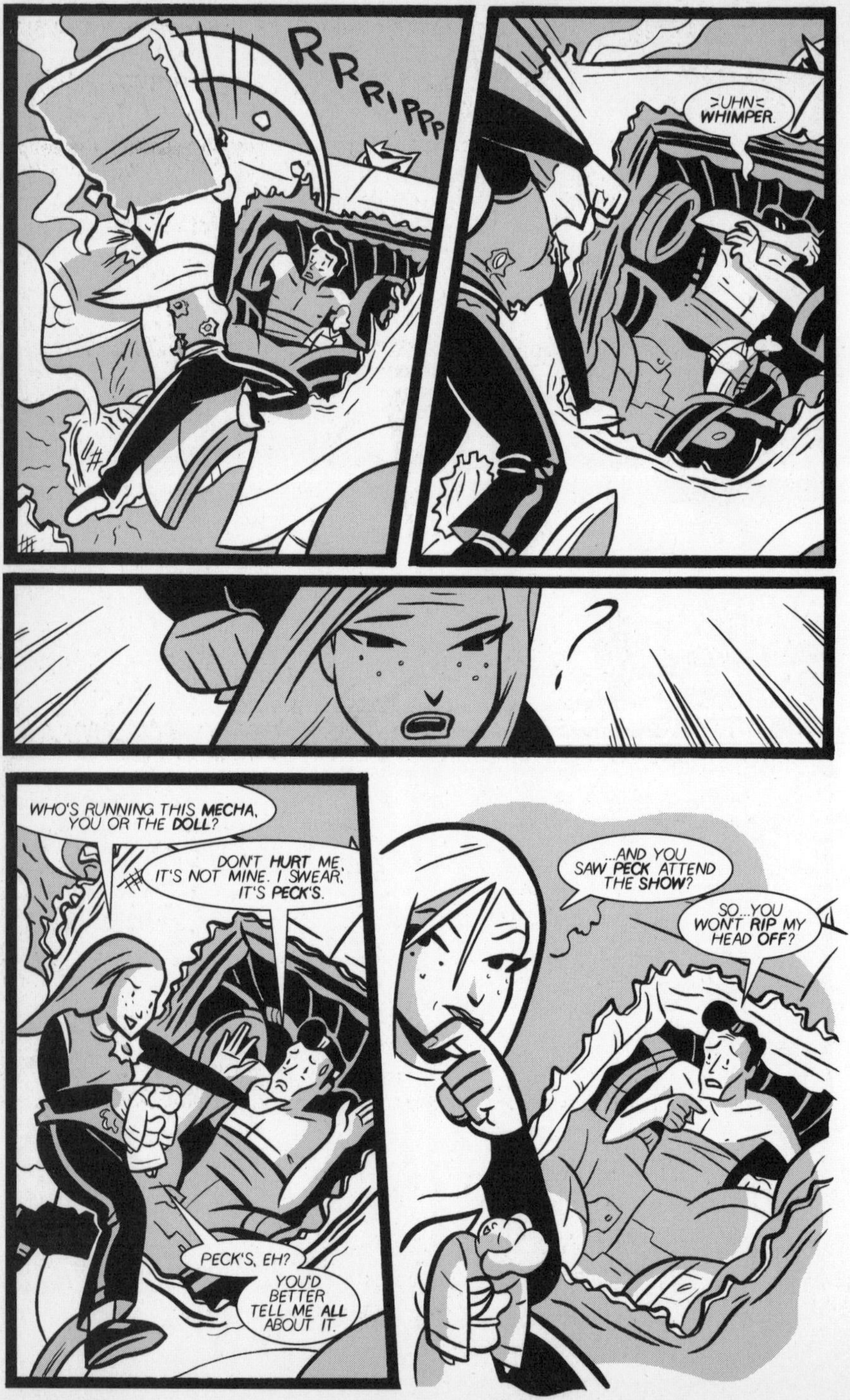
RRRIPPPP
>UHN< WHIMPER.
?
WHO'S RUNNING THIS MECHA, YOU OR THE DOLL?
DON'T HURT ME. IT'S NOT MINE. I SWEAR. IT'S PECK'S.
PECK'S, EH?
YOU'D BETTER TELL ME ALL ABOUT IT.
...AND YOU SAW PECK ATTEND THE SHOW?
SO...YOU WON'T RIP MY HEAD OFF?

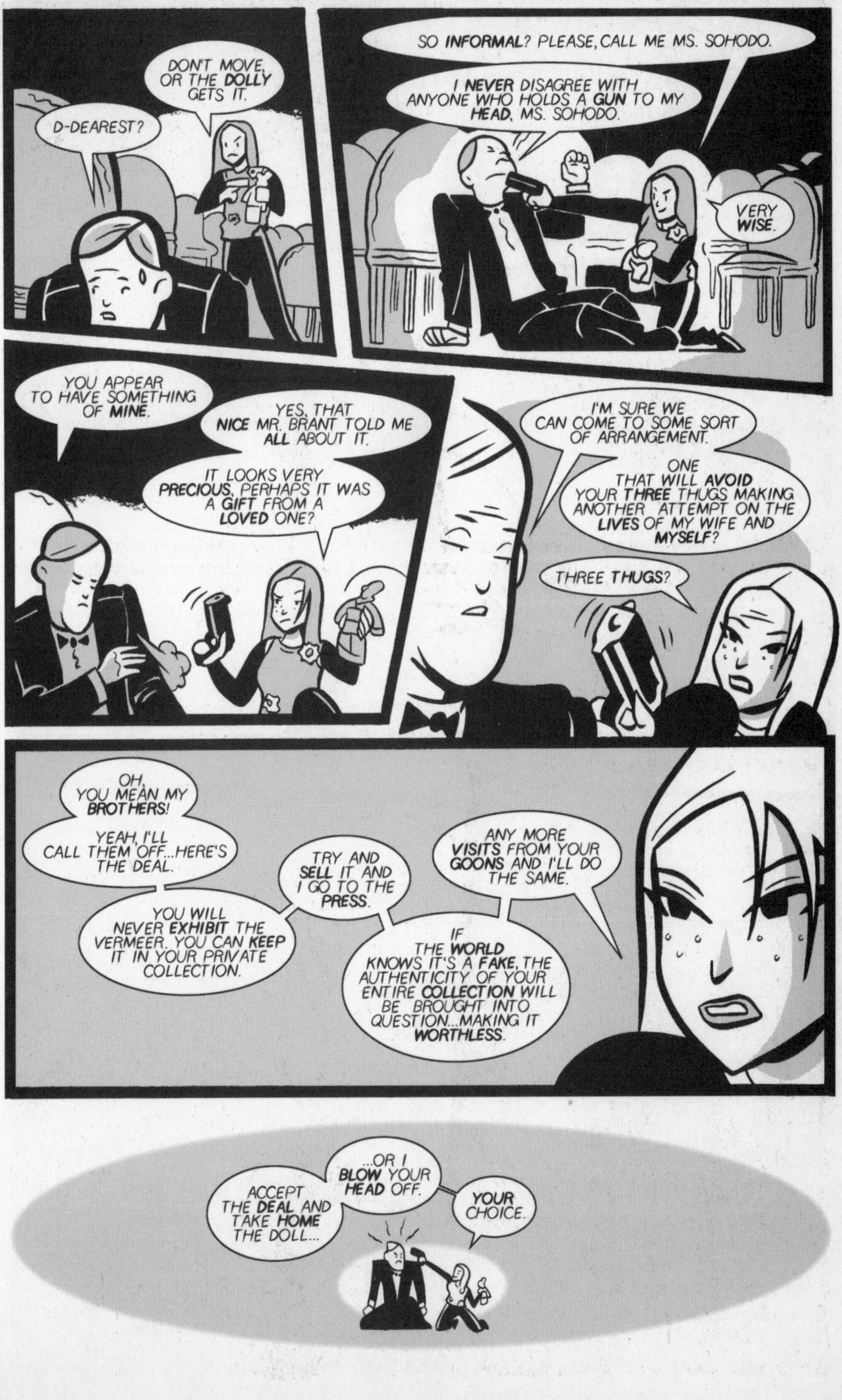
D-DEAREST?
DON'T MOVE, OR THE DOLLY GETS IT.
SO INFORMAL? PLEASE, CALL ME MS. SOHODO.
I NEVER DISAGREE WITH ANYONE WHO HOLDS A GUN TO MY HEAD, MS. SOHODO.
VERY WISE.
YOU APPEAR TO HAVE SOMETHING OF MINE.
YES, THAT NICE MR. BRANT TOLD ME ALL ABOUT IT.
IT LOOKS VERY PRECIOUS, PERHAPS IT WAS A GIFT FROM A LOVED ONE?
I'M SURE WE CAN COME TO SOME SORT OF ARRANGEMENT.
ONE THAT WILL AVOID YOUR THREE THUGS MAKING ANOTHER ATTEMPT ON THE LIVES OF MY WIFE AND MYSELF?
THREE THUGS?
OH, YOU MEAN MY BROTHERS!
YEAH, I'LL CALL THEM OFF...HERE'S THE DEAL.
YOU WILL NEVER EXHIBIT THE VERMEER. YOU CAN KEEP IT IN YOUR PRIVATE COLLECTION.
TRY AND SELL IT AND I GO TO THE PRESS.
IF THE WORLD KNOWS IT'S A FAKE, THE AUTHENTICITY OF YOUR ENTIRE COLLECTION WILL BE BROUGHT INTO QUESTION...MAKING IT WORTHLESS.
ANY MORE VISITS FROM YOUR GOONS AND I'LL DO THE SAME.
ACCEPT THE DEAL AND TAKE HOME THE DOLL...
...OR I BLOW YOUR HEAD OFF.
YOUR CHOICE.

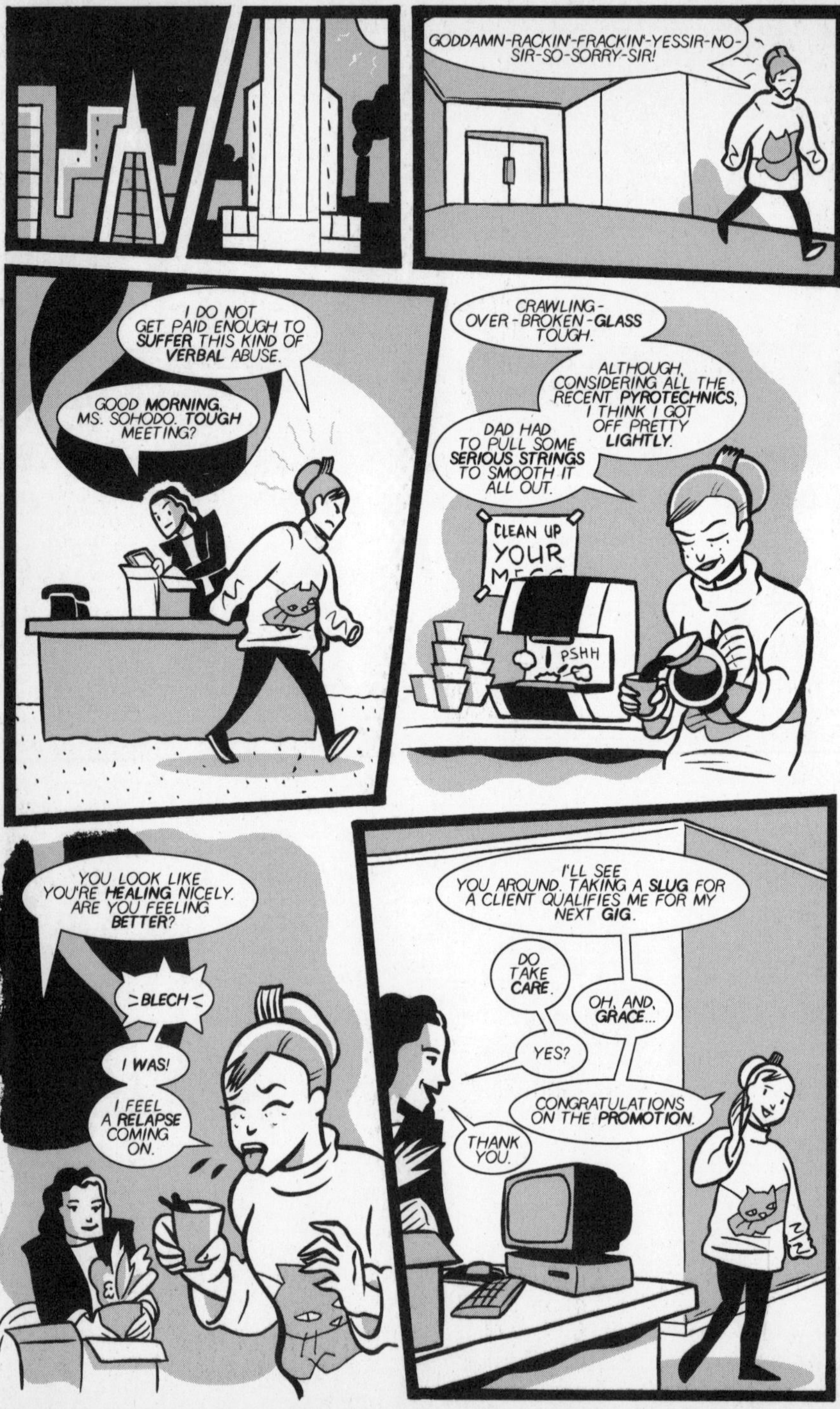
GODDAMN-RACKIN'-FRACKIN'-YESSIR-NO-SIR-SO-SORRY-SIR!
GOOD MORNING, MS. SOHODO. TOUGH MEETING?
I DO NOT GET PAID ENOUGH TO SUFFER THIS KIND OF VERBAL ABUSE.
CRAWLING-OVER-BROKEN-GLASS TOUGH.
ALTHOUGH, CONSIDERING ALL THE RECENT PYROTECHNICS, I THINK I GOT OFF PRETTY LIGHTLY.
DAD HAD TO PULL SOME SERIOUS STRINGS TO SMOOTH IT ALL OUT.
CLEAN UP YOUR
PSHH
YOU LOOK LIKE YOU'RE HEALING NICELY. ARE YOU FEELING BETTER?
BLECH
I WAS!
I FEEL A RELAPSE COMING ON.
I'LL SEE YOU AROUND. TAKING A SLUG FOR A CLIENT QUALIFIES ME FOR MY NEXT GIG.
DO TAKE CARE.
OH, AND, GRACE...
YES?
CONGRATULATIONS ON THE PROMOTION.
THANK YOU.

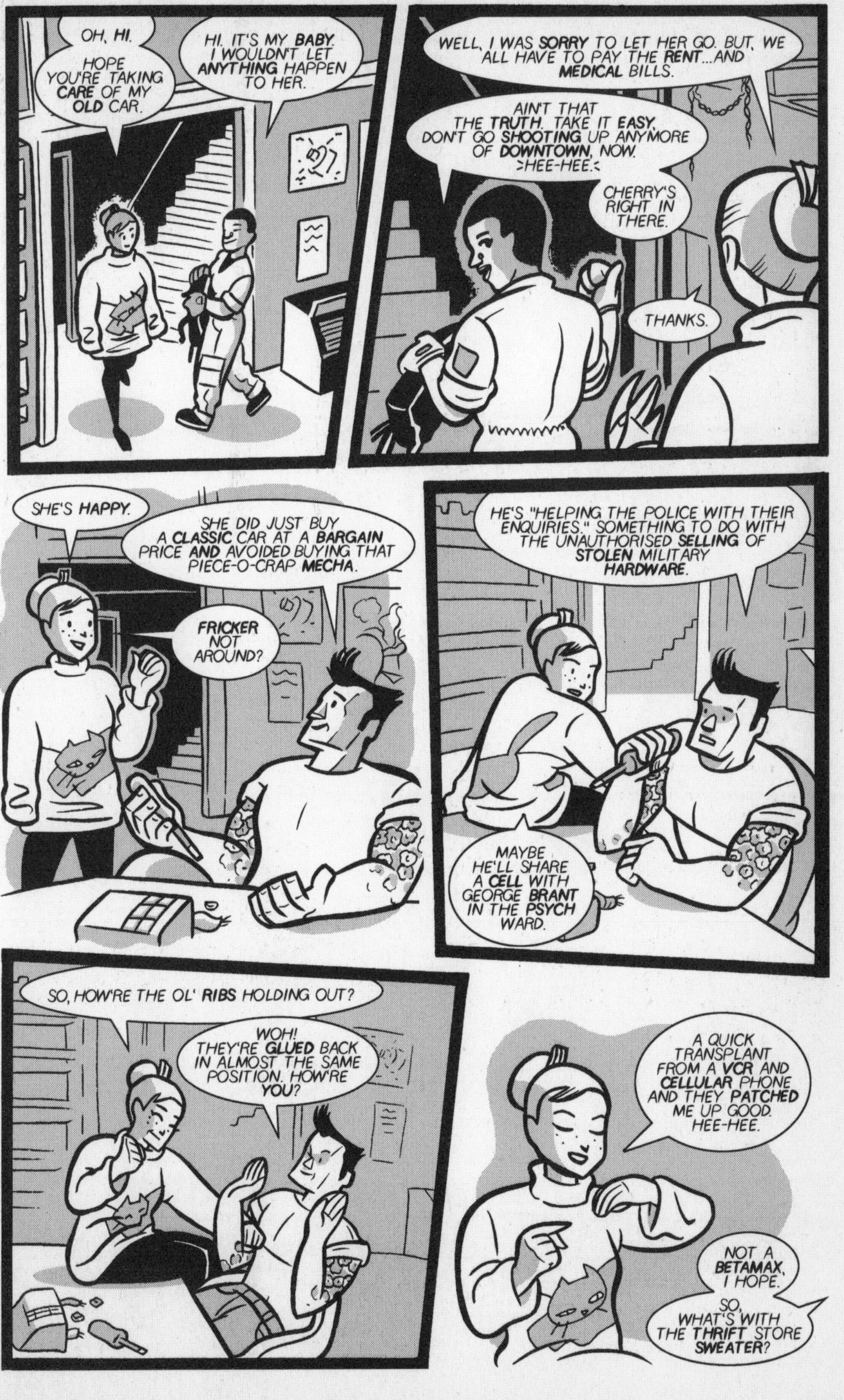
OH, HI.
HOPE YOU'RE TAKING CARE OF MY OLD CAR.
HI. IT'S MY BABY. I WOULDN'T LET ANYTHING HAPPEN TO HER.
WELL, I WAS SORRY TO LET HER GO. BUT, WE ALL HAVE TO PAY THE RENT...AND MEDICAL BILLS.
AIN'T THAT THE TRUTH. TAKE IT EASY. DON'T GO SHOOTING UP ANYMORE OF DOWNTOWN, NOW. >HEE-HEE.<
CHERRY'S RIGHT IN THERE.
THANKS.
SHE'S HAPPY.
SHE DID JUST BUY A CLASSIC CAR AT A BARGAIN PRICE AND AVOIDED BUYING THAT PIECE-O-CRAP MECHA.
FRICKER NOT AROUND?
HE'S "HELPING THE POLICE WITH THEIR ENQUIRIES." SOMETHING TO DO WITH THE UNAUTHORISED SELLING OF STOLEN MILITARY HARDWARE.
MAYBE HE'LL SHARE A CELL WITH GEORGE BRANT IN THE PSYCH WARD.
SO, HOW'RE THE OL' RIBS HOLDING OUT?
WOH! THEY'RE GLUED BACK IN ALMOST THE SAME POSITION. HOW'RE YOU?
A QUICK TRANSPLANT FROM A VCR AND CELLULAR PHONE AND THEY PATCHED ME UP GOOD. HEE-HEE.
NOT A BETAMAX, I HOPE.
SO, WHAT'S WITH THE THRIFT STORE SWEATER?

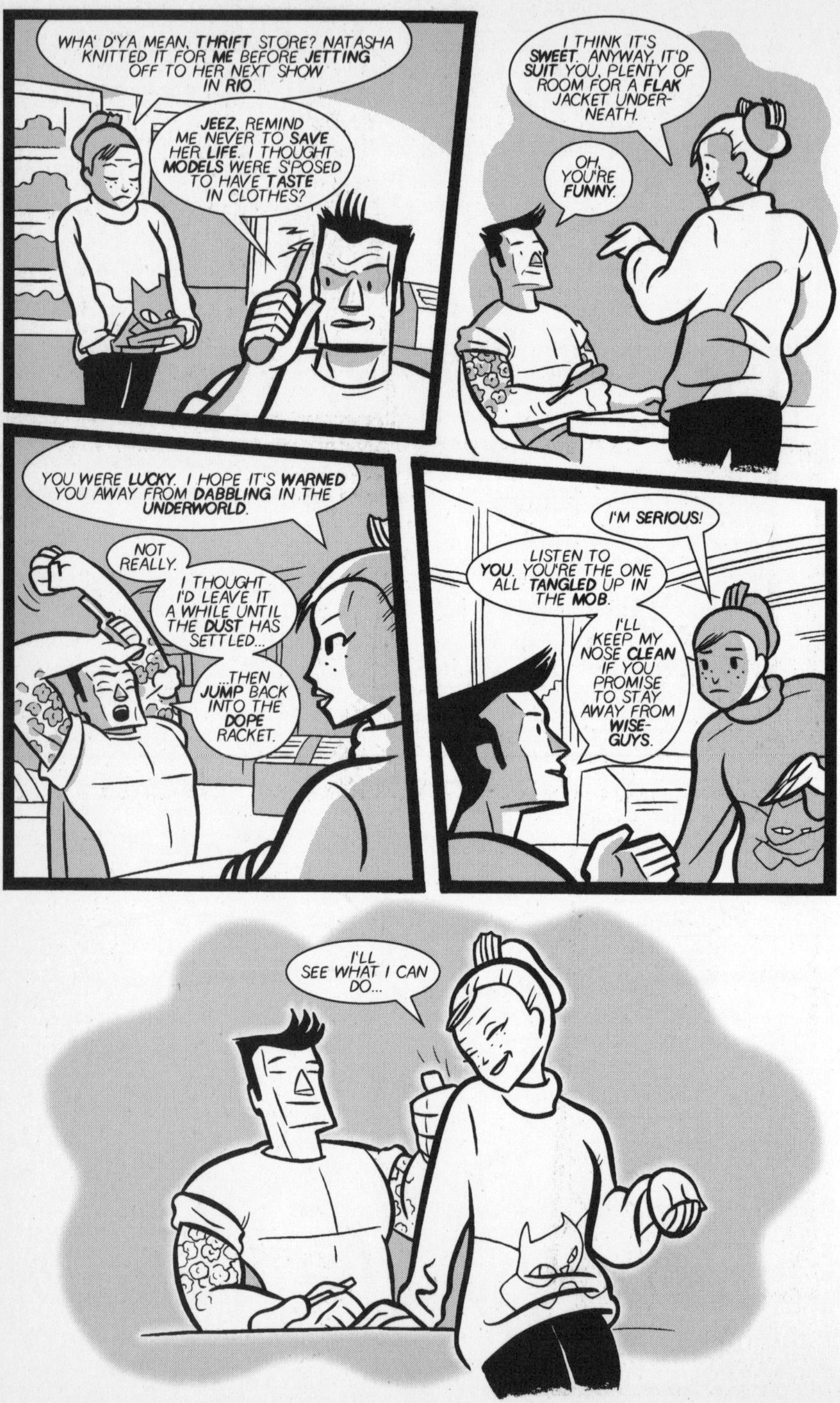
WHA' D'YA MEAN, THRIFT STORE? NATASHA KNITTED IT FOR ME BEFORE JETTING OFF TO HER NEXT SHOW IN RIO.
JEEZ, REMIND ME NEVER TO SAVE HER LIFE. I THOUGHT MODELS WERE S'POSED TO HAVE TASTE IN CLOTHES?
I THINK IT'S SWEET. ANYWAY, IT'D SUIT YOU, PLENTY OF ROOM FOR A FLAK JACKET UNDER-NEATH.
OH, YOU'RE FUNNY.
YOU WERE LUCKY. I HOPE IT'S WARNED YOU AWAY FROM DABBLING IN THE UNDERWORLD.
NOT REALLY.
I THOUGHT I'D LEAVE IT A WHILE UNTIL THE DUST HAS SETTLED...
...THEN JUMP BACK INTO THE DOPE RACKET.
I'M SERIOUS!
LISTEN TO YOU. YOU'RE THE ONE ALL TANGLED UP IN THE MOB.
I'LL KEEP MY NOSE CLEAN IF YOU PROMISE TO STAY AWAY FROM WISE-GUYS.
I'LL SEE WHAT I CAN DO...

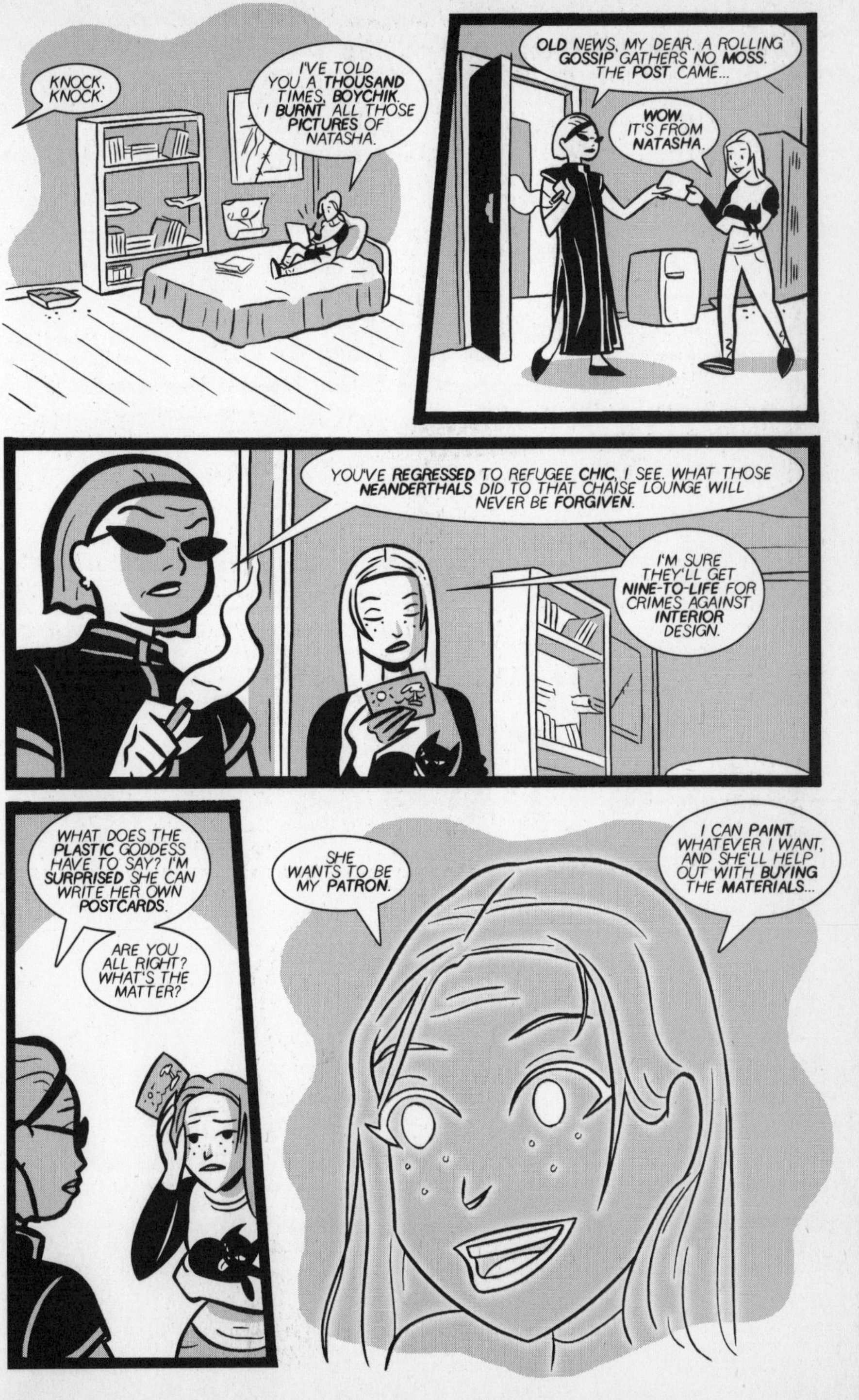
KNOCK, KNOCK.
I'VE TOLD YOU A THOUSAND TIMES, BOYCHIK. I BURNT ALL THOSE PICTURES OF NATASHA.
OLD NEWS, MY DEAR. A ROLLING GOSSIP GATHERS NO MOSS. THE POST CAME...
WOW. IT'S FROM NATASHA.
YOU'VE REGRESSED TO REFUGEE CHIC, I SEE. WHAT THOSE NEANDERTHALS DID TO THAT CHAISE LOUNGE WILL NEVER BE FORGIVEN.
I'M SURE THEY'LL GET NINE-TO-LIFE FOR CRIMES AGAINST INTERIOR DESIGN.
WHAT DOES THE PLASTIC GODDESS HAVE TO SAY? I'M SURPRISED SHE CAN WRITE HER OWN POSTCARDS.
ARE YOU ALL RIGHT? WHAT'S THE MATTER?
SHE WANTS TO BE MY PATRON.
I CAN PAINT WHATEVER I WANT, AND SHE'LL HELP OUT WITH BUYING THE MATERIALS...

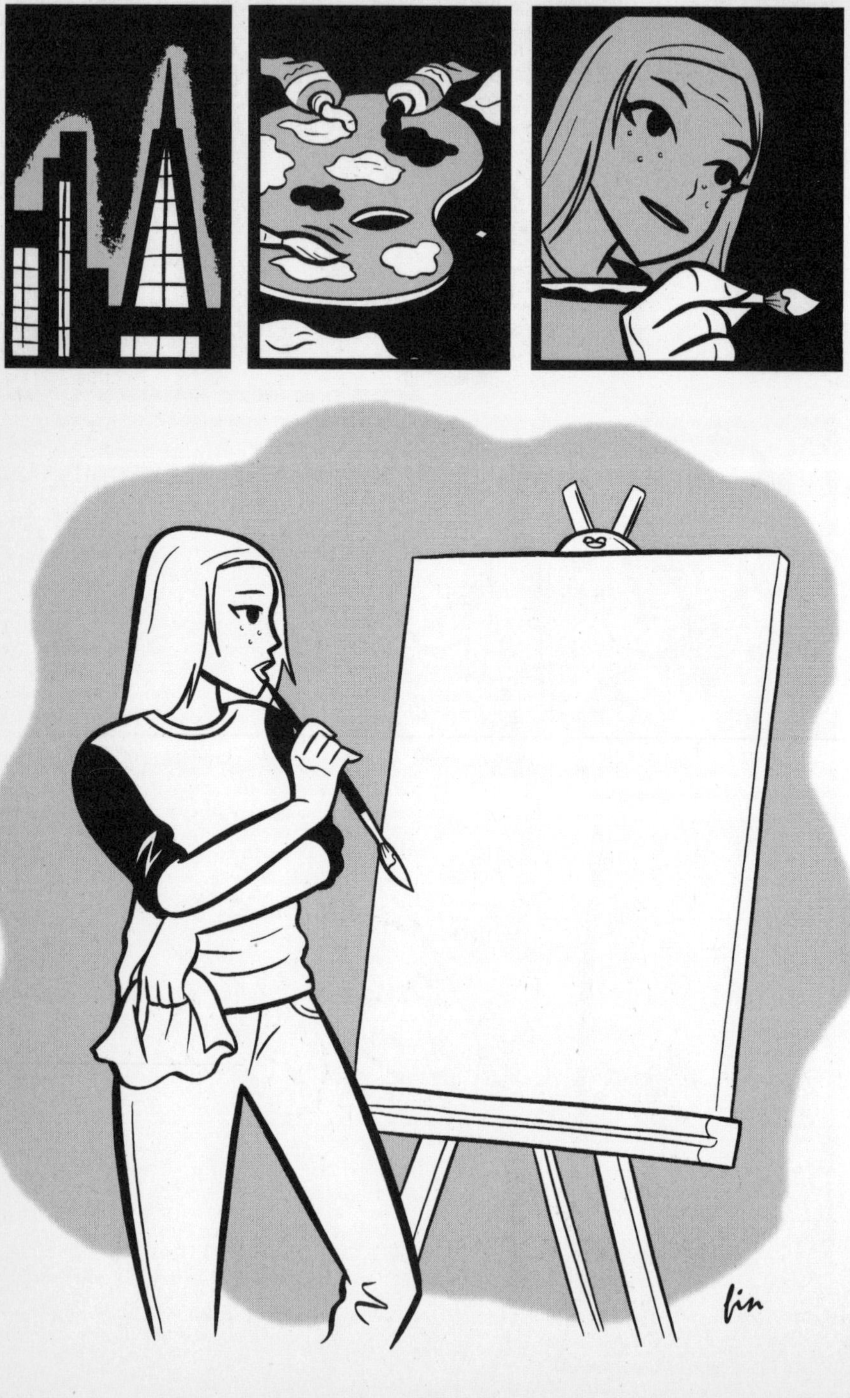

geisha ™

out of tune

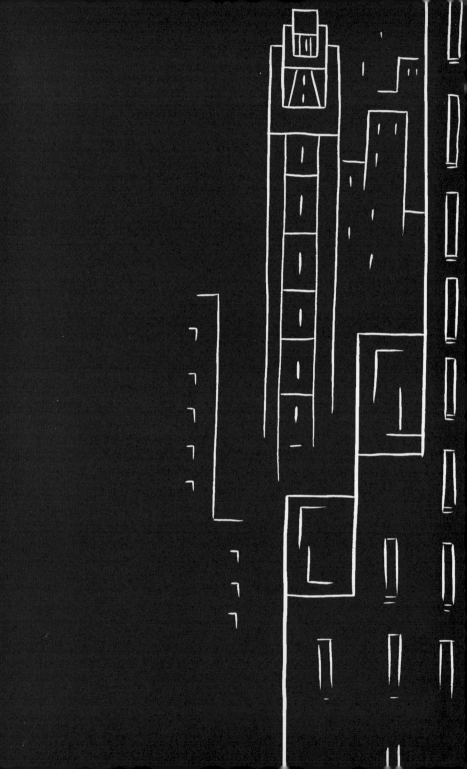

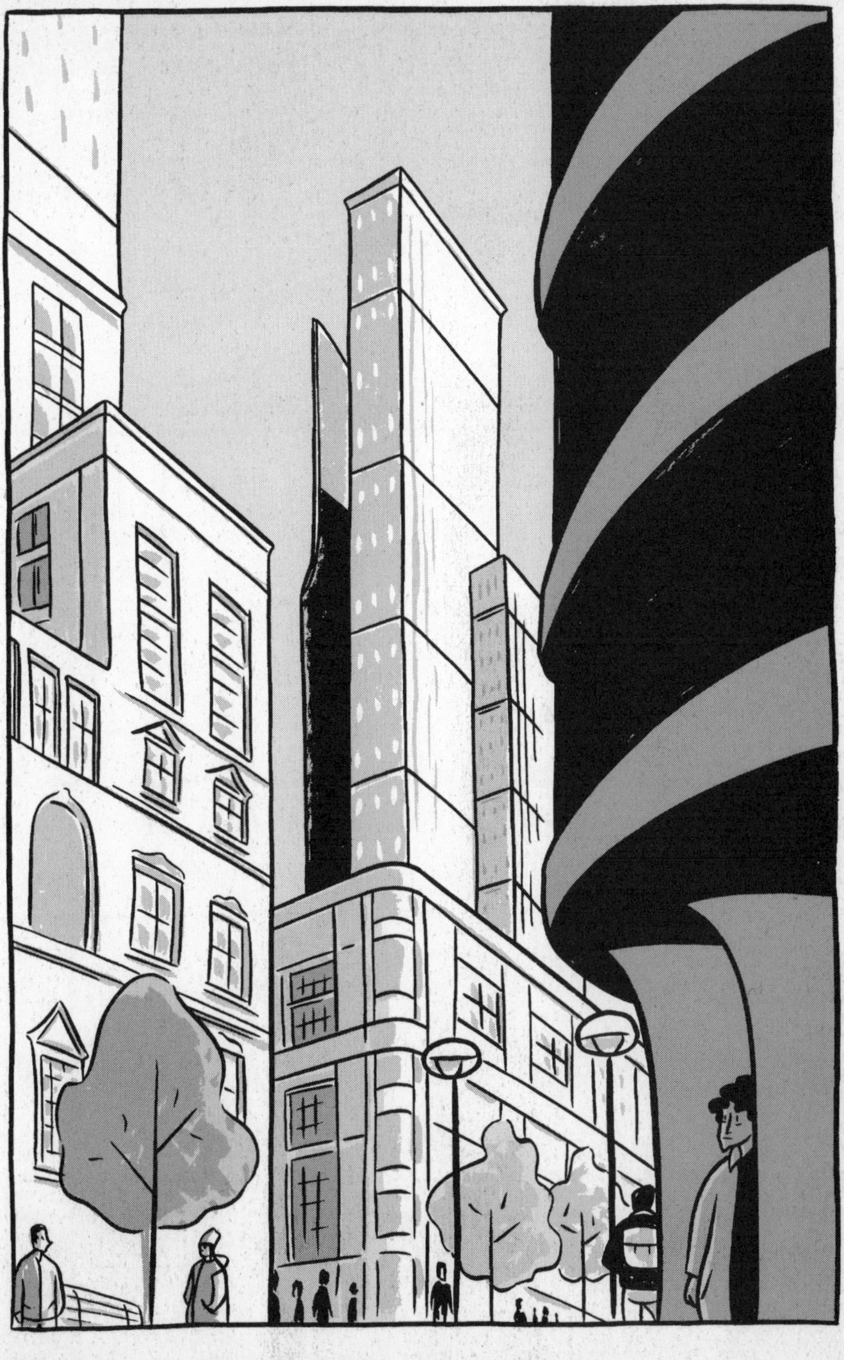

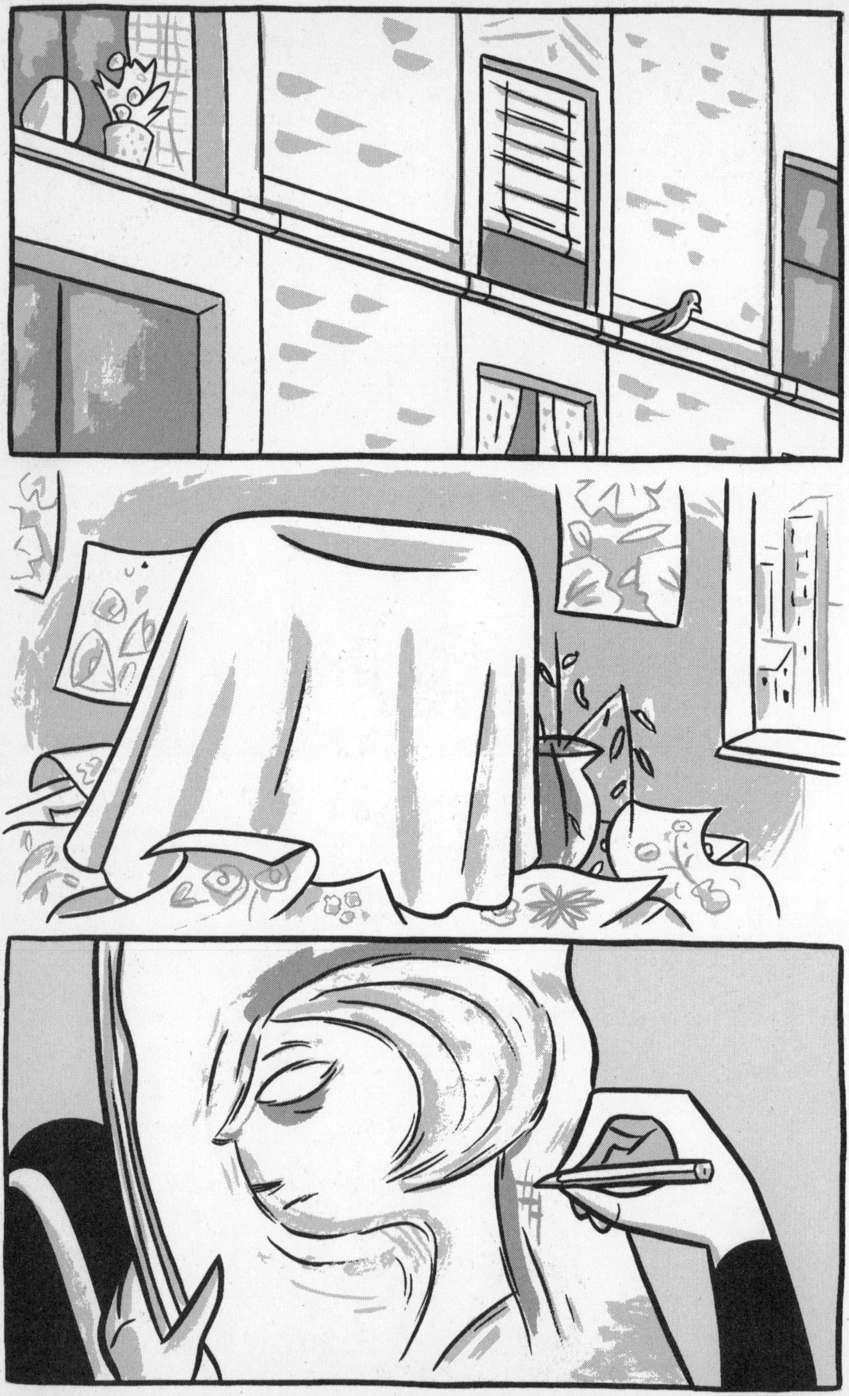

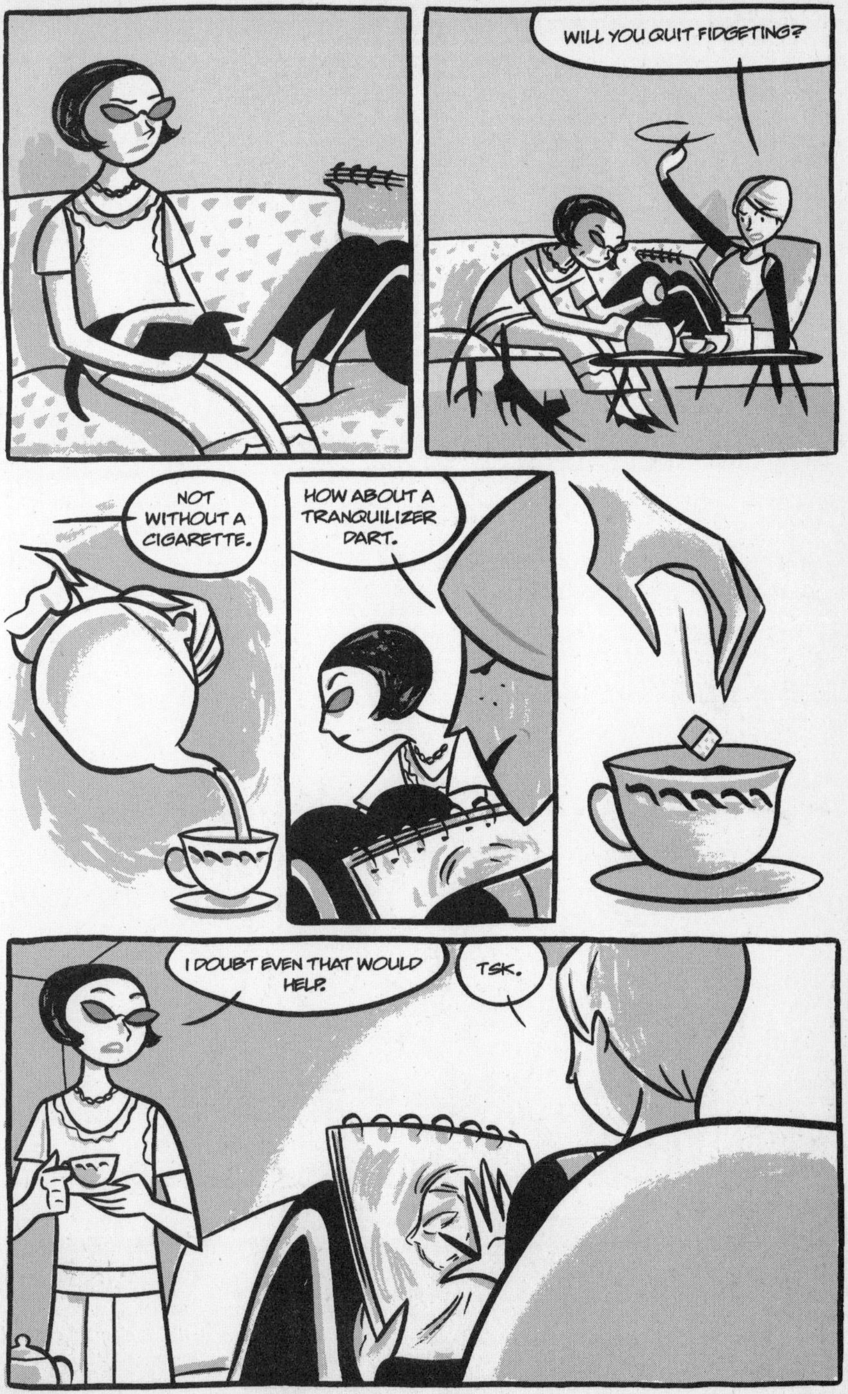
WILL YOU QUIT FIDGETING?
NOT WITHOUT A CIGARETTE.
HOW ABOUT A TRANQUILIZER DART.
I DOUBT EVEN THAT WOULD HELP.
TSK.

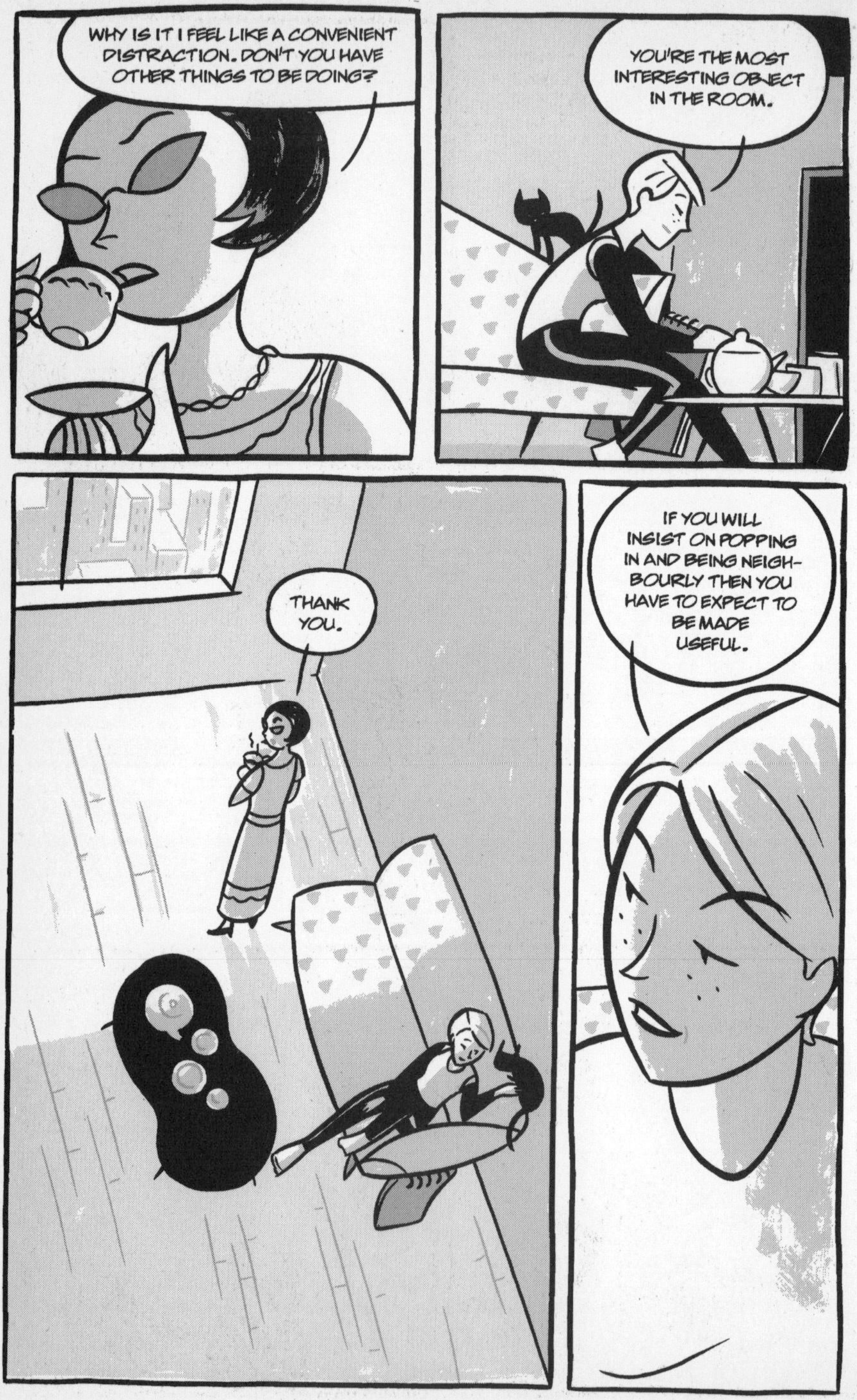
WHY IS IT I FEEL LIKE A CONVENIENT DISTRACTION. DON'T YOU HAVE OTHER THINGS TO BE DOING?
YOU'RE THE MOST INTERESTING OBJECT IN THE ROOM.
THANK YOU.
IF YOU WILL INSIST ON POPPING IN AND BEING NEIGH-BOURLY THEN YOU HAVE TO EXPECT TO BE MADE USEFUL.

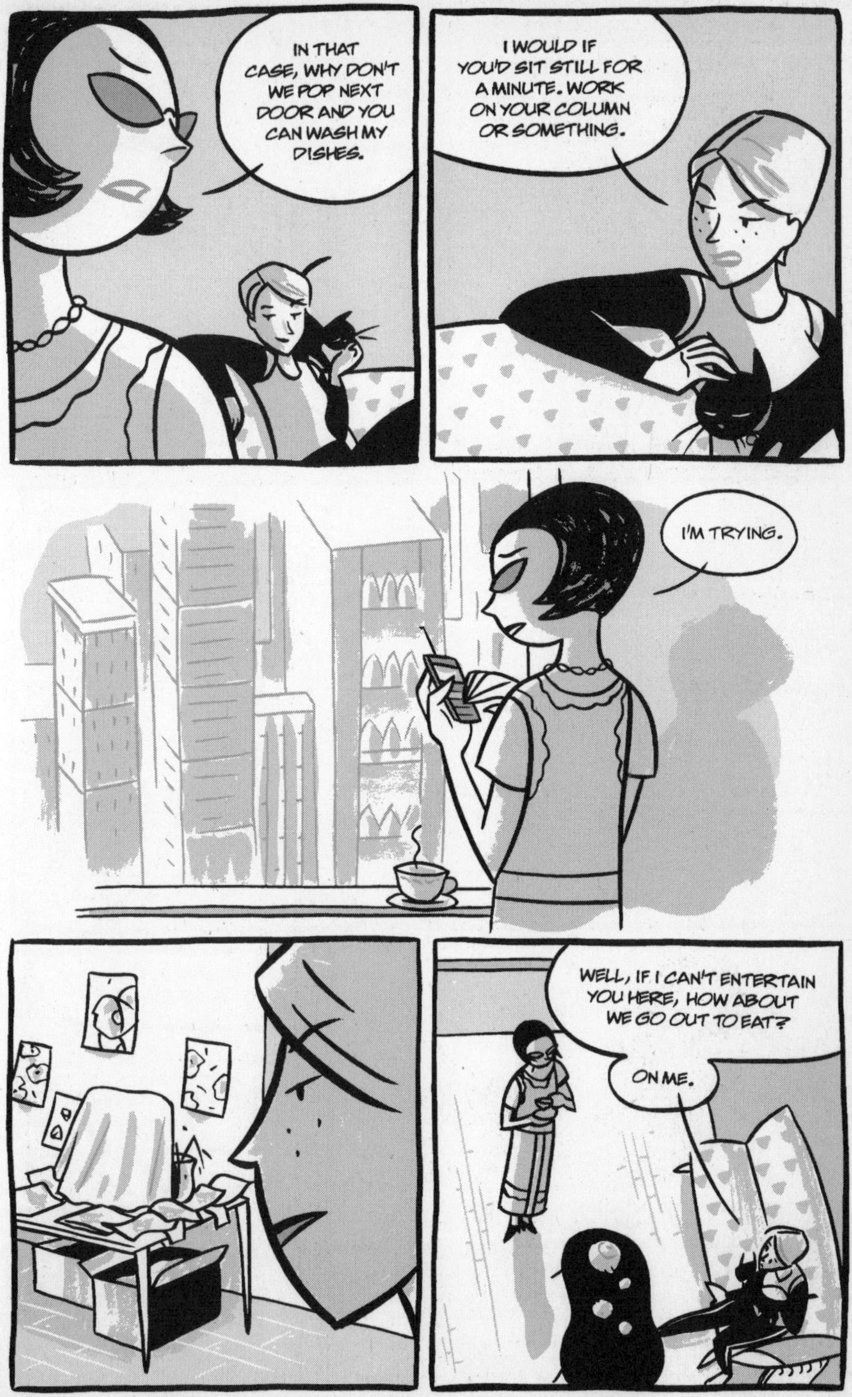
IN THAT CASE, WHY DON'T WE POP NEXT DOOR AND YOU CAN WASH MY DISHES.
I WOULD IF YOU'D SIT STILL FOR A MINUTE. WORK ON YOUR COLUMN OR SOMETHING.
I'M TRYING.
WELL, IF I CAN'T ENTERTAIN YOU HERE, HOW ABOUT WE GO OUT TO EAT?
ON ME.

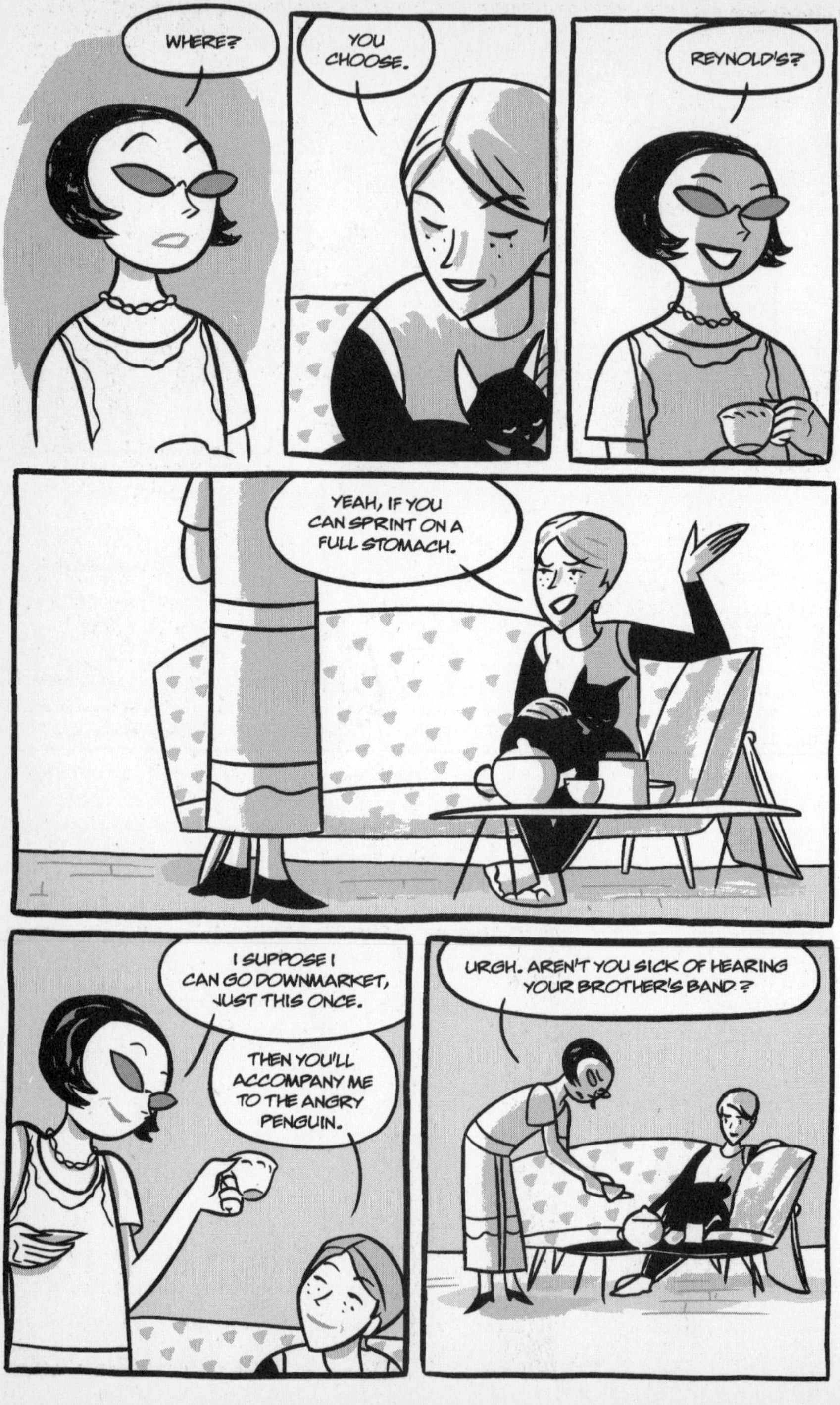
WHERE?
YOU CHOOSE.
REYNOLD'S?
YEAH, IF YOU CAN SPRINT ON A FULL STOMACH.
I SUPPOSE I CAN GO DOWNMARKET, JUST THIS ONCE.
THEN YOU'LL ACCOMPANY ME TO THE ANGRY PENGUIN.
URGH. AREN'T YOU SICK OF HEARING YOUR BROTHER'S BAND?

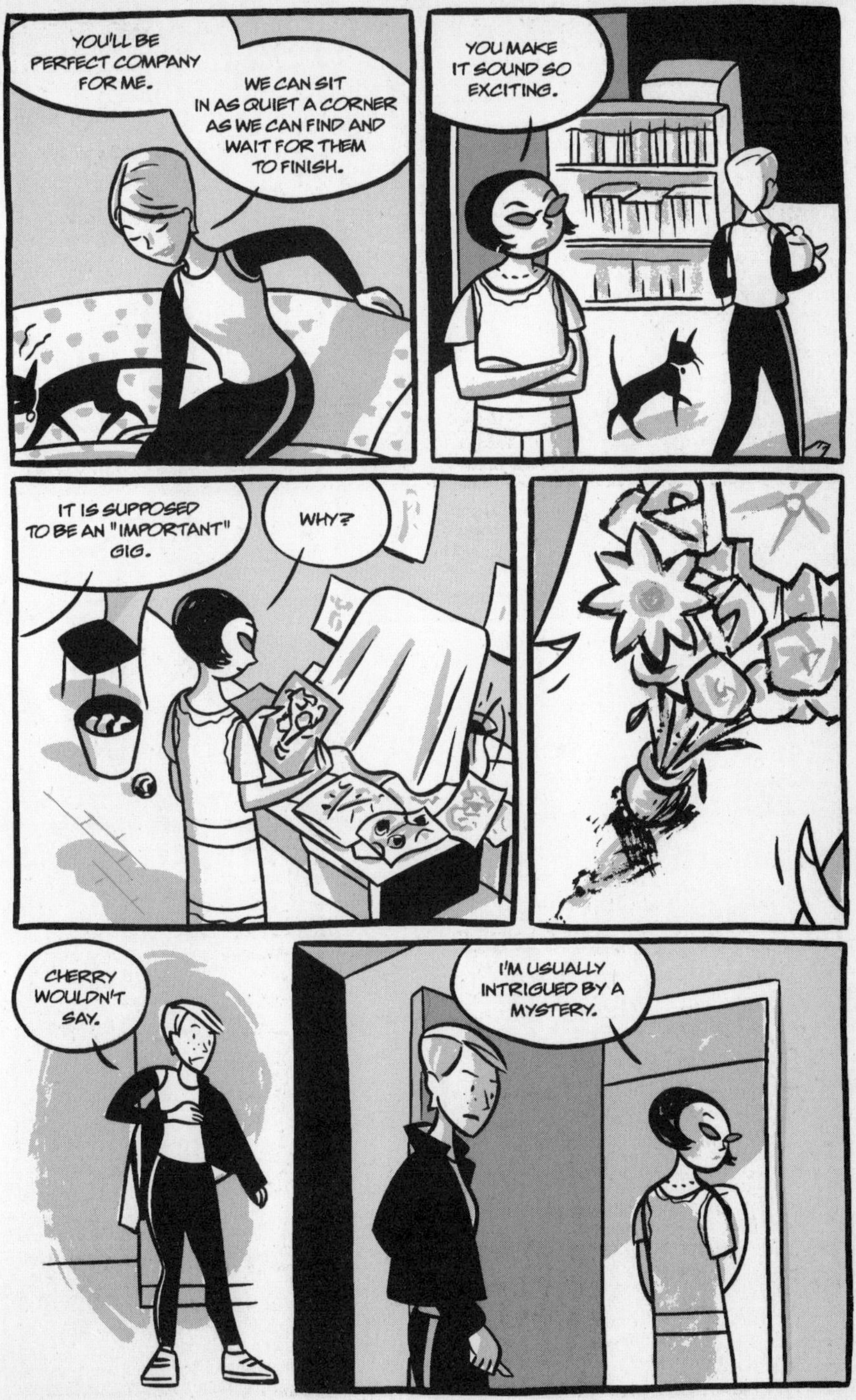
YOU'LL BE PERFECT COMPANY FOR ME.
WE CAN SIT IN AS QUIET A CORNER AS WE CAN FIND AND WAIT FOR THEM TO FINISH.
YOU MAKE IT SOUND SO EXCITING.
IT IS SUPPOSED TO BE AN "IMPORTANT" GIG.
WHY?
CHERRY WOULDN'T SAY.
I'M USUALLY INTRIGUED BY A MYSTERY.

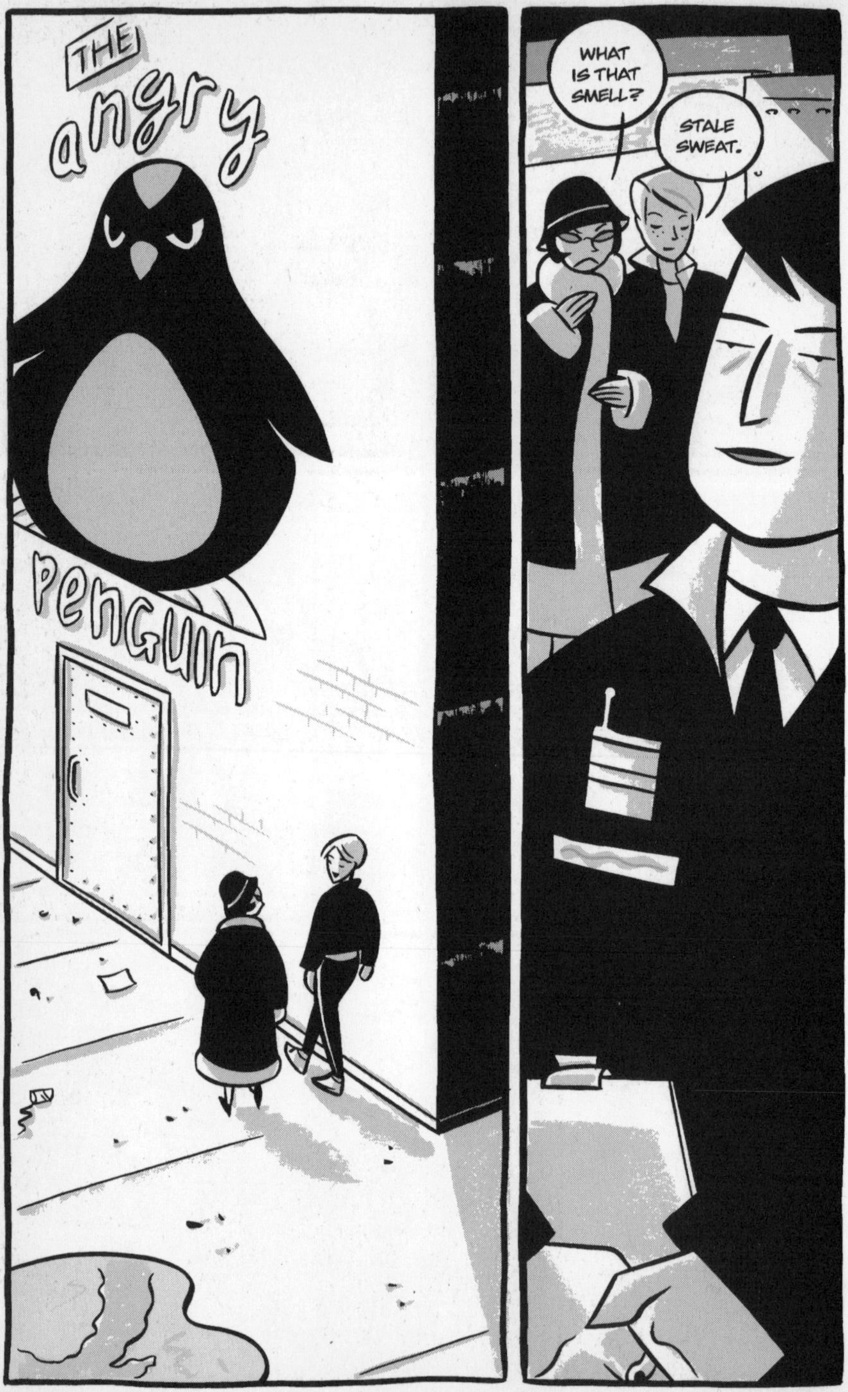
THE angry penguin
WHAT IS THAT SMELL?
STALE SWEAT.

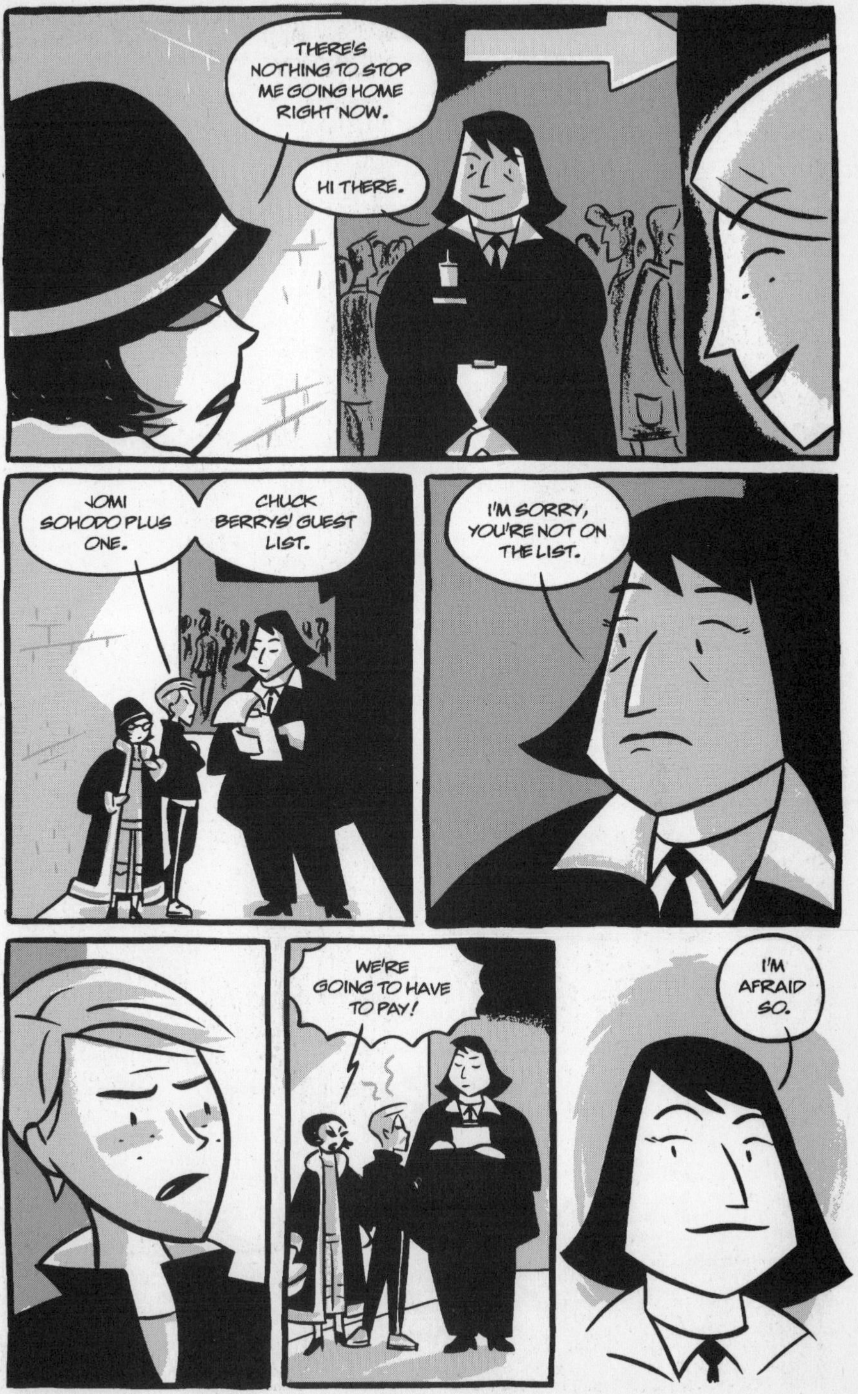
THERE'S NOTHING TO STOP ME GOING HOME RIGHT NOW.
HI THERE.
JOMI SOHODO PLUS ONE.
CHUCK BERRYS' GUEST LIST.
I'M SORRY, YOU'RE NOT ON THE LIST.
WE'RE GOING TO HAVE TO PAY!
I'M AFRAID SO.

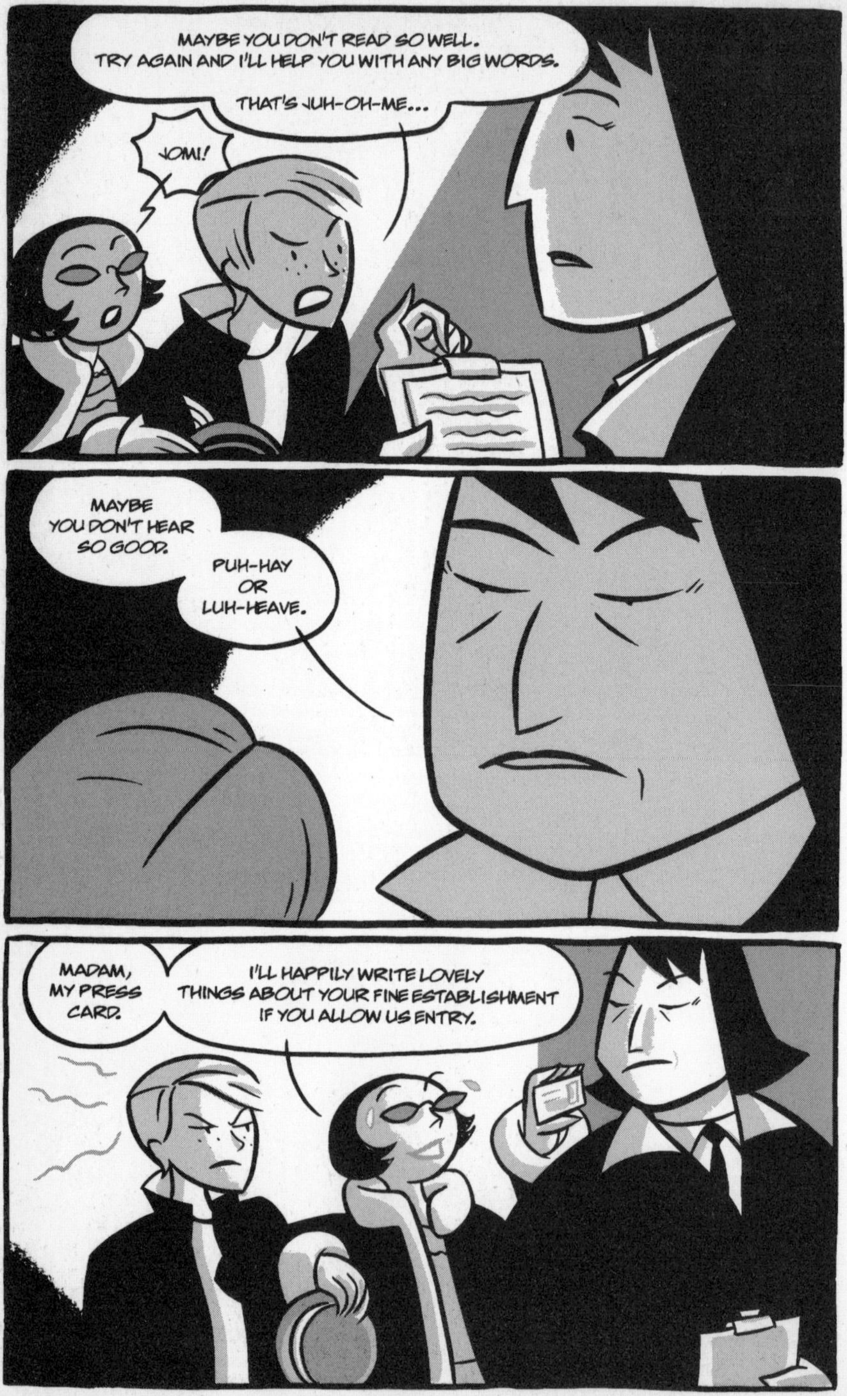
MAYBE YOU DON'T READ SO WELL. TRY AGAIN AND I'LL HELP YOU WITH ANY BIG WORDS.
THAT'S JUH-OH-ME...
JOMI!
MAYBE YOU DON'T HEAR SO GOOD.
PUH-HAY OR LUH-HEAVE.
MADAM, MY PRESS CARD.
I'LL HAPPILY WRITE LOVELY THINGS ABOUT YOUR FINE ESTABLISHMENT IF YOU ALLOW US ENTRY.

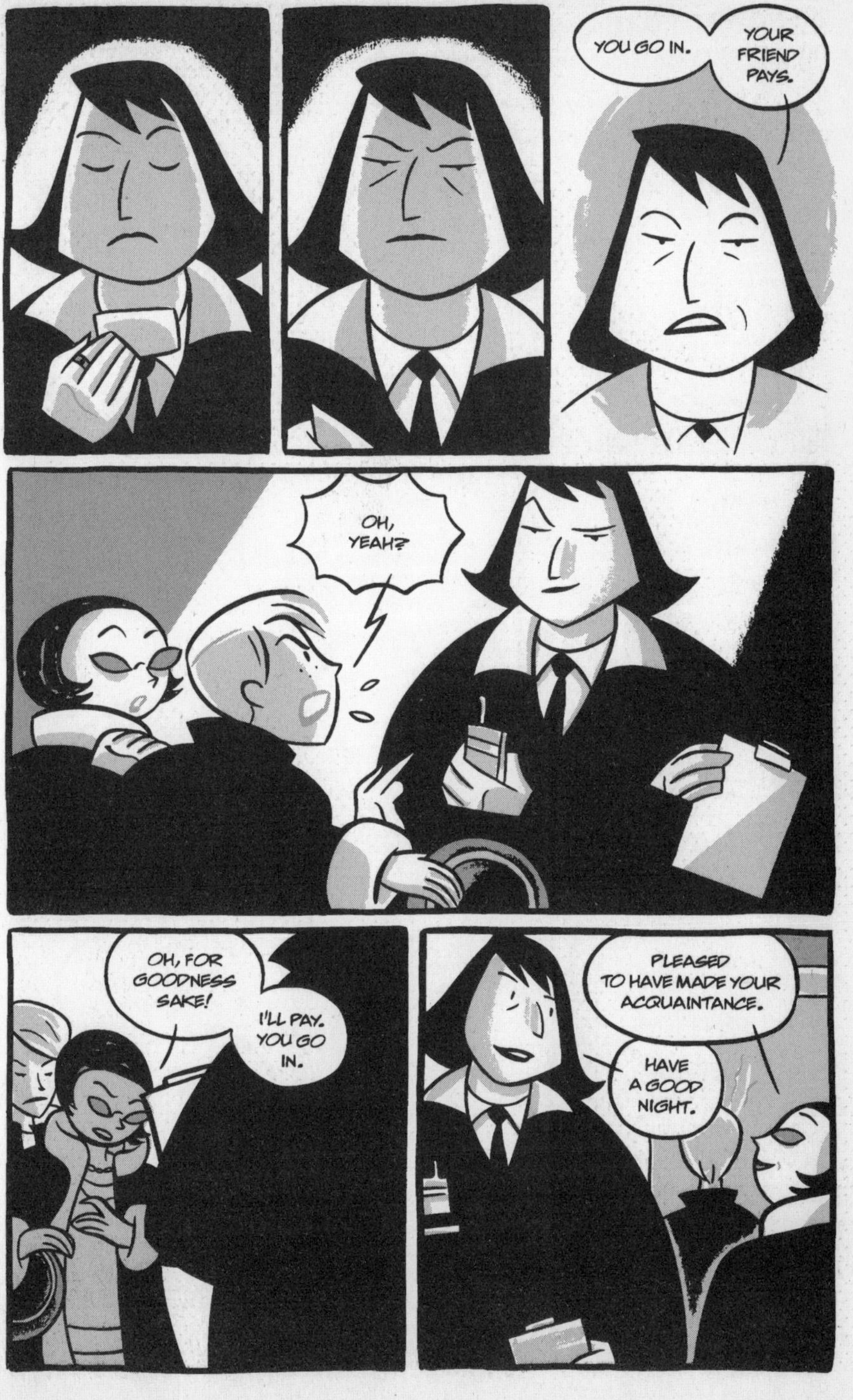
YOU GO IN.
YOUR FRIEND PAYS.
OH, YEAH?
OH, FOR GOODNESS SAKE!
I'LL PAY. YOU GO IN.
PLEASED TO HAVE MADE YOUR ACQUAINTANCE.
HAVE A GOOD NIGHT.

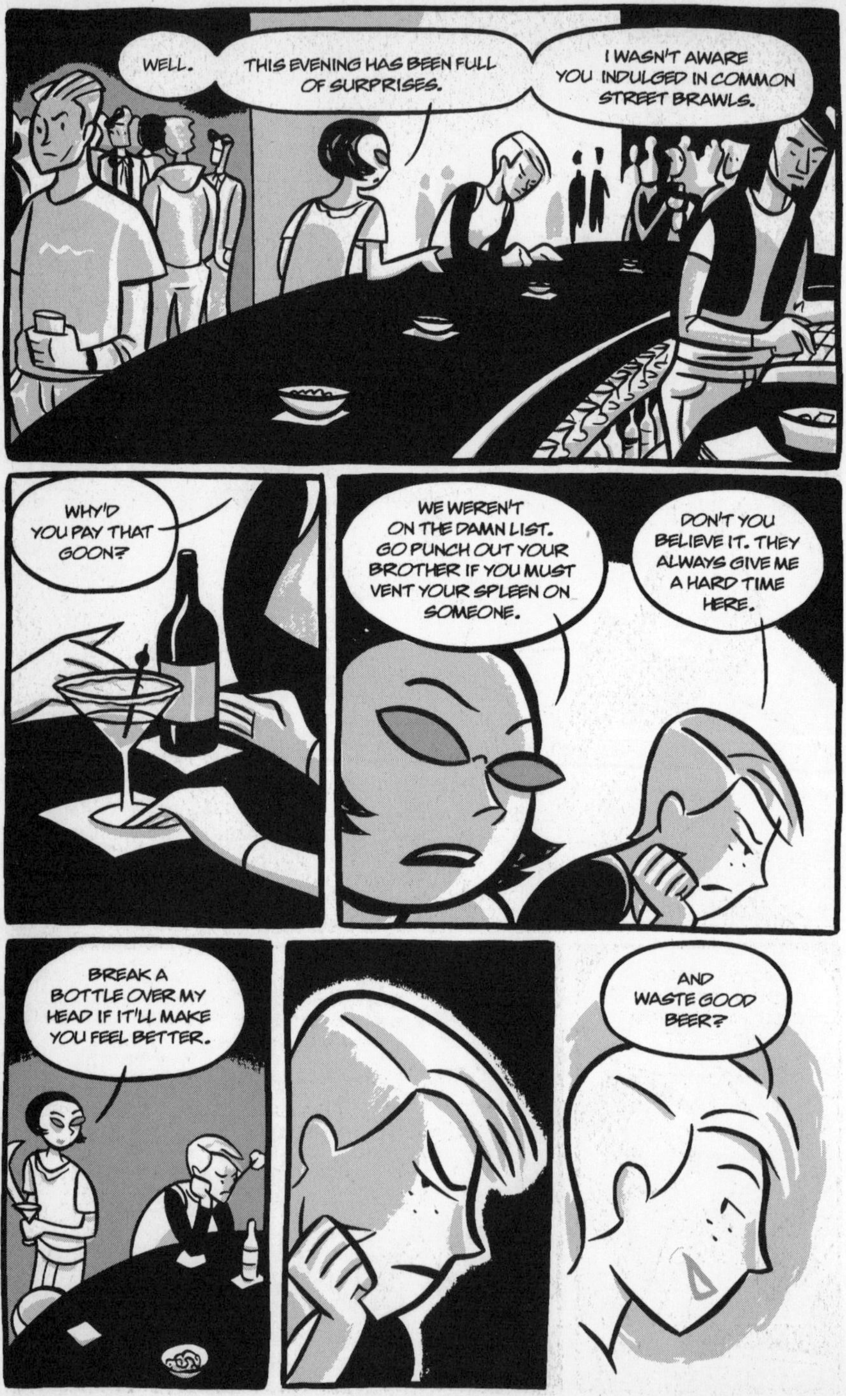
WELL.
THIS EVENING HAS BEEN FULL OF SURPRISES.
I WASN'T AWARE YOU INDULGED IN COMMON STREET BRAWLS.
WHY'D YOU PAY THAT GOON?
WE WEREN'T ON THE DAMN LIST. GO PUNCH OUT YOUR BROTHER IF YOU MUST VENT YOUR SPLEEN ON SOMEONE.
DON'T YOU BELIEVE IT. THEY ALWAYS GIVE ME A HARD TIME HERE.
BREAK A BOTTLE OVER MY HEAD IF IT'LL MAKE YOU FEEL BETTER.
AND WASTE GOOD BEER?

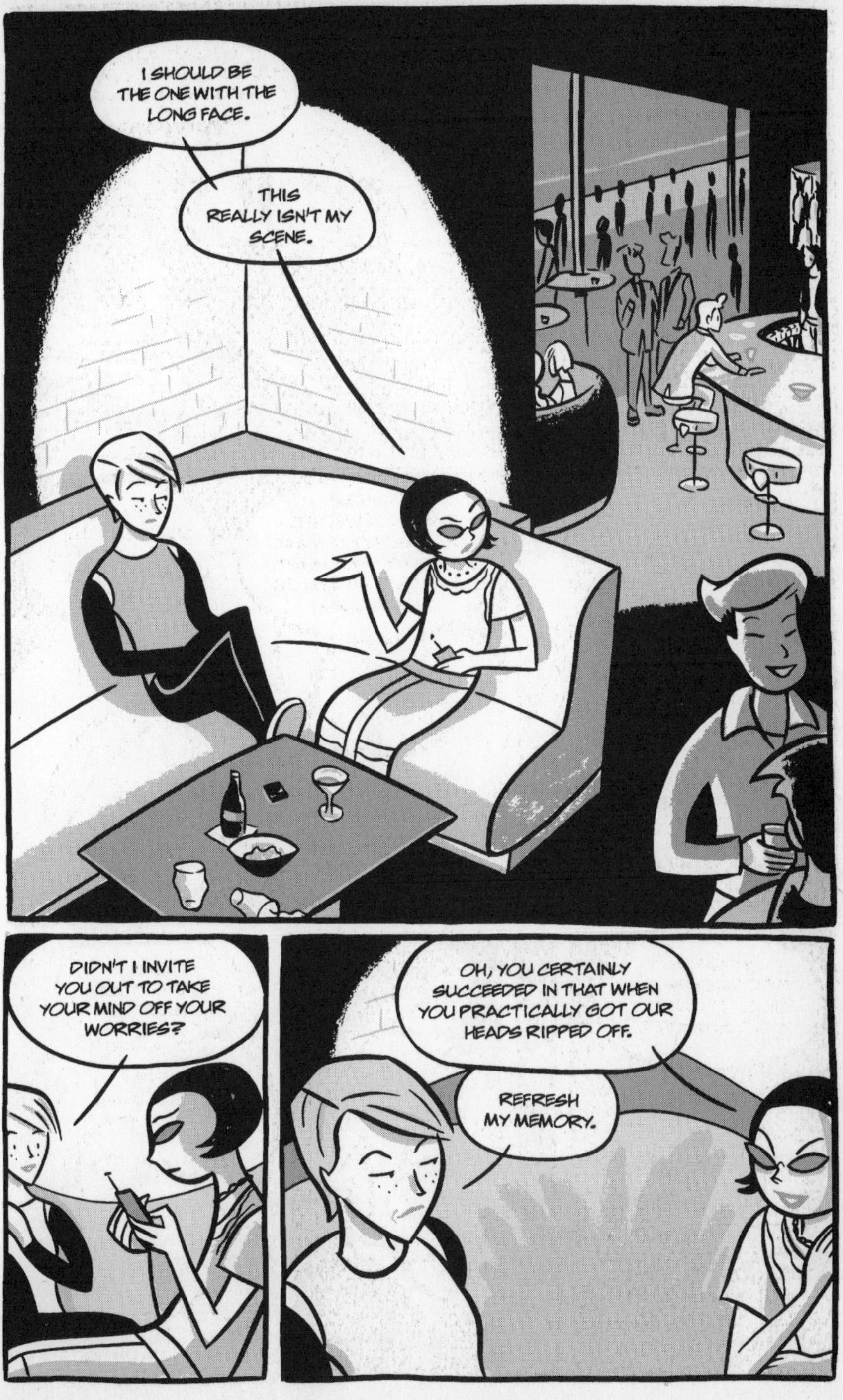
I SHOULD BE THE ONE WITH THE LONG FACE.
THIS REALLY ISN'T MY SCENE.
DIDN'T I INVITE YOU OUT TO TAKE YOUR MIND OFF YOUR WORRIES?
OH, YOU CERTAINLY SUCCEEDED IN THAT WHEN YOU PRACTICALLY GOT OUR HEADS RIPPED OFF.
REFRESH MY MEMORY.

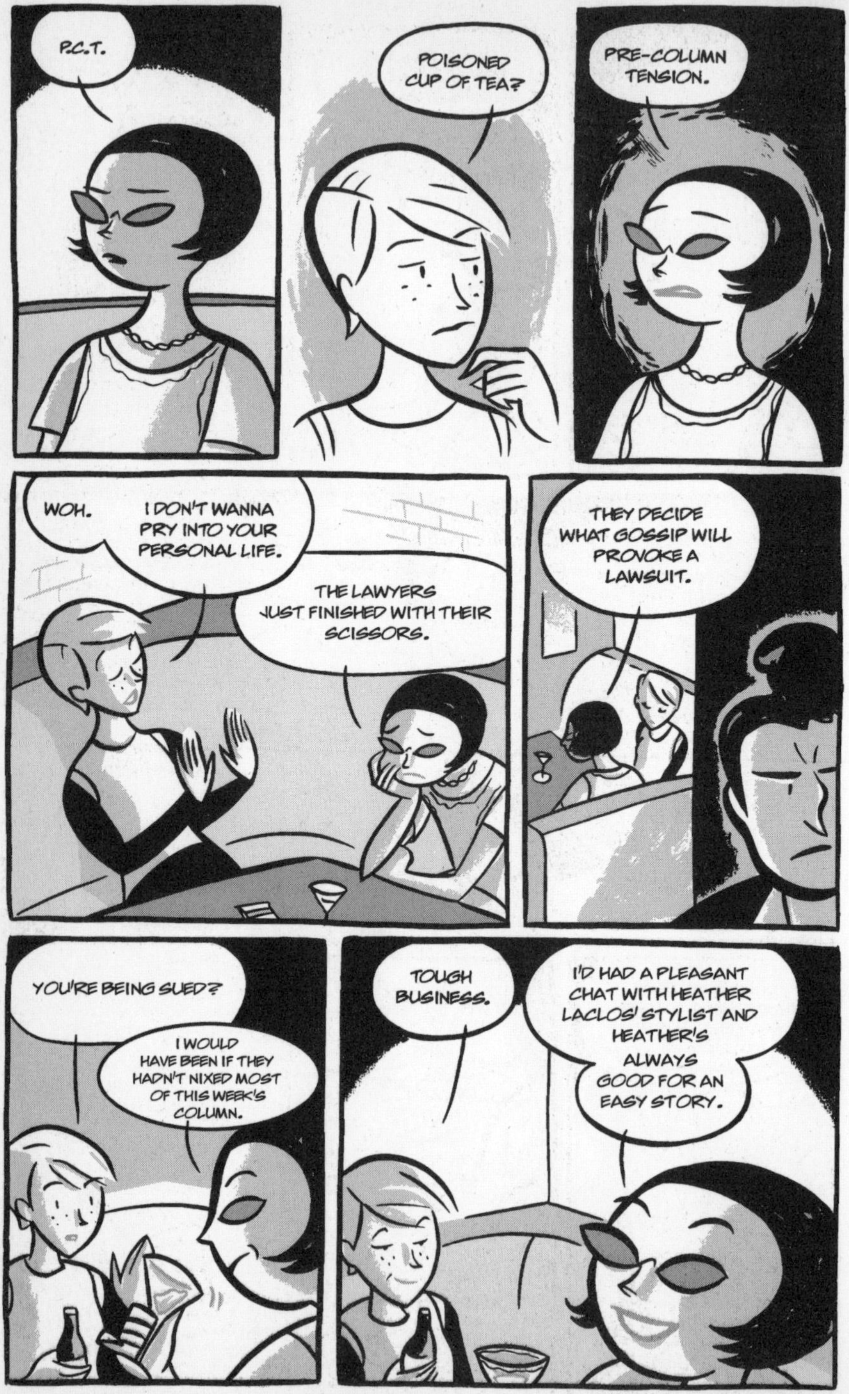
P.C.T.
POISONED CUP OF TEA?
PRE-COLUMN TENSION.
WOH.
I DON'T WANNA PRY INTO YOUR PERSONAL LIFE.
THE LAWYERS JUST FINISHED WITH THEIR SCISSORS.
THEY DECIDE WHAT GOSSIP WILL PROVOKE A LAWSUIT.
YOU'RE BEING SUED?
I WOULD HAVE BEEN IF THEY HADN'T NIXED MOST OF THIS WEEK'S COLUMN.
TOUGH BUSINESS.
I'D HAD A PLEASANT CHAT WITH HEATHER LACLOS' STYLIST AND HEATHER'S ALWAYS GOOD FOR AN EASY STORY.

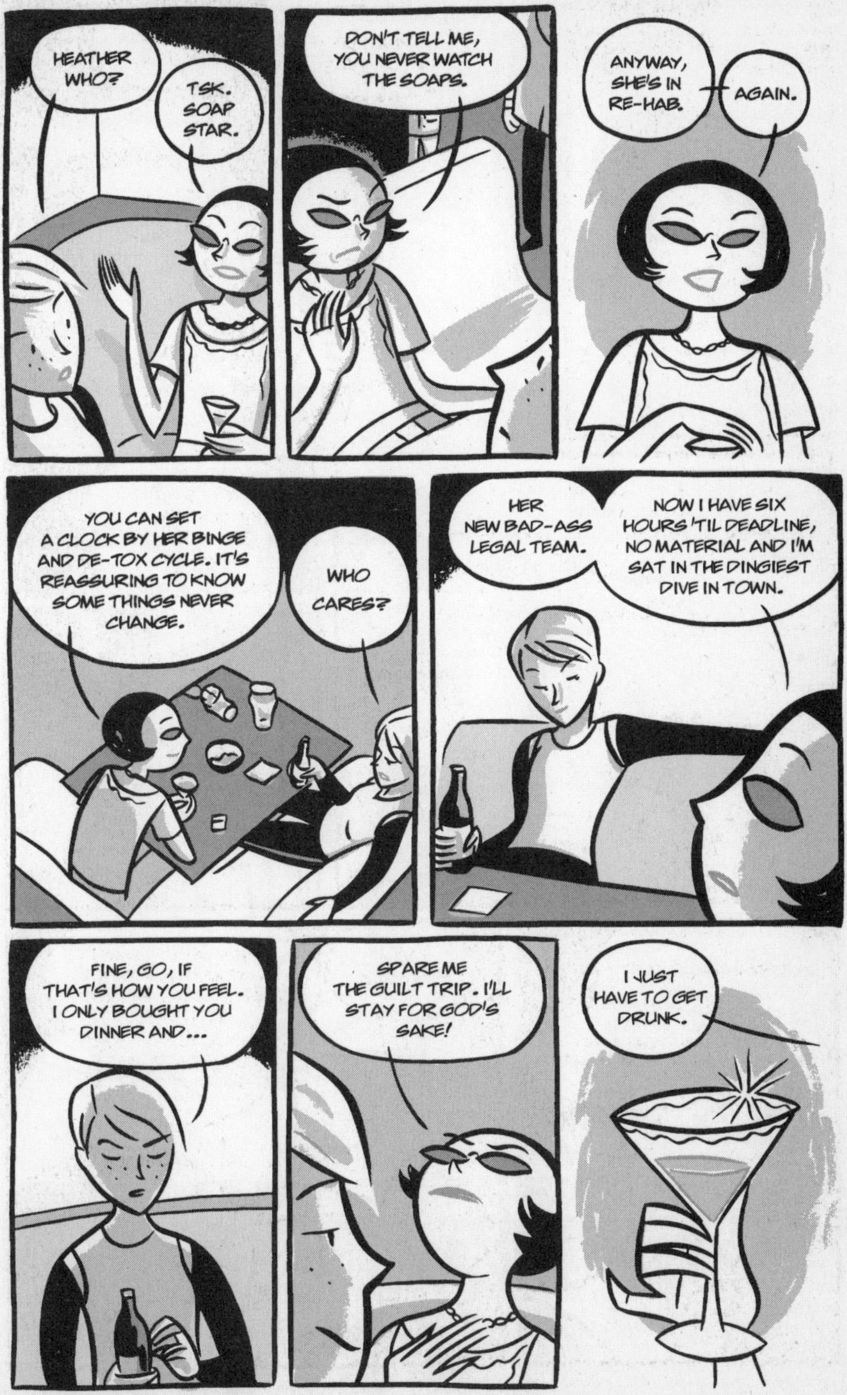
HEATHER WHO?
TSK. SOAP STAR.
DON'T TELL ME, YOU NEVER WATCH THE SOAPS.
ANYWAY, SHE'S IN RE-HAB.
AGAIN.
YOU CAN SET A CLOCK BY HER BINGE AND DE-TOX CYCLE. IT'S REASSURING TO KNOW SOME THINGS NEVER CHANGE.
WHO CARES?
HER NEW BAD-ASS LEGAL TEAM.
NOW I HAVE SIX HOURS 'TIL DEADLINE, NO MATERIAL AND I'M SAT IN THE DINGIEST DIVE IN TOWN.
FINE, GO, IF THAT'S HOW YOU FEEL. I ONLY BOUGHT YOU DINNER AND...
SPARE ME THE GUILT TRIP. I'LL STAY FOR GOD'S SAKE!
I JUST HAVE TO GET DRUNK.

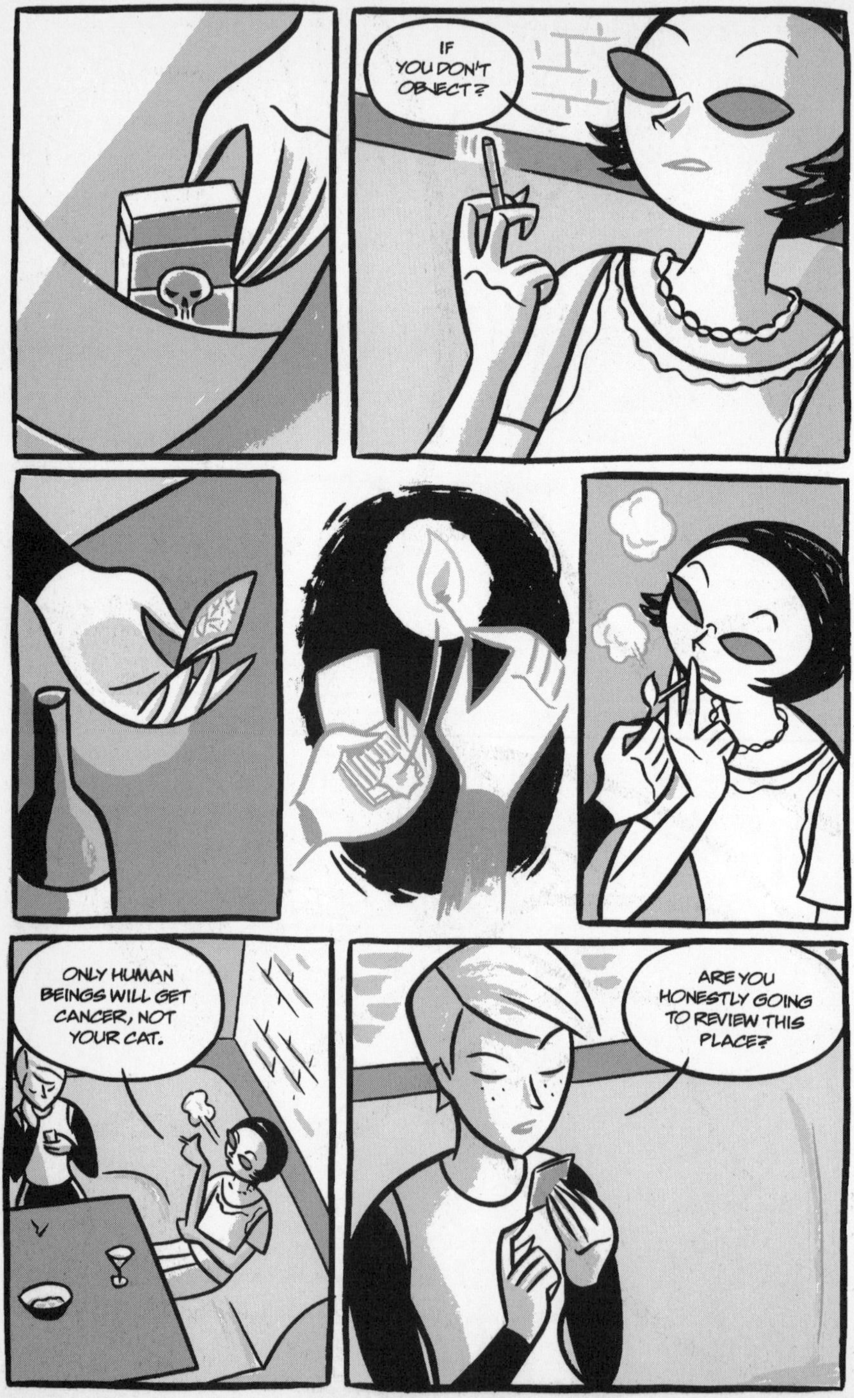
IF YOU DON'T OBJECT?
ONLY HUMAN BEINGS WILL GET CANCER, NOT YOUR CAT.
ARE YOU HONESTLY GOING TO REVIEW THIS PLACE?

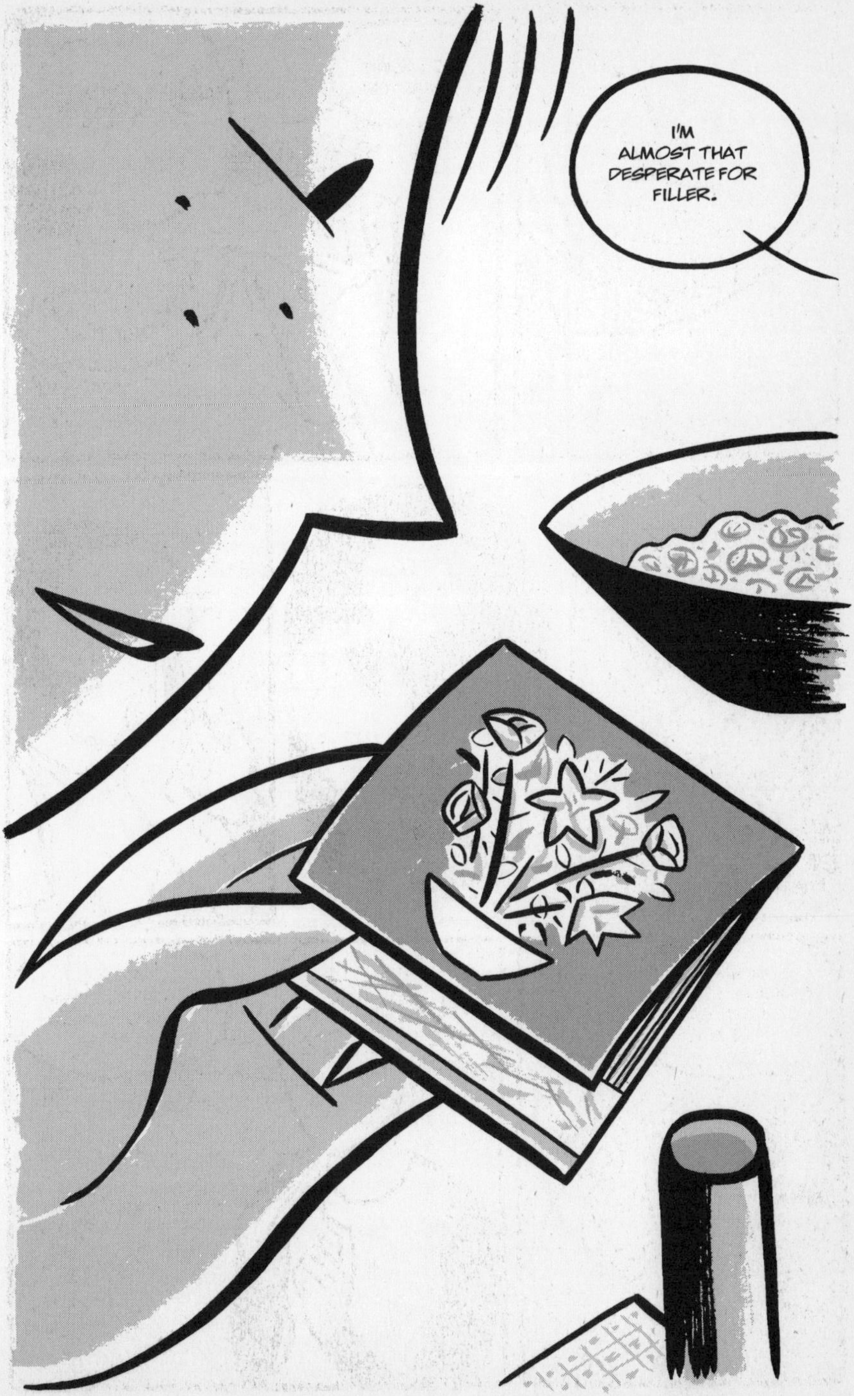
I'M ALMOST THAT DESPERATE FOR FILLER.

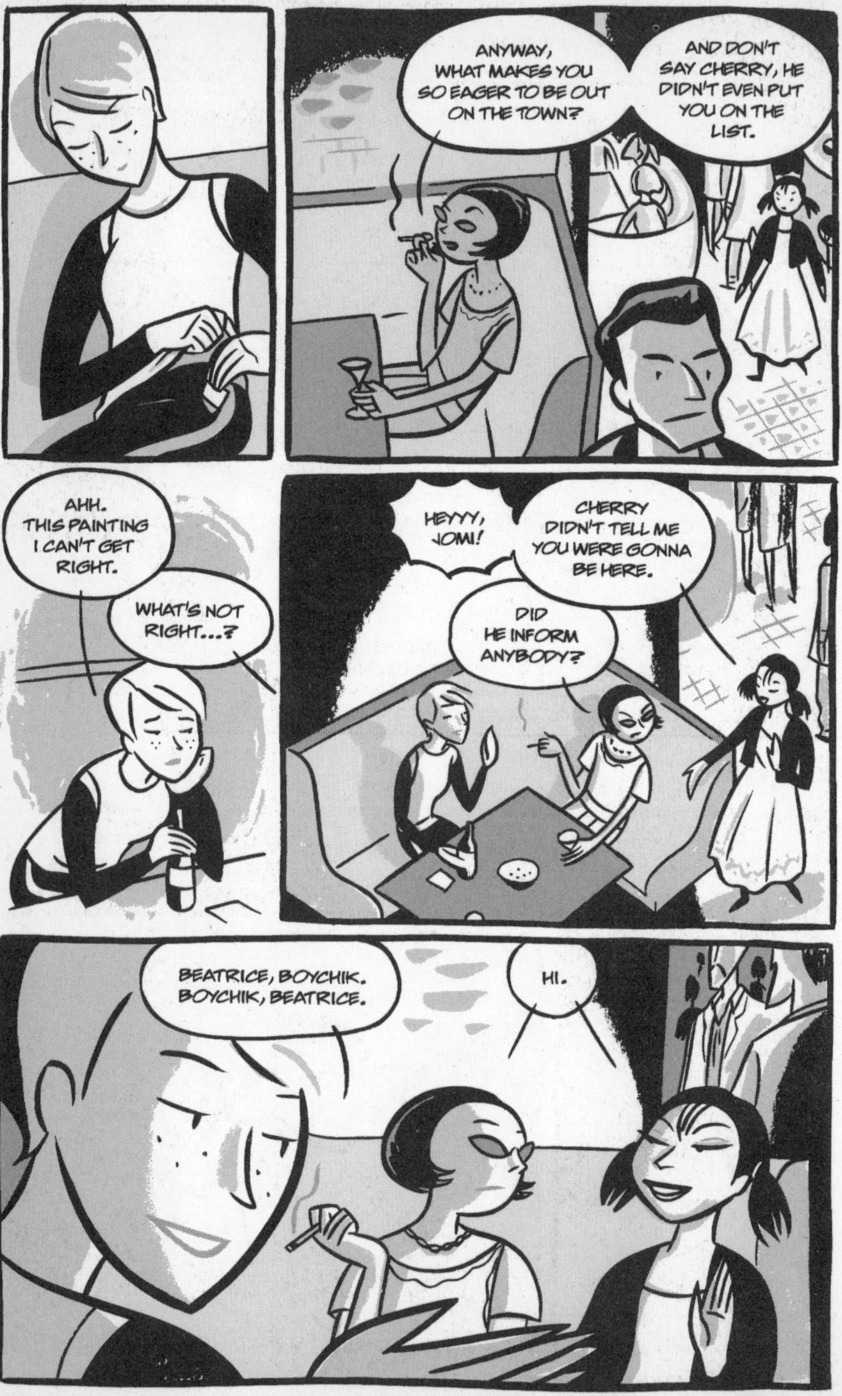
ANYWAY, WHAT MAKES YOU SO EAGER TO BE OUT ON THE TOWN?
AND DON'T SAY CHERRY, HE DIDN'T EVEN PUT YOU ON THE LIST.
AHH. THIS PAINTING I CAN'T GET RIGHT.
WHAT'S NOT RIGHT...?
HEYYY, JOMI!
CHERRY DIDN'T TELL ME YOU WERE GONNA BE HERE.
DID HE INFORM ANYBODY?
BEATRICE, BOYCHIK. BOYCHIK, BEATRICE.
HI.

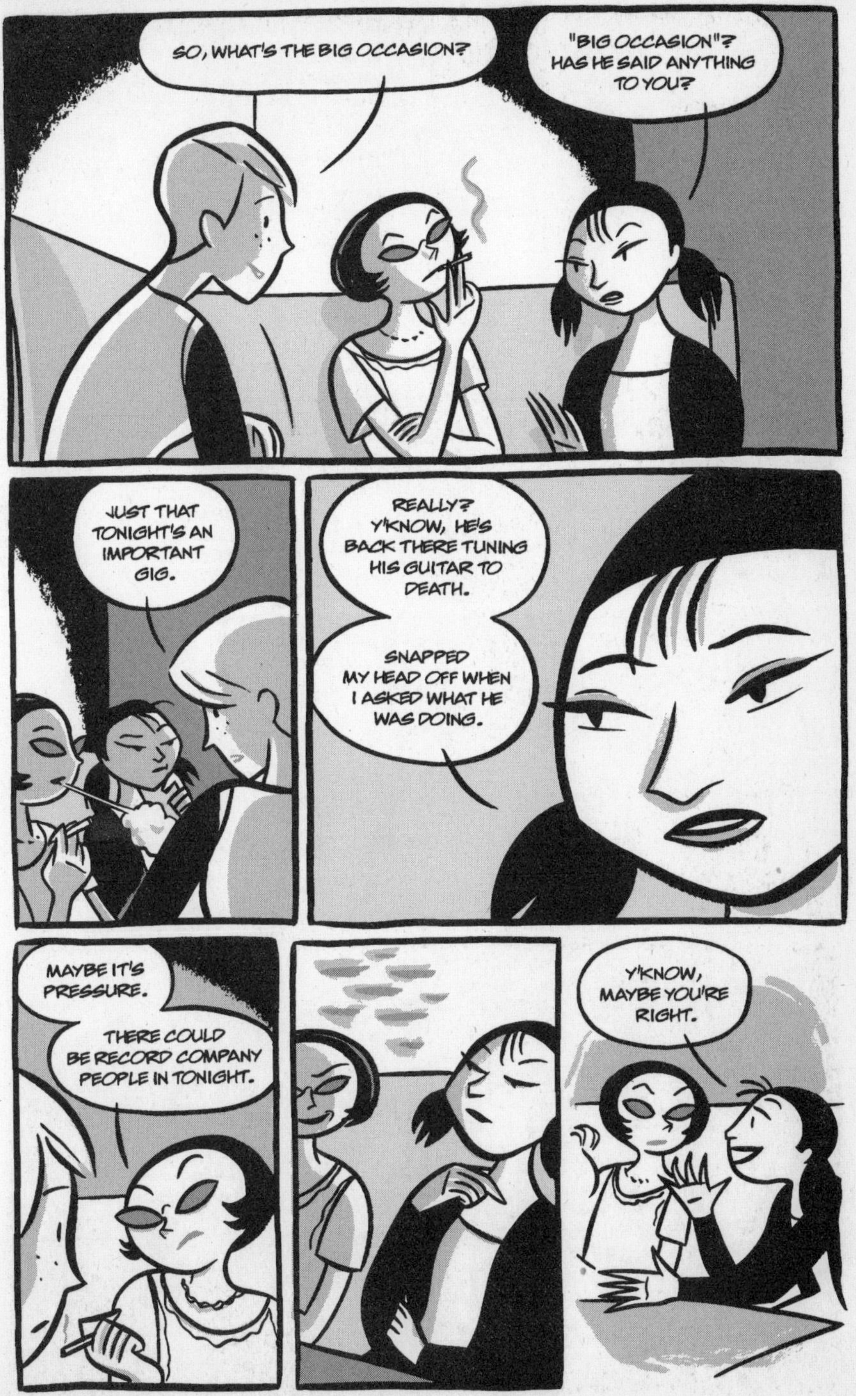
SO, WHAT'S THE BIG OCCASION?
"BIG OCCASION"? HAS HE SAID ANYTHING TO YOU?
JUST THAT TONIGHT'S AN IMPORTANT GIG.
REALLY? Y'KNOW, HE'S BACK THERE TUNING HIS GUITAR TO DEATH.
SNAPPED MY HEAD OFF WHEN I ASKED WHAT HE WAS DOING.
MAYBE IT'S PRESSURE.
THERE COULD BE RECORD COMPANY PEOPLE IN TONIGHT.
Y'KNOW, MAYBE YOU'RE RIGHT.

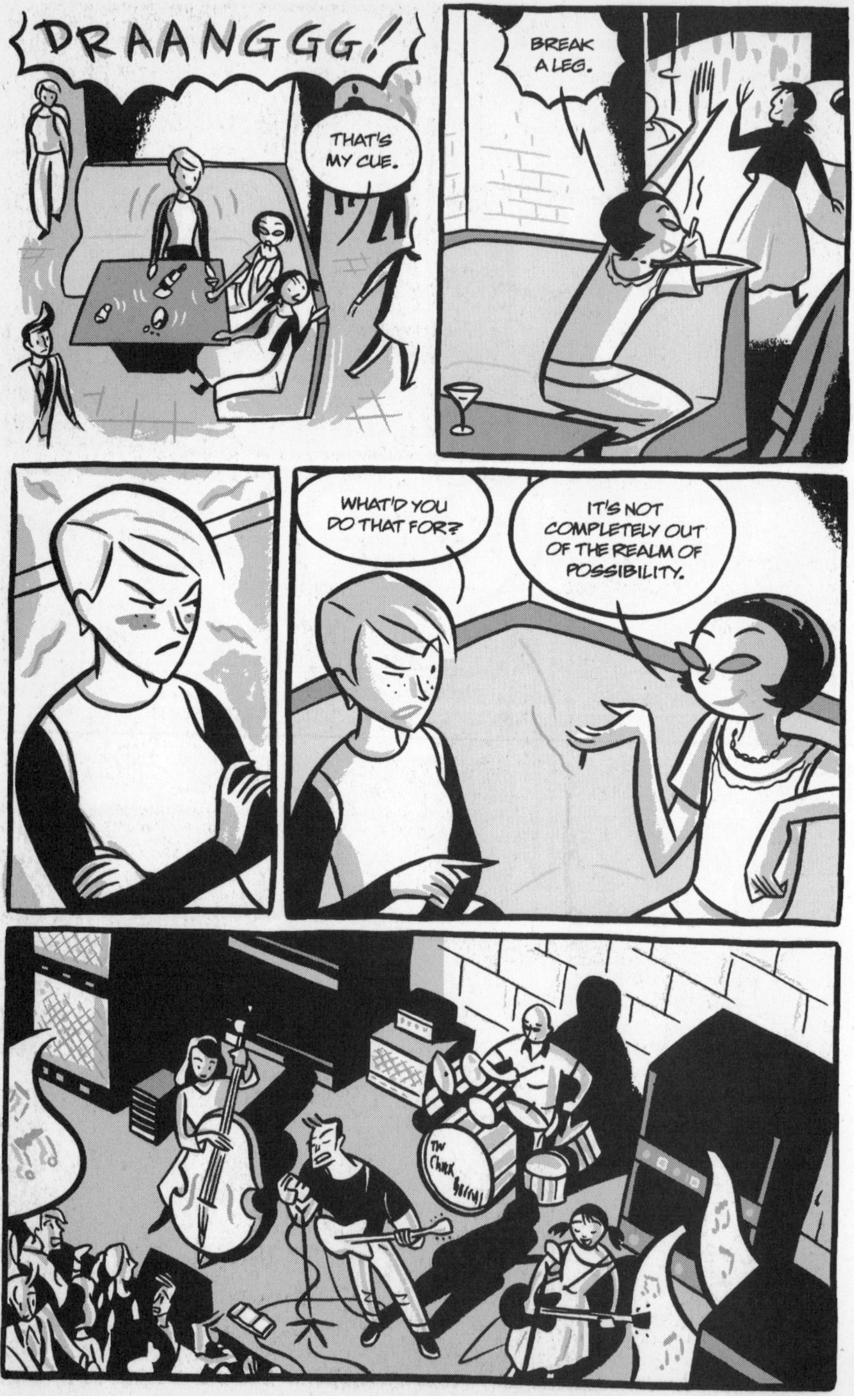
DRAANGGG!
THAT'S MY CUE.
BREAK A LEG.
WHAT'D YOU DO THAT FOR?
IT'S NOT COMPLETELY OUT OF THE REALM OF POSSIBILITY.

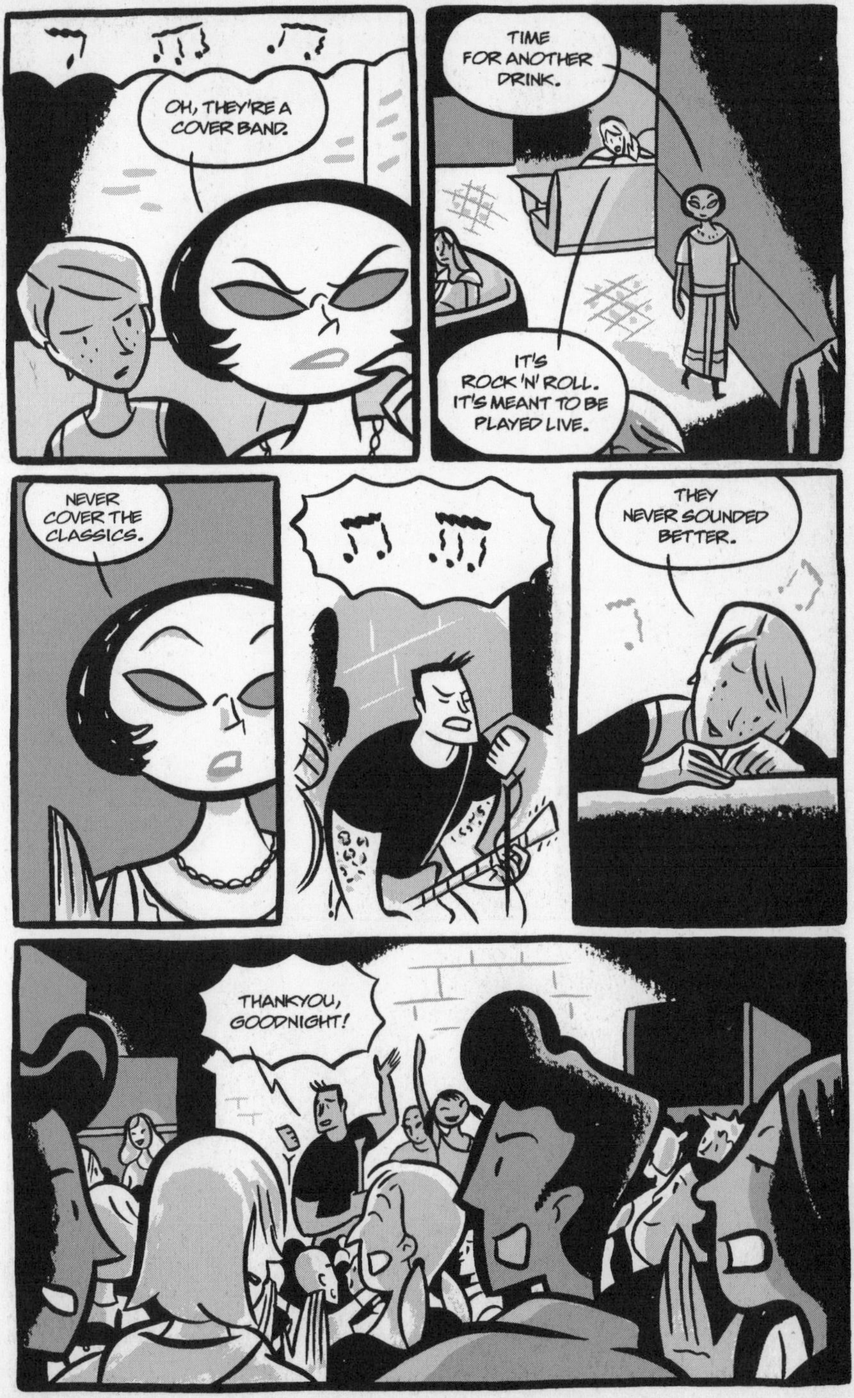

OH, THEY'RE A COVER BAND.
TIME FOR ANOTHER DRINK.
IT'S ROCK 'N' ROLL. IT'S MEANT TO BE PLAYED LIVE.
NEVER COVER THE CLASSICS.
THEY NEVER SOUNDED BETTER.
THANKYOU, GOODNIGHT!

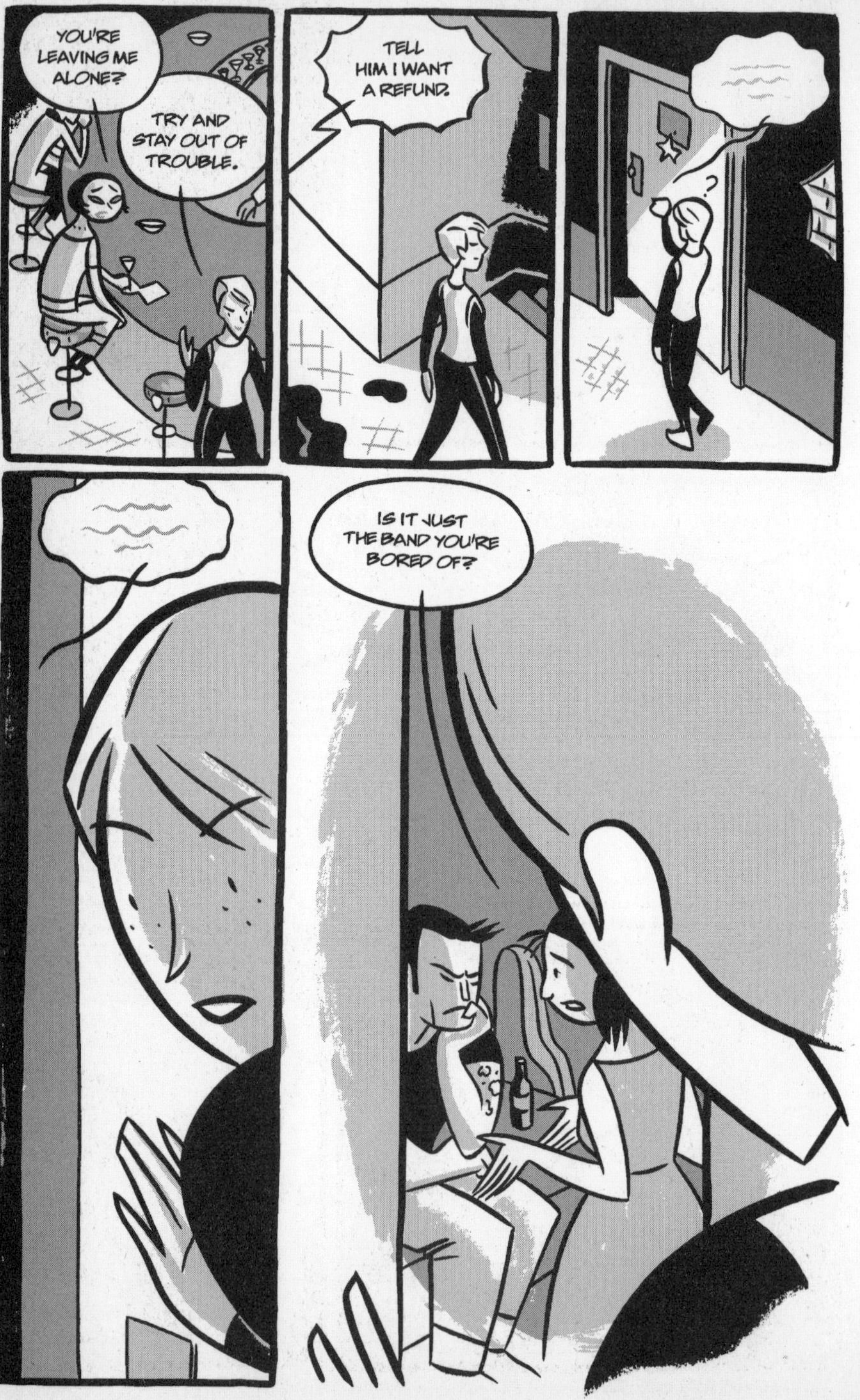
YOU'RE LEAVING ME ALONE?
TRY AND STAY OUT OF TROUBLE.
TELL HIM I WANT A REFUND.
IS IT JUST THE BAND YOU'RE BORED OF?

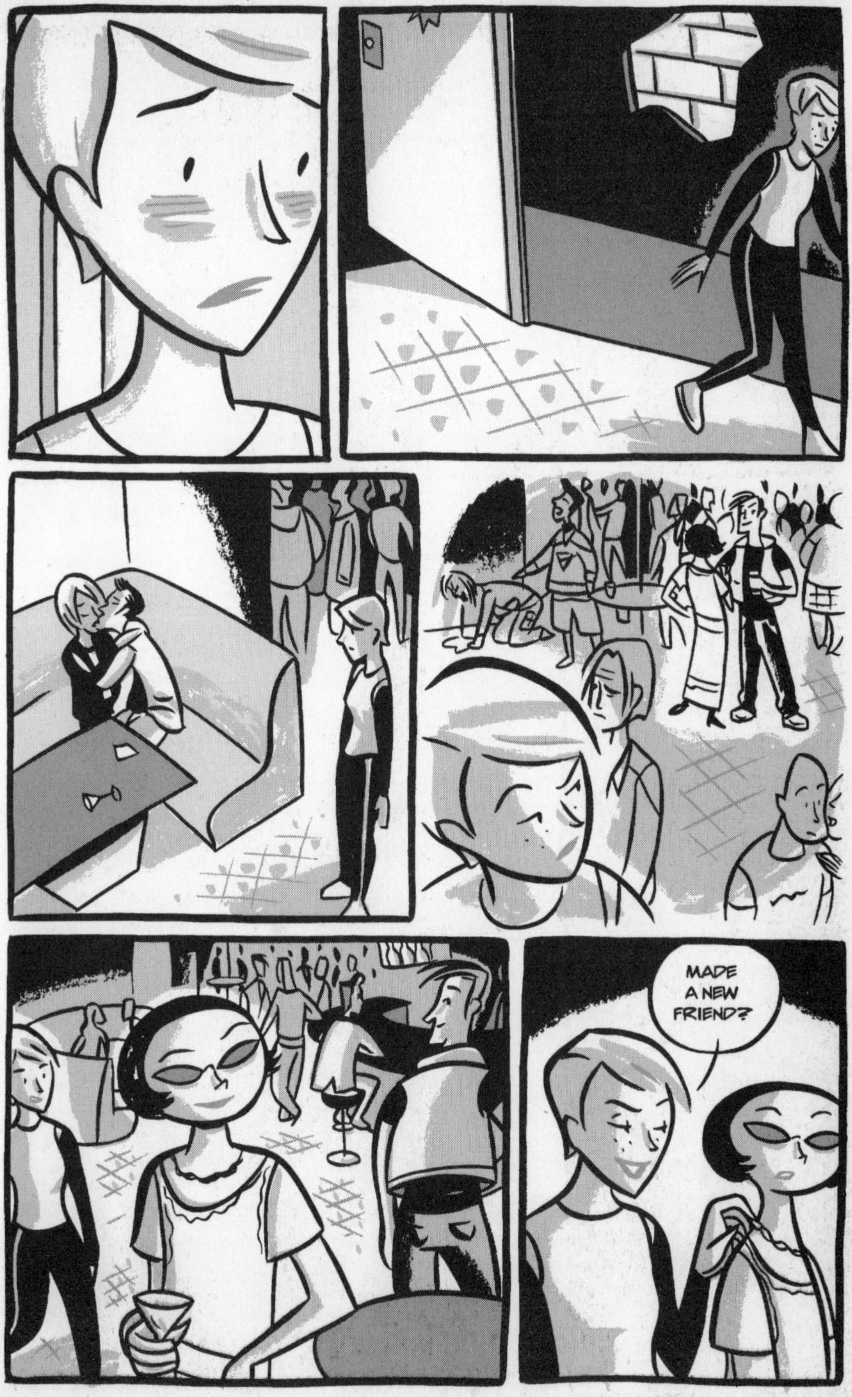
MADE A NEW FRIEND?

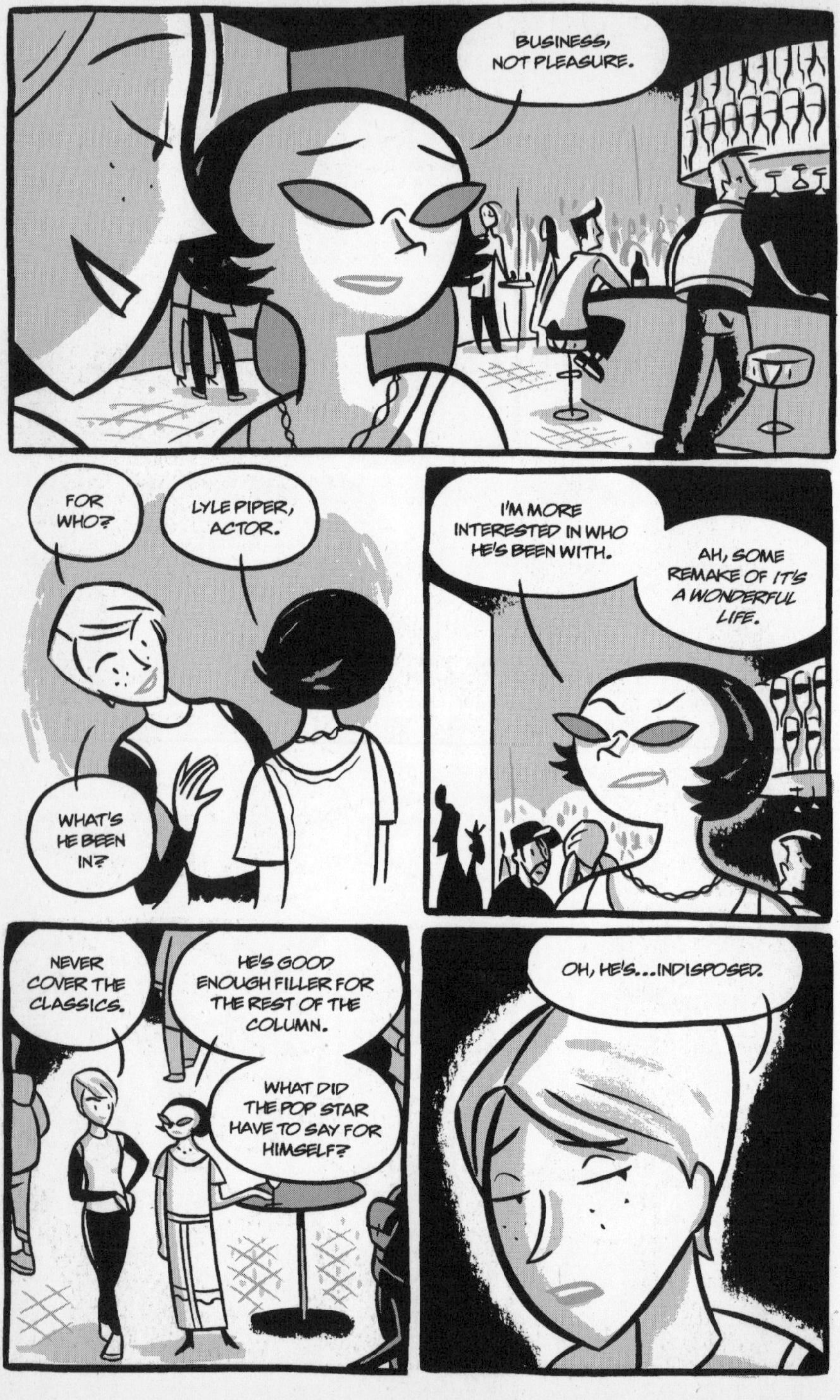
BUSINESS, NOT PLEASURE.
FOR WHO?
LYLE PIPER, ACTOR.
WHAT'S HE BEEN IN?
I'M MORE INTERESTED IN WHO HE'S BEEN WITH.
AH, SOME REMAKE OF IT'S A WONDERFUL LIFE.
NEVER COVER THE CLASSICS.
HE'S GOOD ENOUGH FILLER FOR THE REST OF THE COLUMN.
WHAT DID THE POP STAR HAVE TO SAY FOR HIMSELF?
OH, HE'S...INDISPOSED.

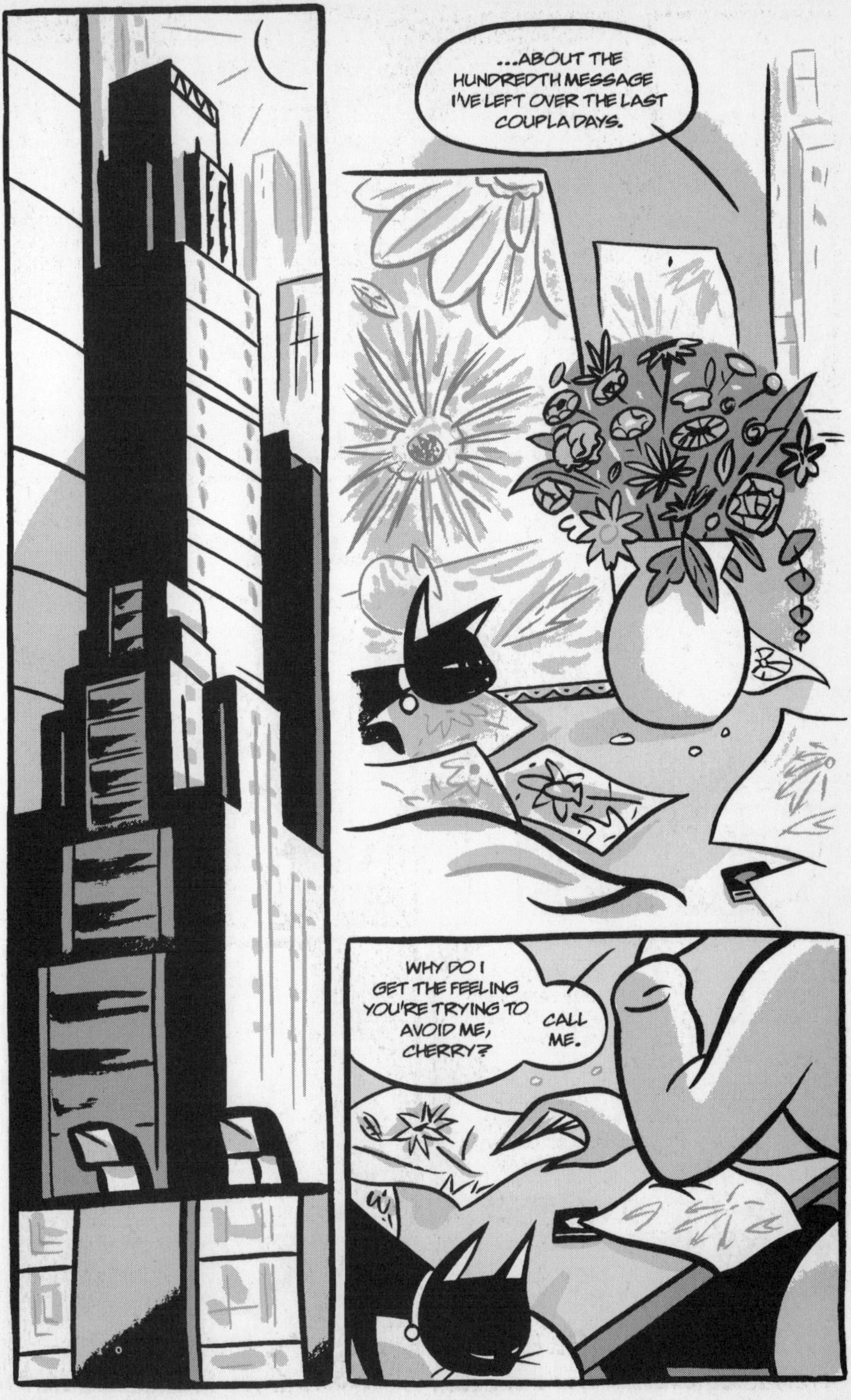
...ABOUT THE HUNDREDTH MESSAGE I'VE LEFT OVER THE LAST COUPLA DAYS.
WHY DO I GET THE FEELING YOU'RE TRYING TO AVOID ME, CHERRY?
CALL ME.

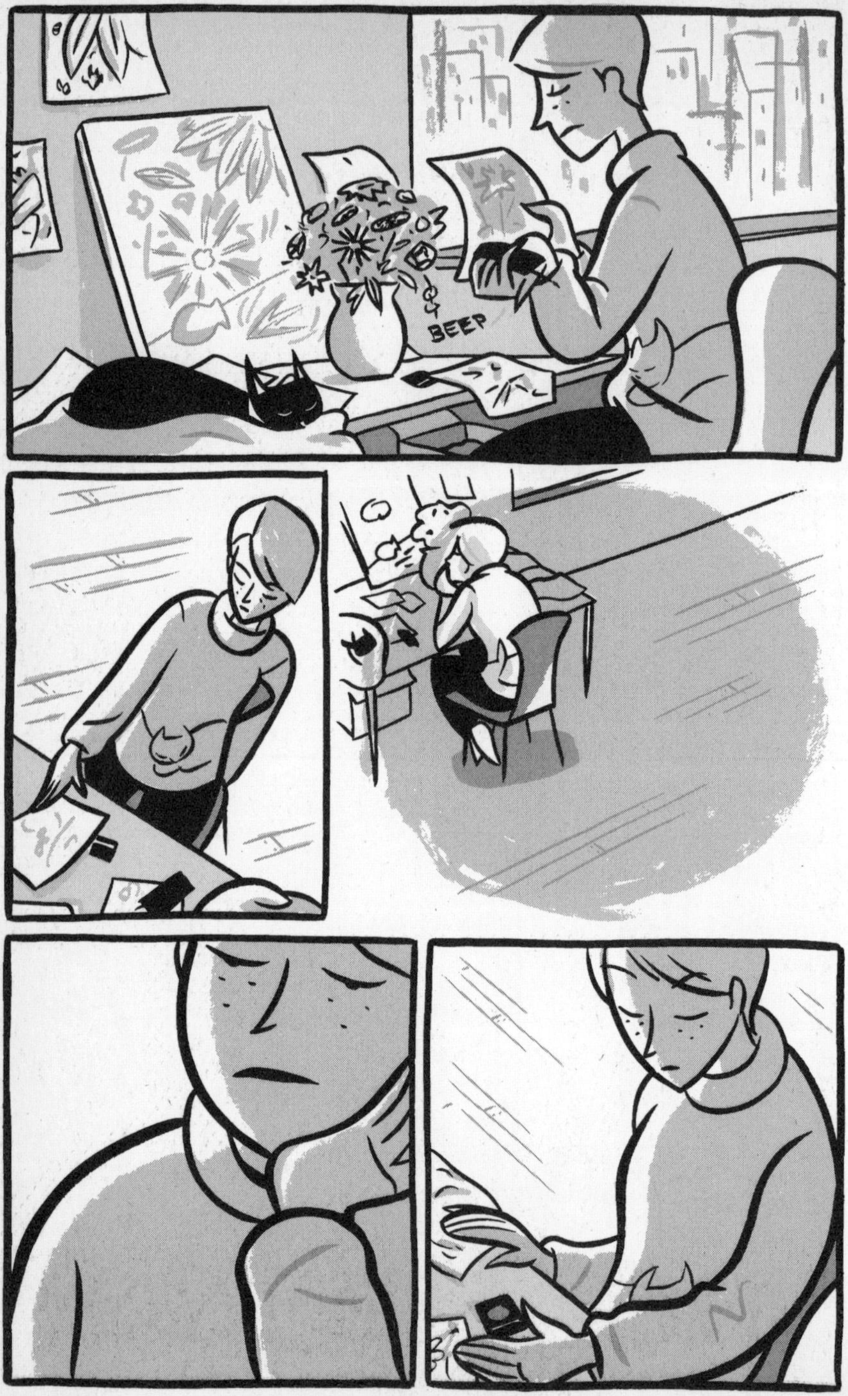
BEEP

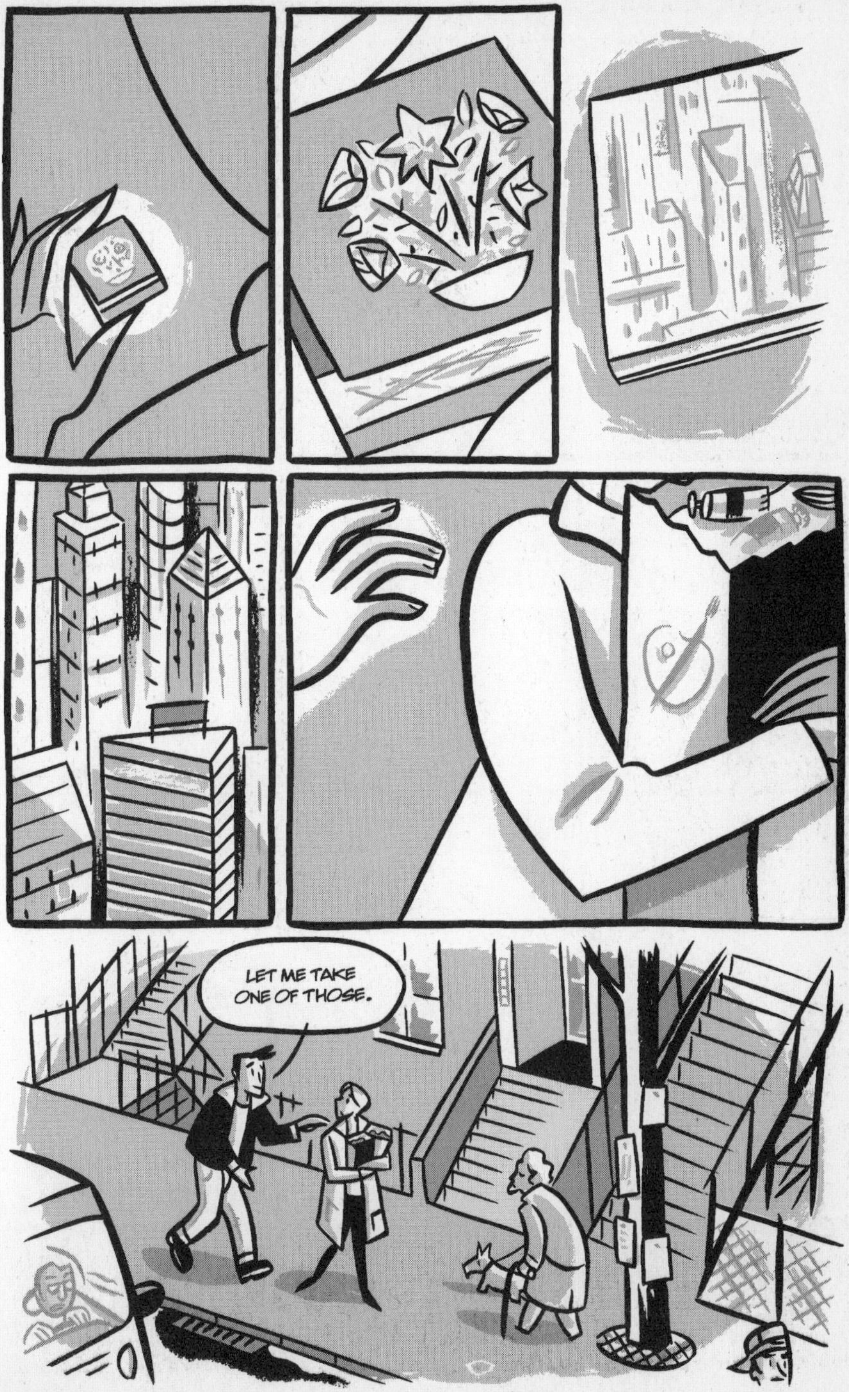
LET ME TAKE ONE OF THOSE.

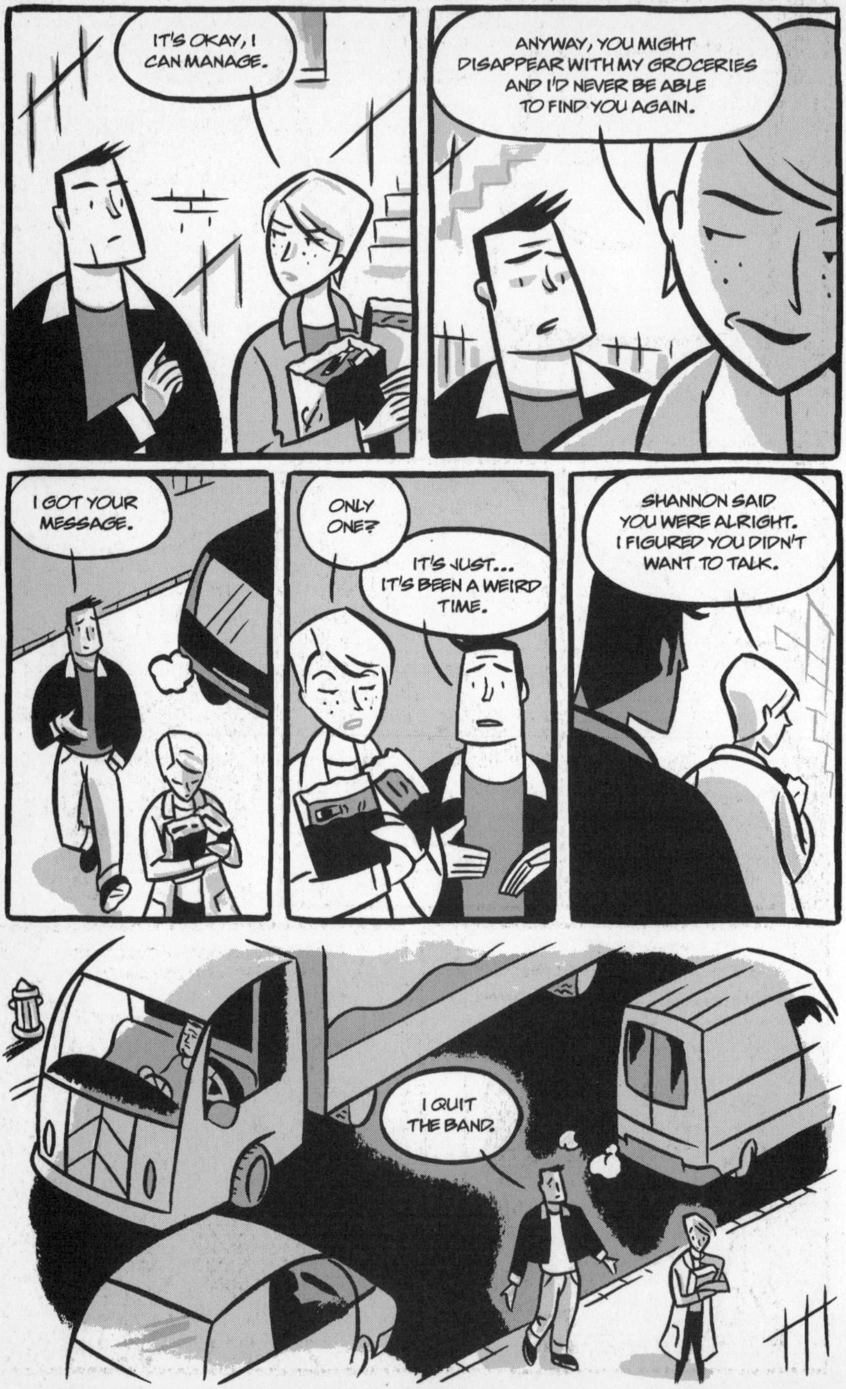
IT'S OKAY, I CAN MANAGE.
ANYWAY, YOU MIGHT DISAPPEAR WITH MY GROCERIES AND I'D NEVER BE ABLE TO FIND YOU AGAIN.
I GOT YOUR MESSAGE.
ONLY ONE?
IT'S JUST... IT'S BEEN A WEIRD TIME.
SHANNON SAID YOU WERE ALRIGHT. I FIGURED YOU DIDN'T WANT TO TALK.
I QUIT THE BAND.

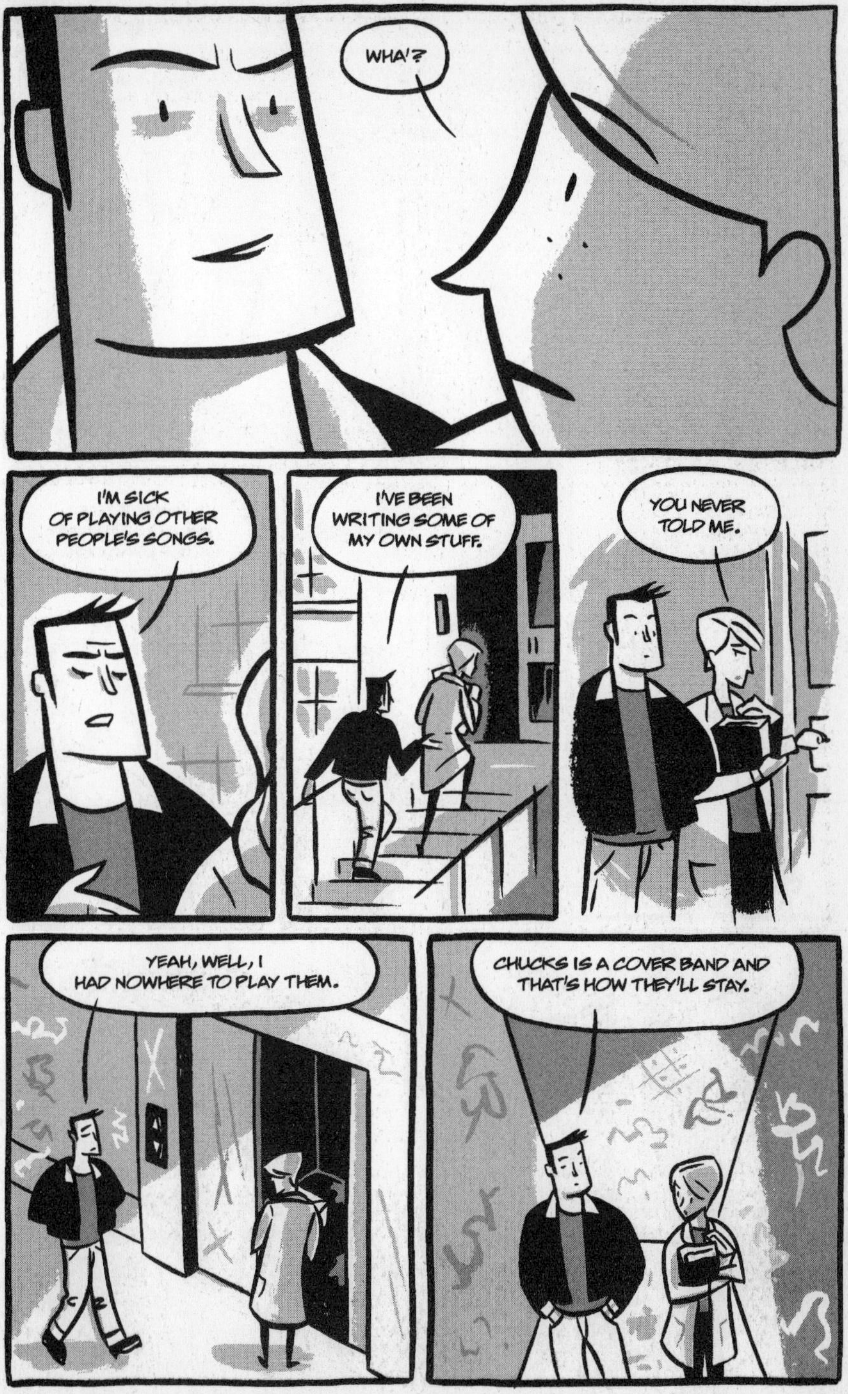
WHA'?
I'M SICK OF PLAYING OTHER PEOPLE'S SONGS.
I'VE BEEN WRITING SOME OF MY OWN STUFF.
YOU NEVER TOLD ME.
YEAH, WELL, I HAD NOWHERE TO PLAY THEM.
CHUCKS IS A COVER BAND AND THAT'S HOW THEY'LL STAY.

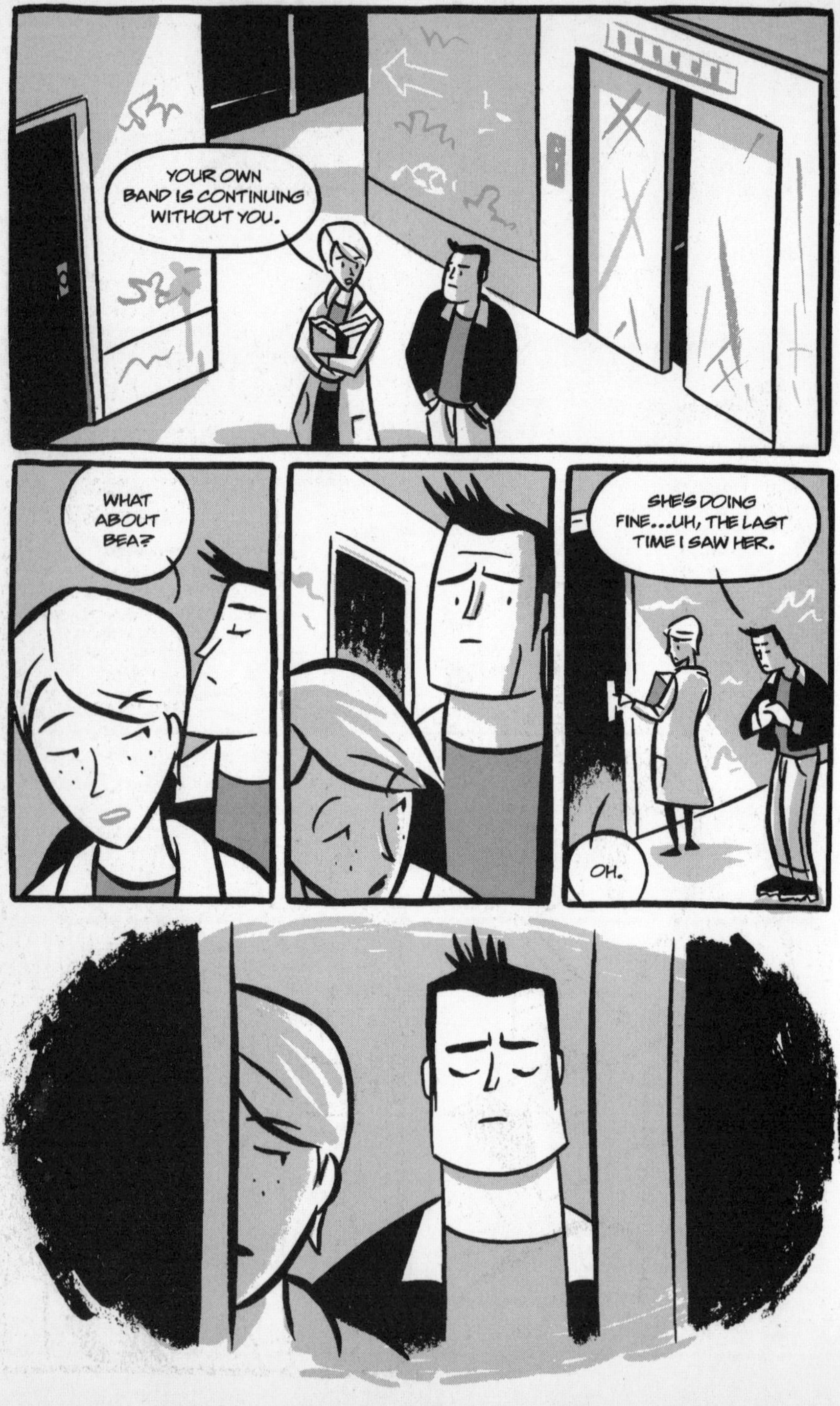
YOUR OWN BAND IS CONTINUING WITHOUT YOU.
WHAT ABOUT BEA?
SHE'S DOING FINE...UH, THE LAST TIME I SAW HER.
OH.

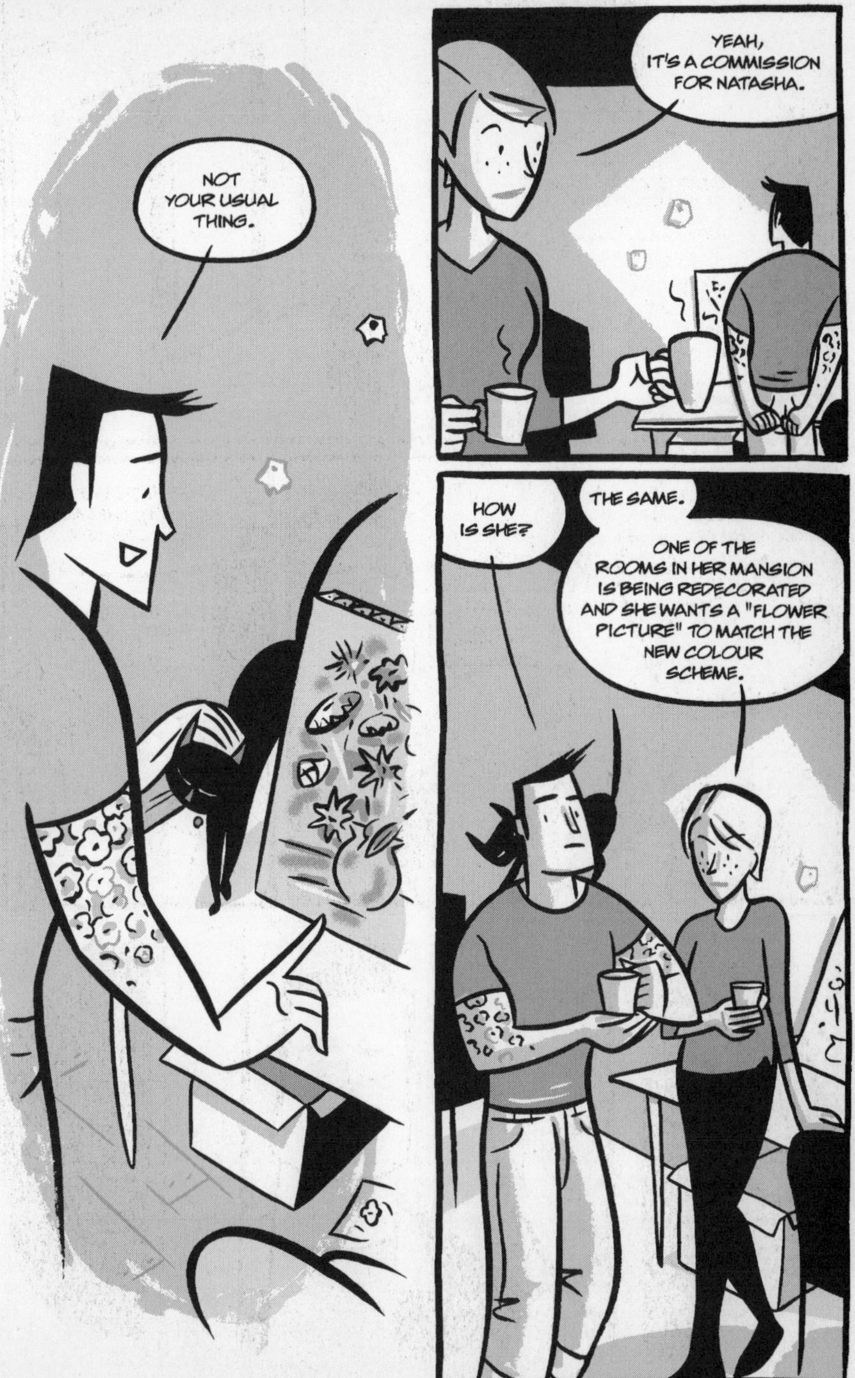
NOT YOUR USUAL THING.
YEAH, IT'S A COMMISSION FOR NATASHA.
HOW IS SHE?
THE SAME.
ONE OF THE ROOMS IN HER MANSION IS BEING REDECORATED AND SHE WANTS A "FLOWER PICTURE" TO MATCH THE NEW COLOUR SCHEME.

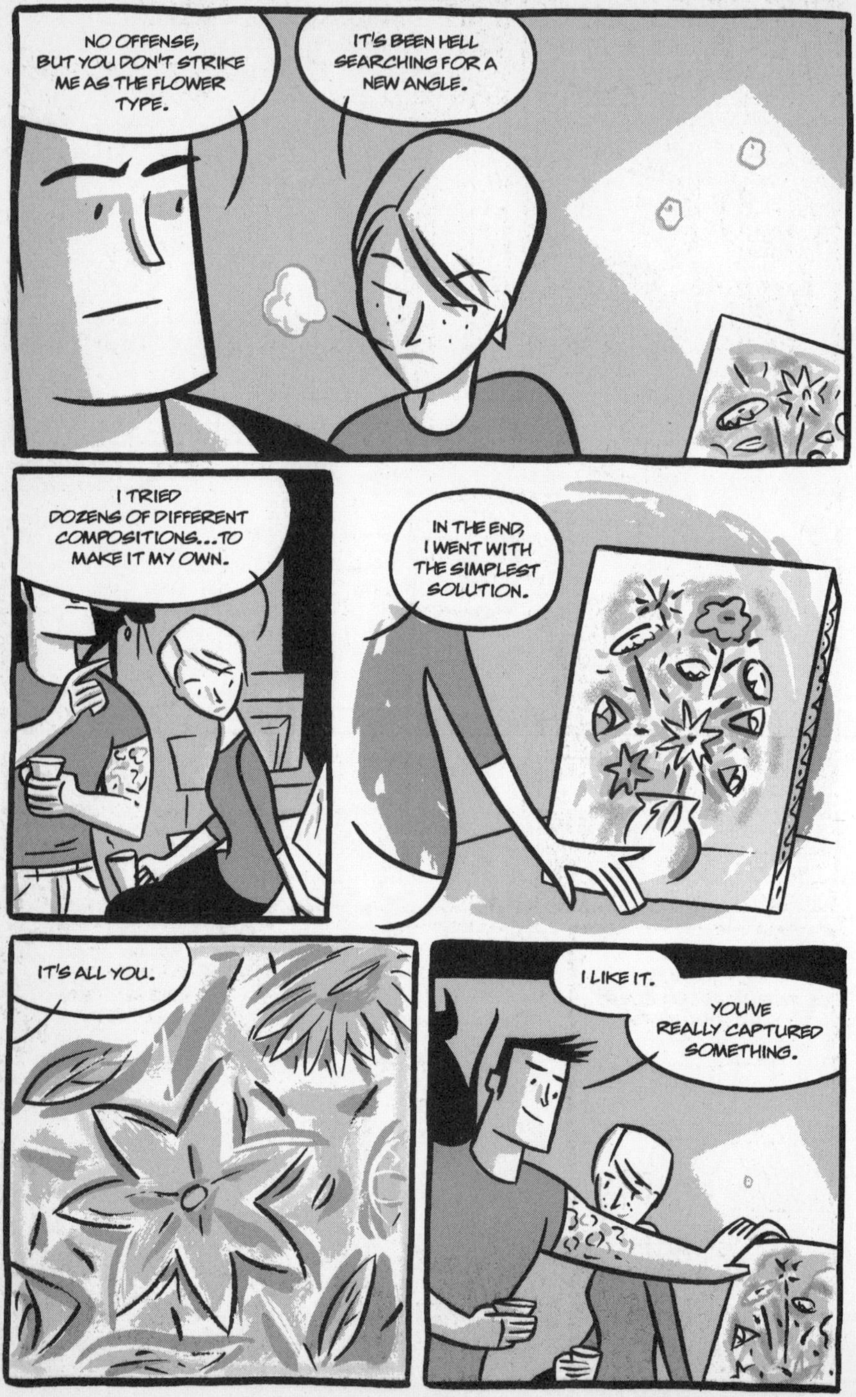
NO OFFENSE, BUT YOU DON'T STRIKE ME AS THE FLOWER TYPE.
IT'S BEEN HELL SEARCHING FOR A NEW ANGLE.
I TRIED DOZENS OF DIFFERENT COMPOSITIONS... TO MAKE IT MY OWN.
IN THE END, I WENT WITH THE SIMPLEST SOLUTION.
IT'S ALL YOU.
I LIKE IT.
YOU'VE REALLY CAPTURED SOMETHING.

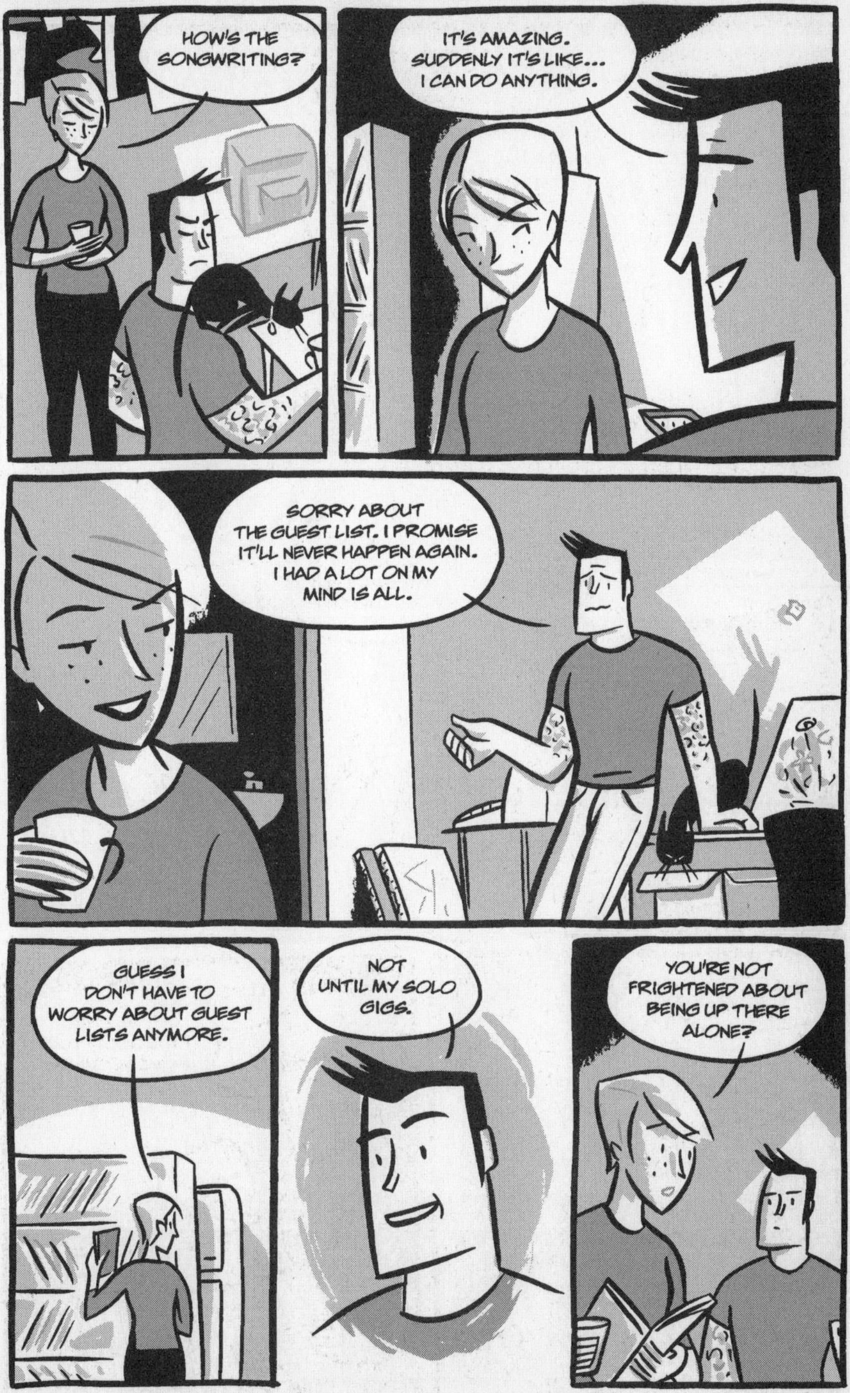
HOW'S THE SONGWRITING?
IT'S AMAZING. SUDDENLY IT'S LIKE... I CAN DO ANYTHING.
SORRY ABOUT THE GUEST LIST. I PROMISE IT'LL NEVER HAPPEN AGAIN. I HAD A LOT ON MY MIND IS ALL.
GUESS I DON'T HAVE TO WORRY ABOUT GUEST LISTS ANYMORE.
NOT UNTIL MY SOLO GIGS.
YOU'RE NOT FRIGHTENED ABOUT BEING UP THERE ALONE?

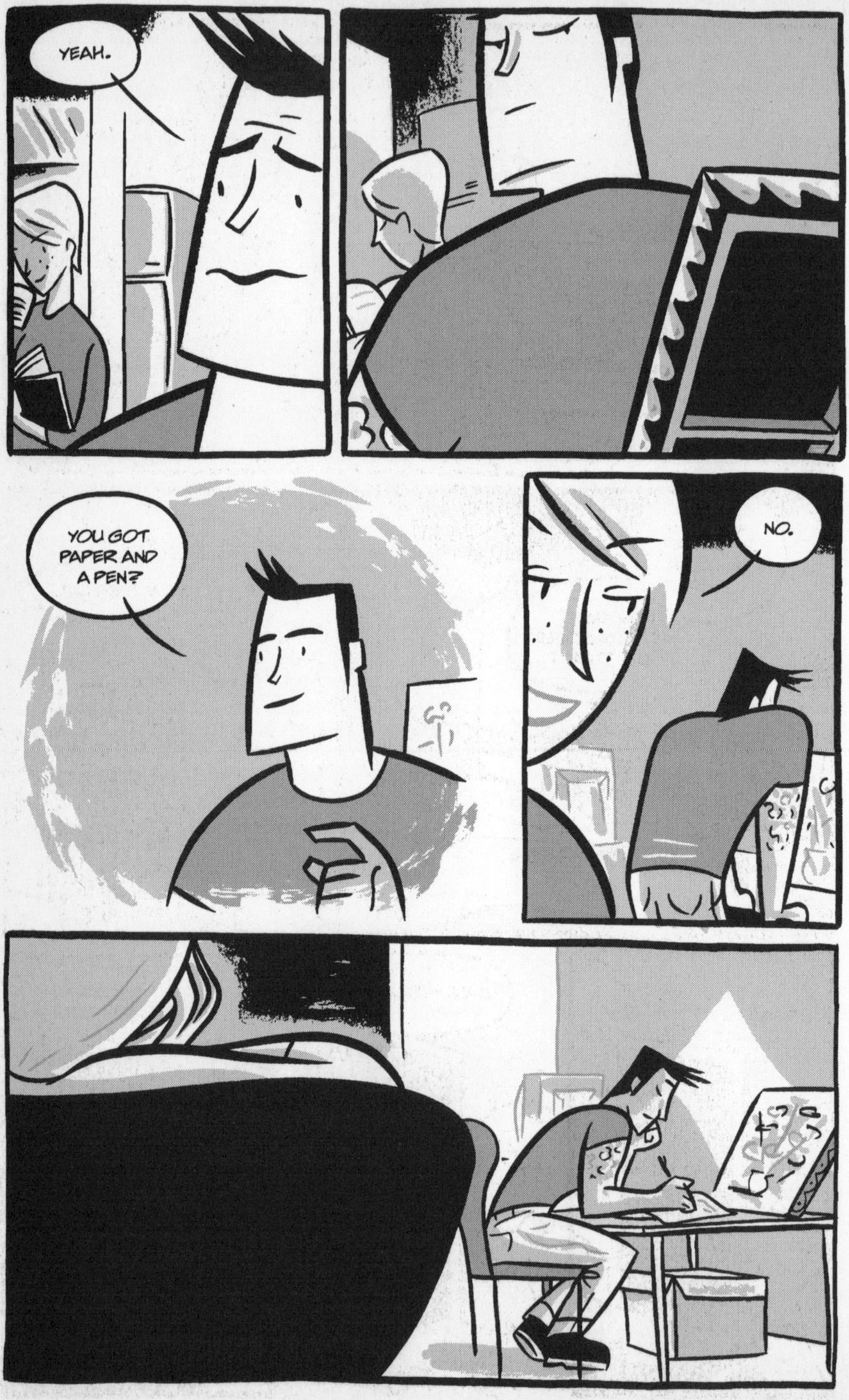
YEAH.
YOU GOT PAPER AND A PEN?
NO.

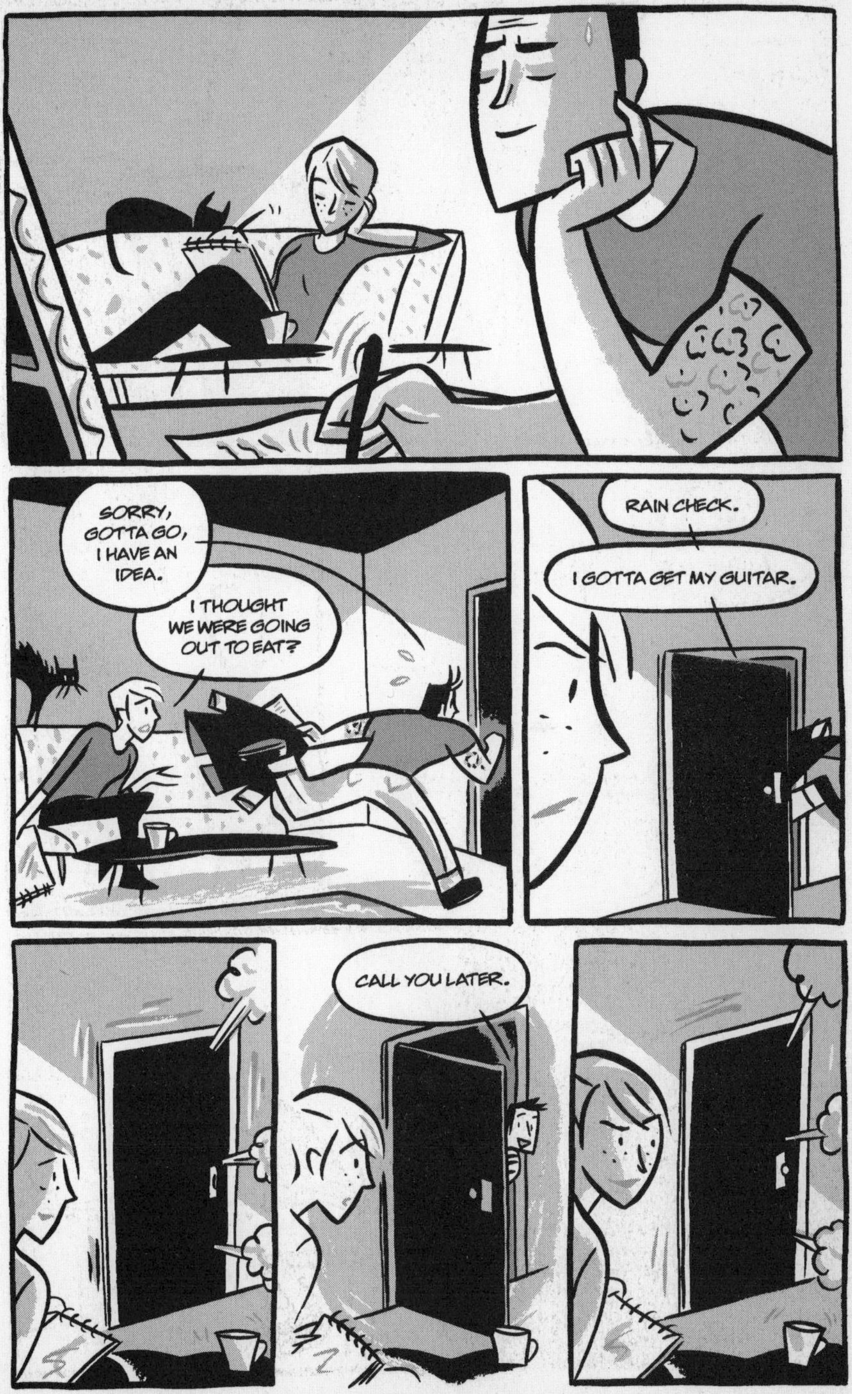
SORRY, GOTTA GO, I HAVE AN IDEA.
I THOUGHT WE WERE GOING OUT TO EAT?
RAIN CHECK.
I GOTTA GET MY GUITAR.
CALL YOU LATER.

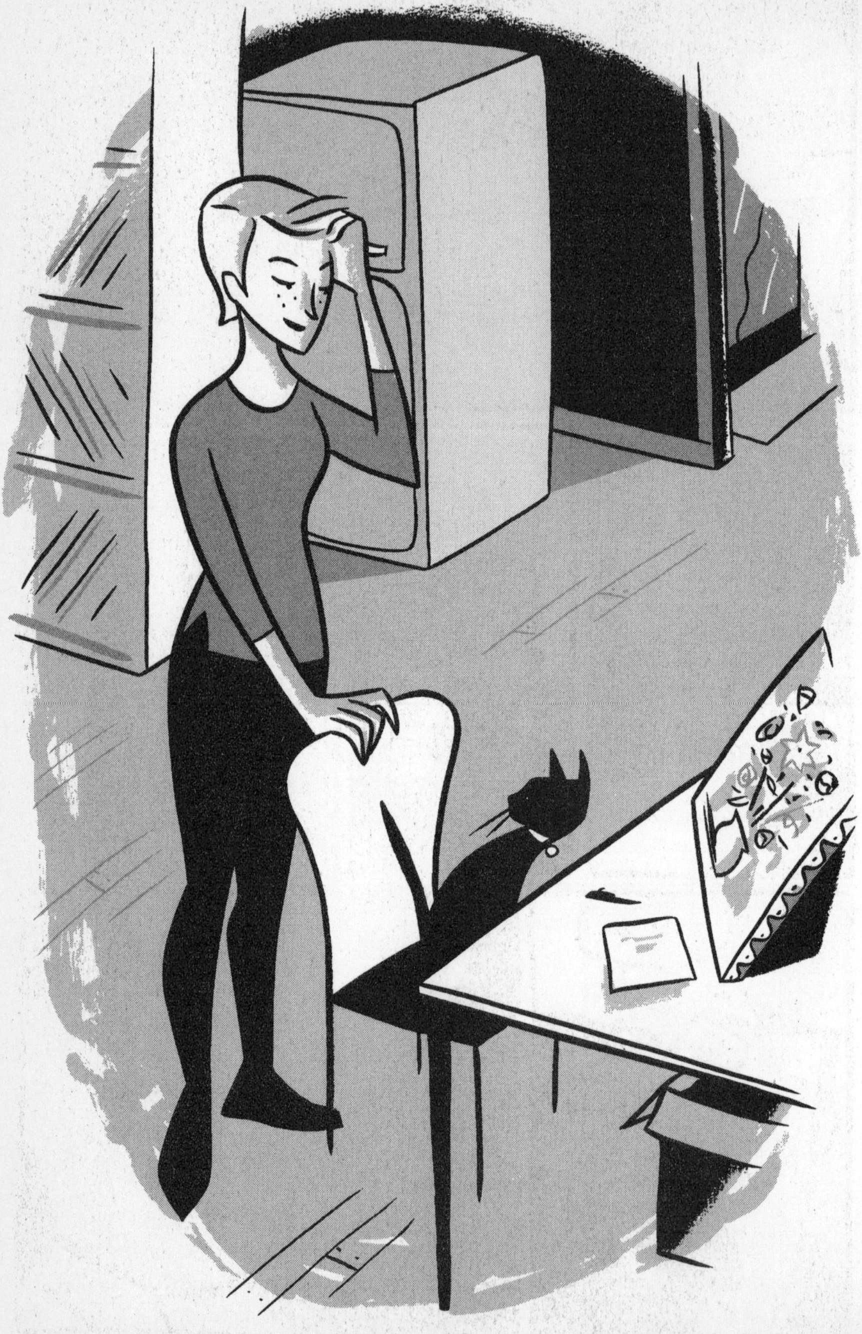

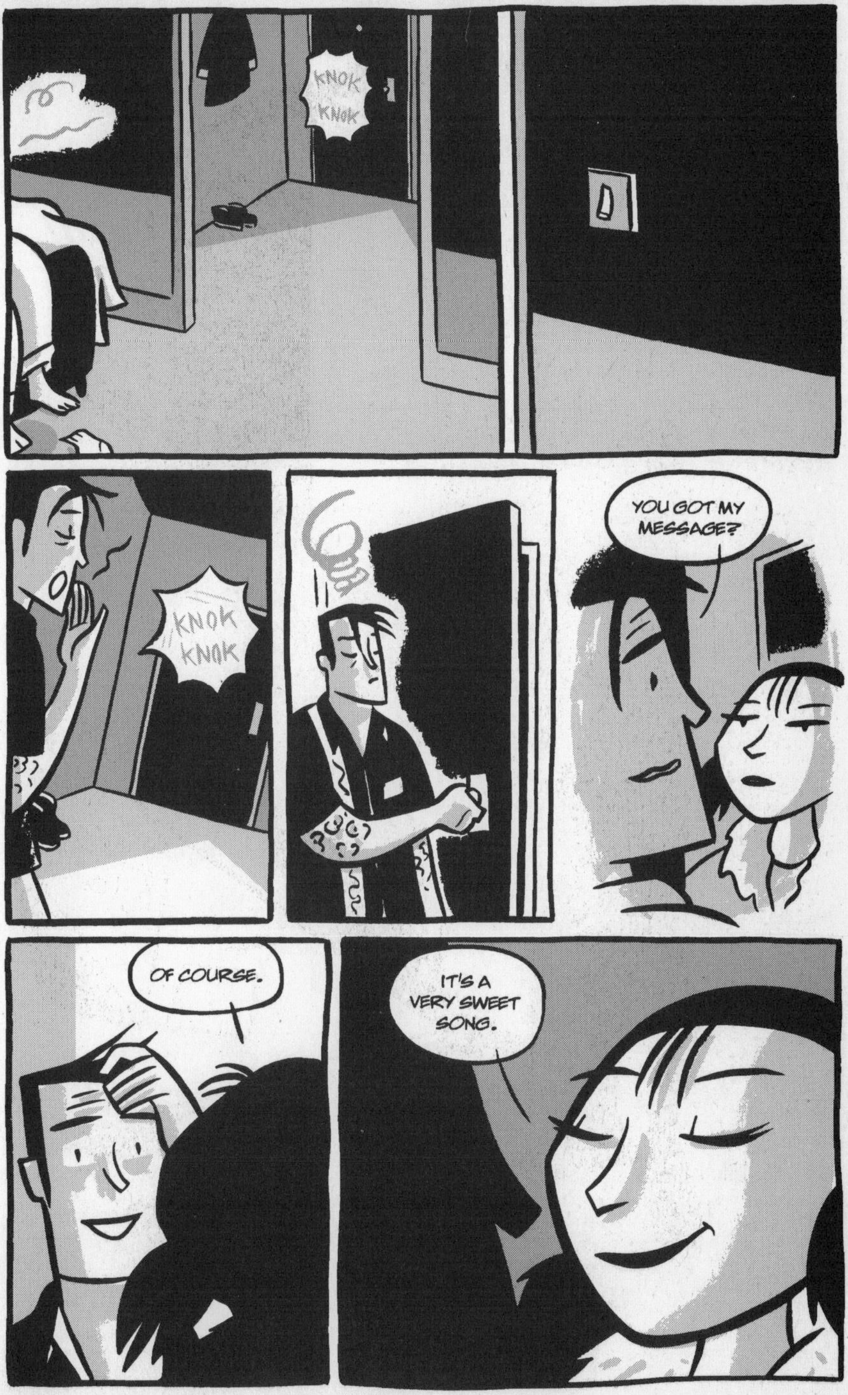
KNOK KNOK
KNOK KNOK
YOU GOT MY MESSAGE?
OF COURSE.
IT'S A VERY SWEET SONG.

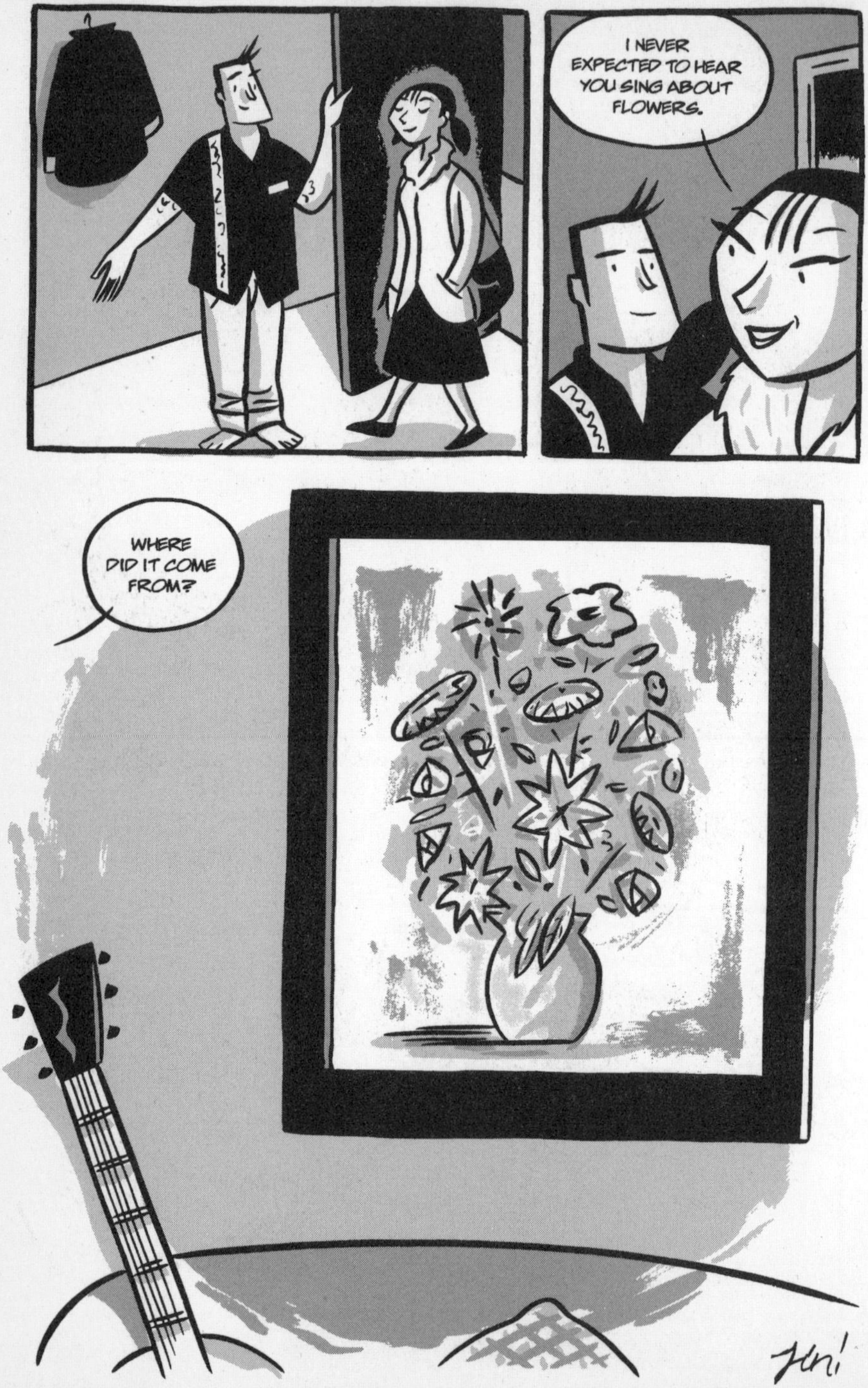
I NEVER EXPECTED TO HEAR YOU SING ABOUT FLOWERS.
WHERE DID IT COME FROM?
Jeni

short stories

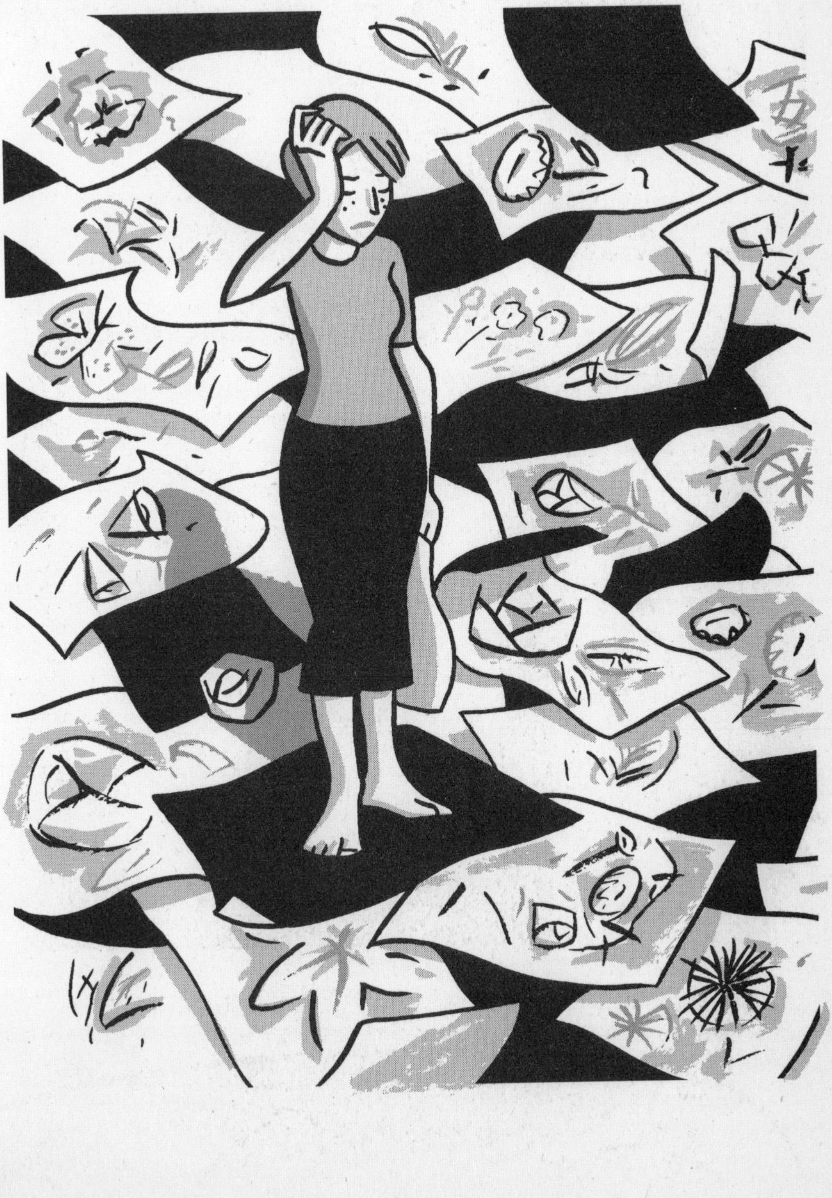

ARAGATO

A GEISHA STORY ANDI '00

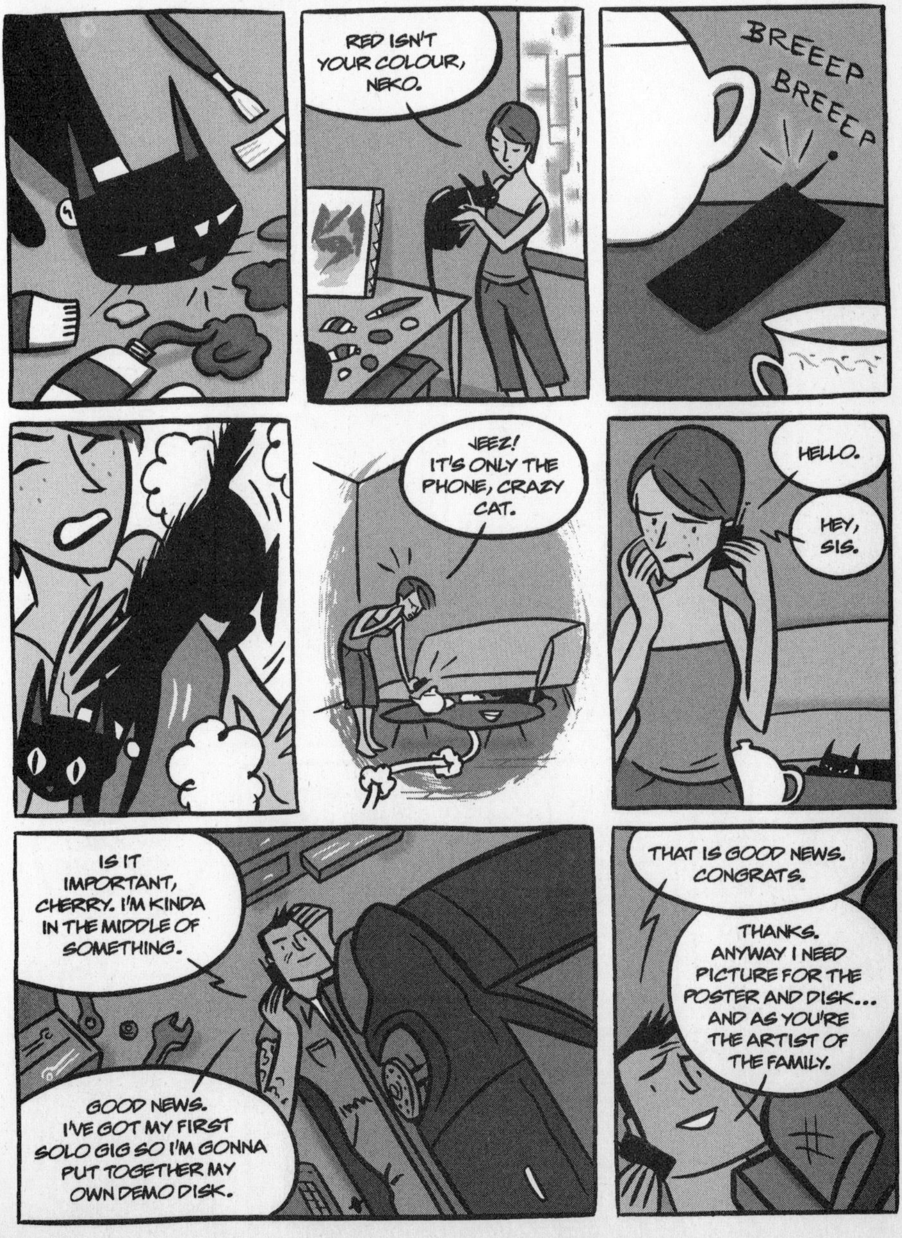
RED ISN'T YOUR COLOUR, NEKO.
BREEEEP BREEEEP
JEEZ! IT'S ONLY THE PHONE, CRAZY CAT.
HELLO.
HEY, SIS.
IS IT IMPORTANT, CHERRY. I'M KINDA IN THE MIDDLE OF SOMETHING.
GOOD NEWS. I'VE GOT MY FIRST SOLO GIG SO I'M GONNA PUT TOGETHER MY OWN DEMO DISK.
THAT IS GOOD NEWS. CONGRATS.
THANKS. ANYWAY I NEED PICTURE FOR THE POSTER AND DISK... AND AS YOU'RE THE ARTIST OF THE FAMILY.

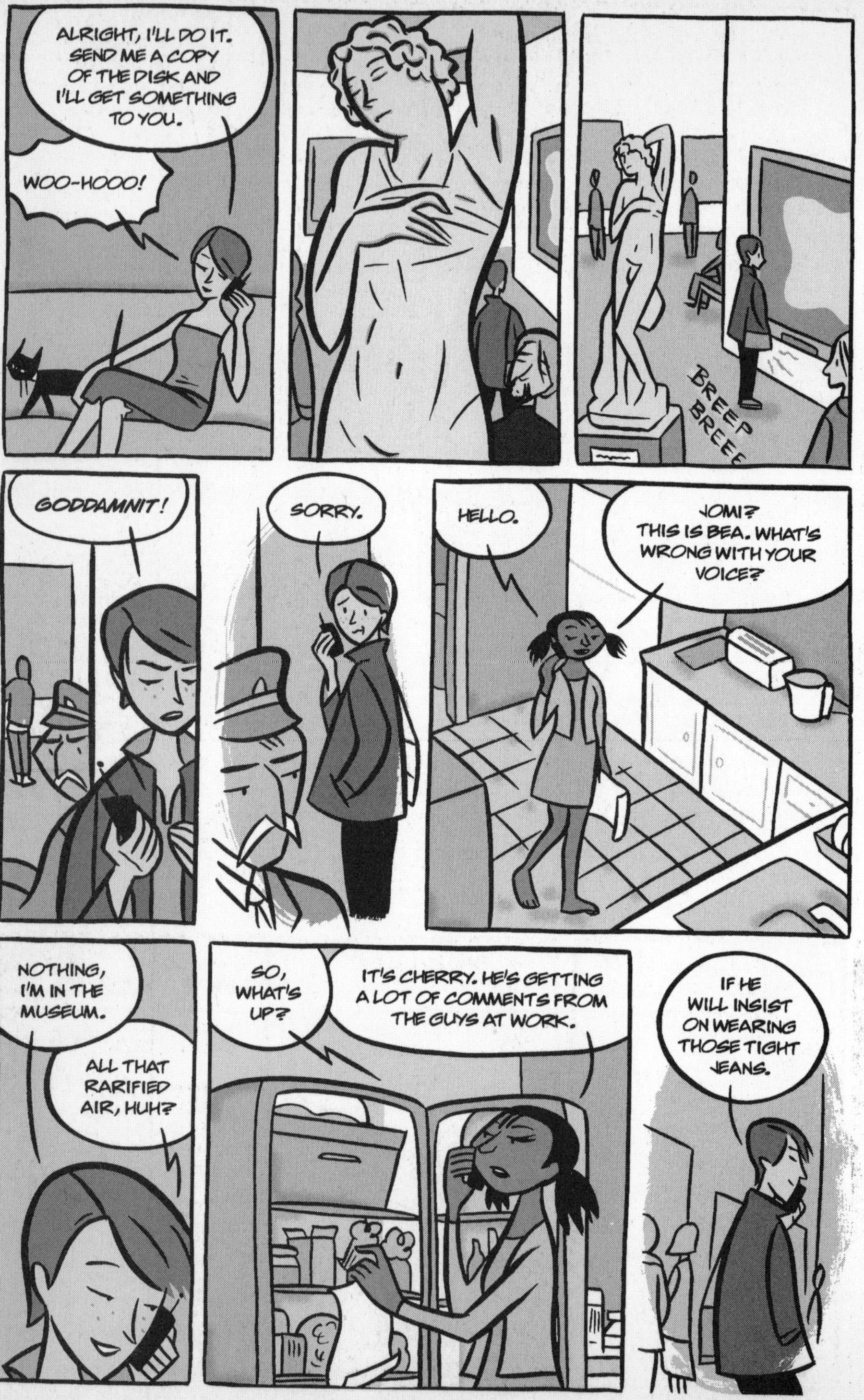
ALRIGHT, I'LL DO IT. SEND ME A COPY OF THE DISK AND I'LL GET SOMETHING TO YOU.
WOO-HOOO!
BREEP BREEE
GODDAMNIT!
SORRY.
HELLO.
JOMI? THIS IS BEA. WHAT'S WRONG WITH YOUR VOICE?
NOTHING, I'M IN THE MUSEUM.
ALL THAT RARIFIED AIR, HUH?
SO, WHAT'S UP?
IT'S CHERRY. HE'S GETTING A LOT OF COMMENTS FROM THE GUYS AT WORK.
IF HE WILL INSIST ON WEARING THOSE TIGHT JEANS.

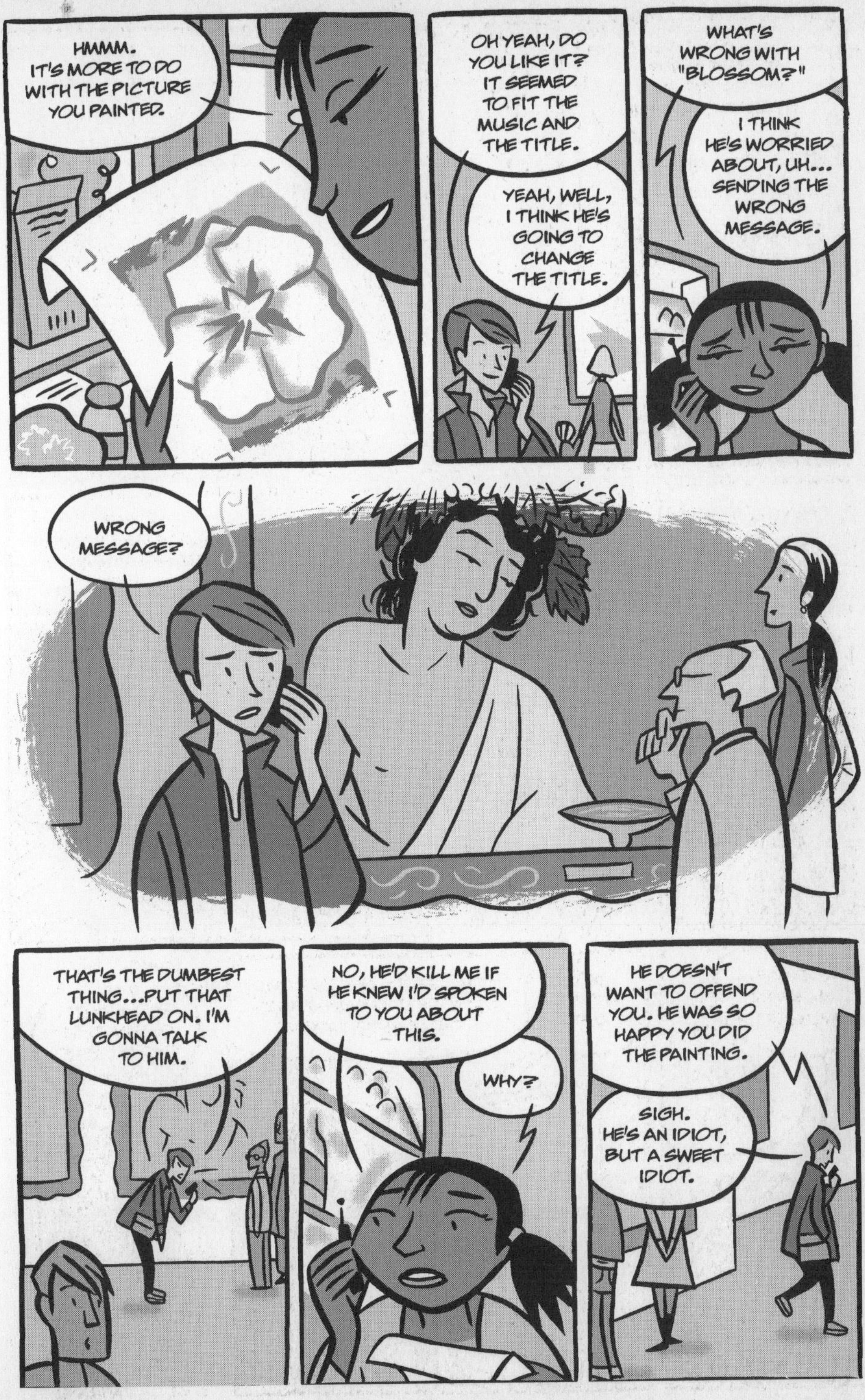
HMMM.
IT'S MORE TO DO WITH THE PICTURE YOU PAINTED.
OH YEAH, DO YOU LIKE IT? IT SEEMED TO FIT THE MUSIC AND THE TITLE.
YEAH, WELL, I THINK HE'S GOING TO CHANGE THE TITLE.
WHAT'S WRONG WITH "BLOSSOM?"
I THINK HE'S WORRIED ABOUT, UH... SENDING THE WRONG MESSAGE.
WRONG MESSAGE?
THAT'S THE DUMBEST THING...PUT THAT LUNKHEAD ON. I'M GONNA TALK TO HIM.
NO, HE'D KILL ME IF HE KNEW I'D SPOKEN TO YOU ABOUT THIS.
WHY?
HE DOESN'T WANT TO OFFEND YOU. HE WAS SO HAPPY YOU DID THE PAINTING.
SIGH.
HE'S AN IDIOT, BUT A SWEET IDIOT.

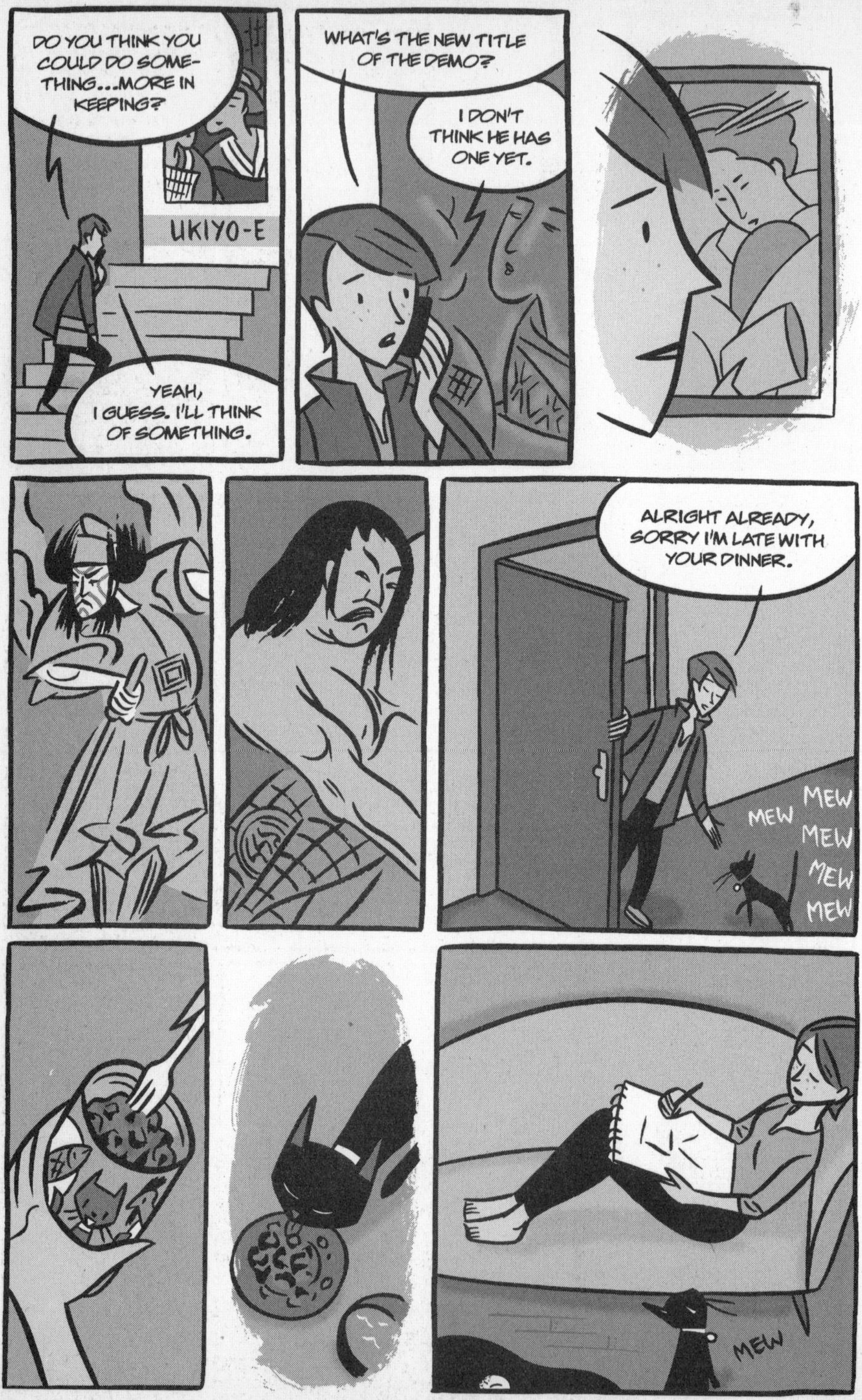
DO YOU THINK YOU COULD DO SOME-THING...MORE IN KEEPING?
UKIYO-E
YEAH, I GUESS. I'LL THINK OF SOMETHING.
WHAT'S THE NEW TITLE OF THE DEMO?
I DON'T THINK HE HAS ONE YET.
ALRIGHT ALREADY, SORRY I'M LATE WITH YOUR DINNER.
MEW MEW MEW MEW MEW
MEW

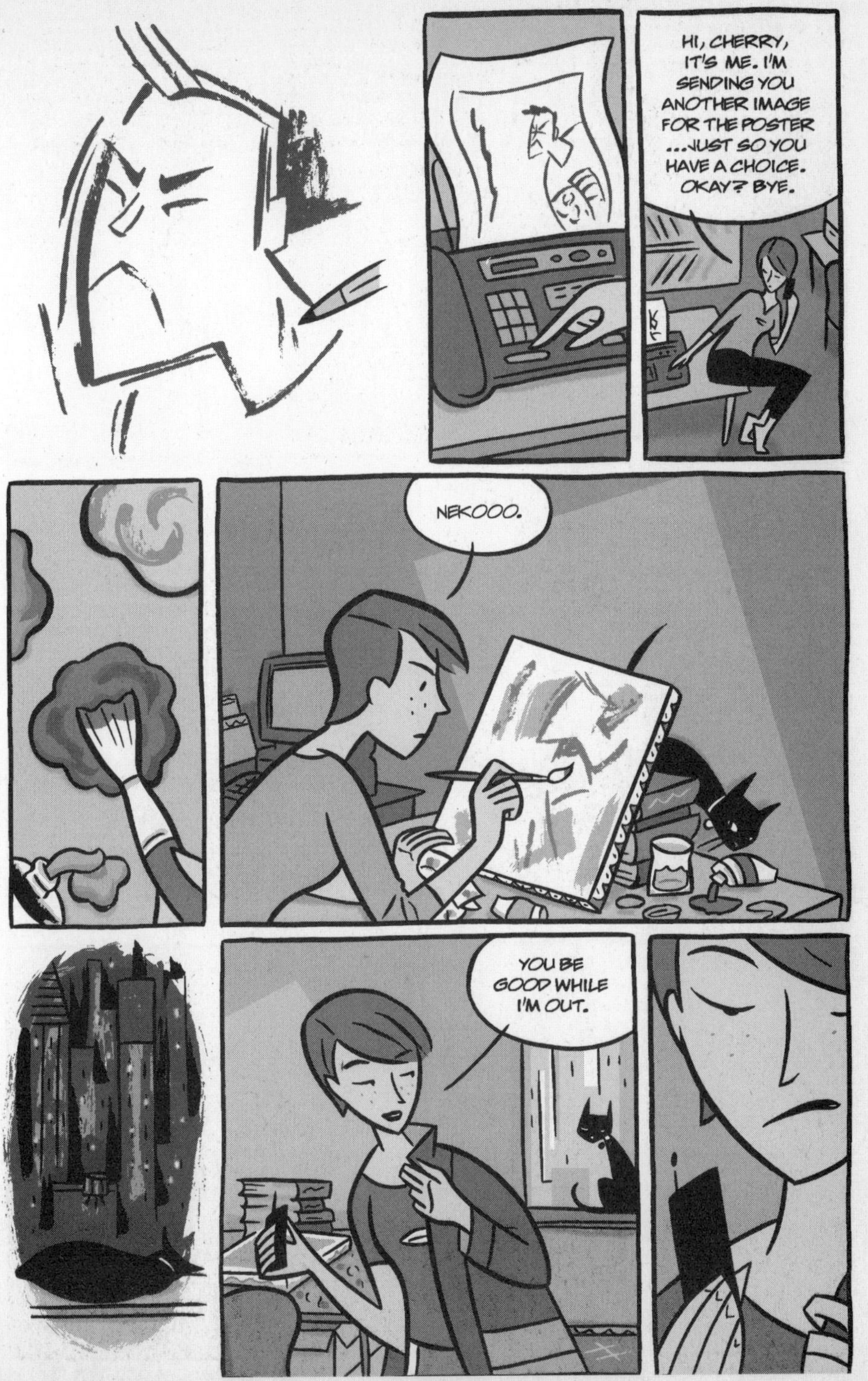
HI, CHERRY, IT'S ME. I'M SENDING YOU ANOTHER IMAGE FOR THE POSTER ...JUST SO YOU HAVE A CHOICE. OKAY? BYE.
NEKOOO.
YOU BE GOOD WHILE I'M OUT.

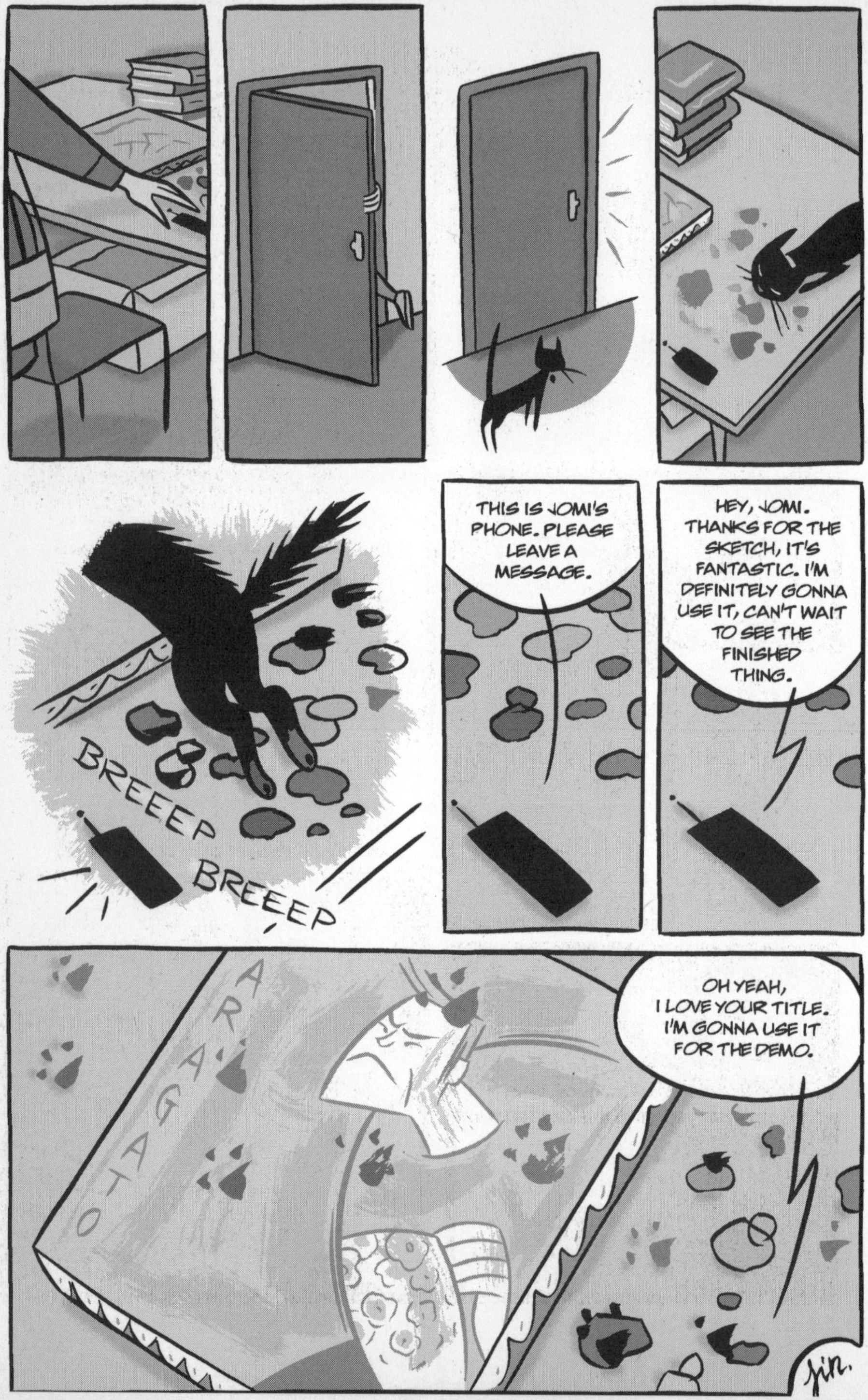
BREEEP
BREEEP
THIS IS JOMI'S PHONE. PLEASE LEAVE A MESSAGE.
HEY, JOMI. THANKS FOR THE SKETCH, IT'S FANTASTIC. I'M DEFINITELY GONNA USE IT, CAN'T WAIT TO SEE THE FINISHED THING.
ARAGATO
OH YEAH, I LOVE YOUR TITLE. I'M GONNA USE IT FOR THE DEMO.
fin.

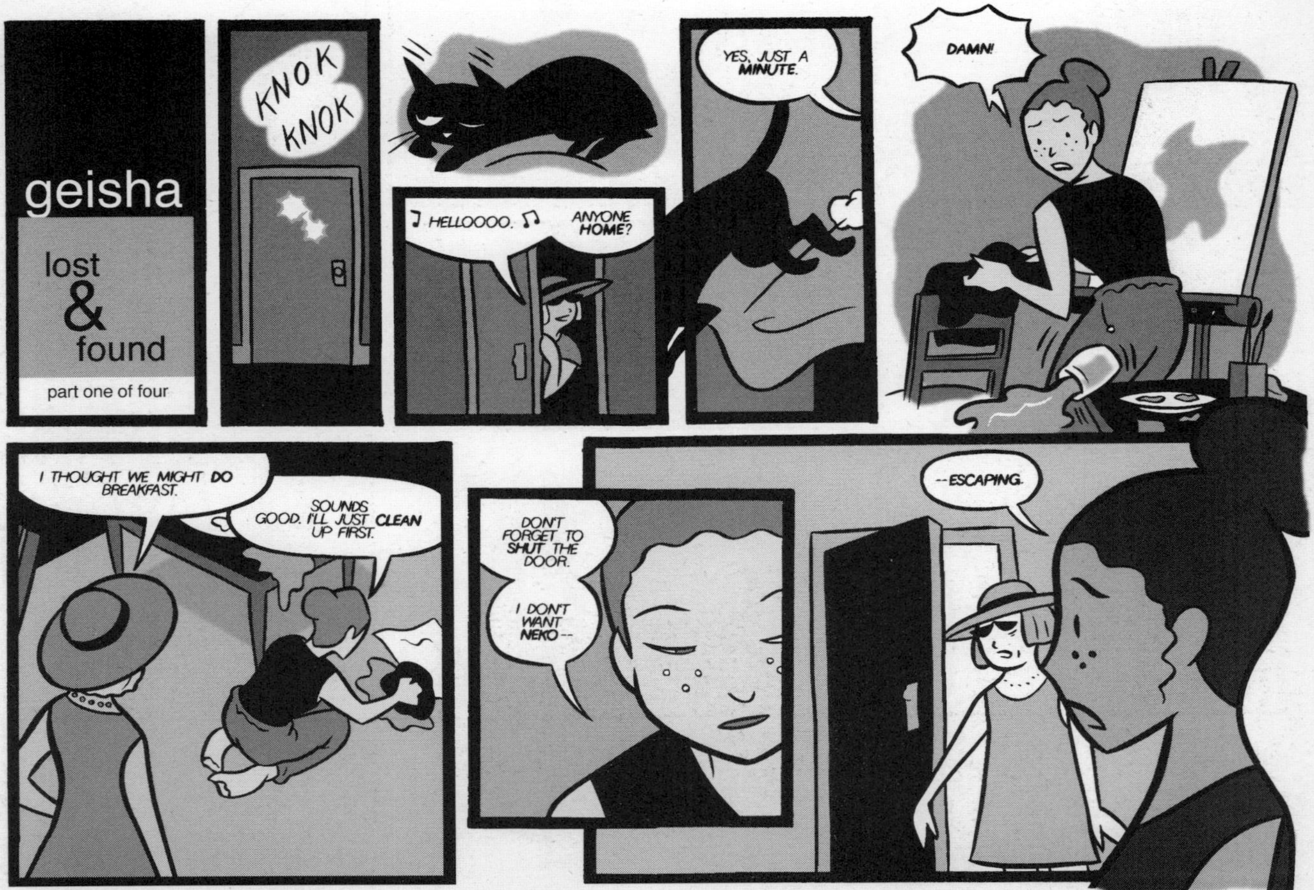
geisha
lost & found
part one of four
KNOK KNOK
♪ HELLOOOO. ♫
ANYONE HOME?
YES, JUST A MINUTE.
DAMN!
I THOUGHT WE MIGHT DO BREAKFAST.
SOUNDS GOOD. I'LL JUST CLEAN UP FIRST.
DON'T FORGET TO SHUT THE DOOR.
I DON'T WANT NEKO--
--ESCAPING.

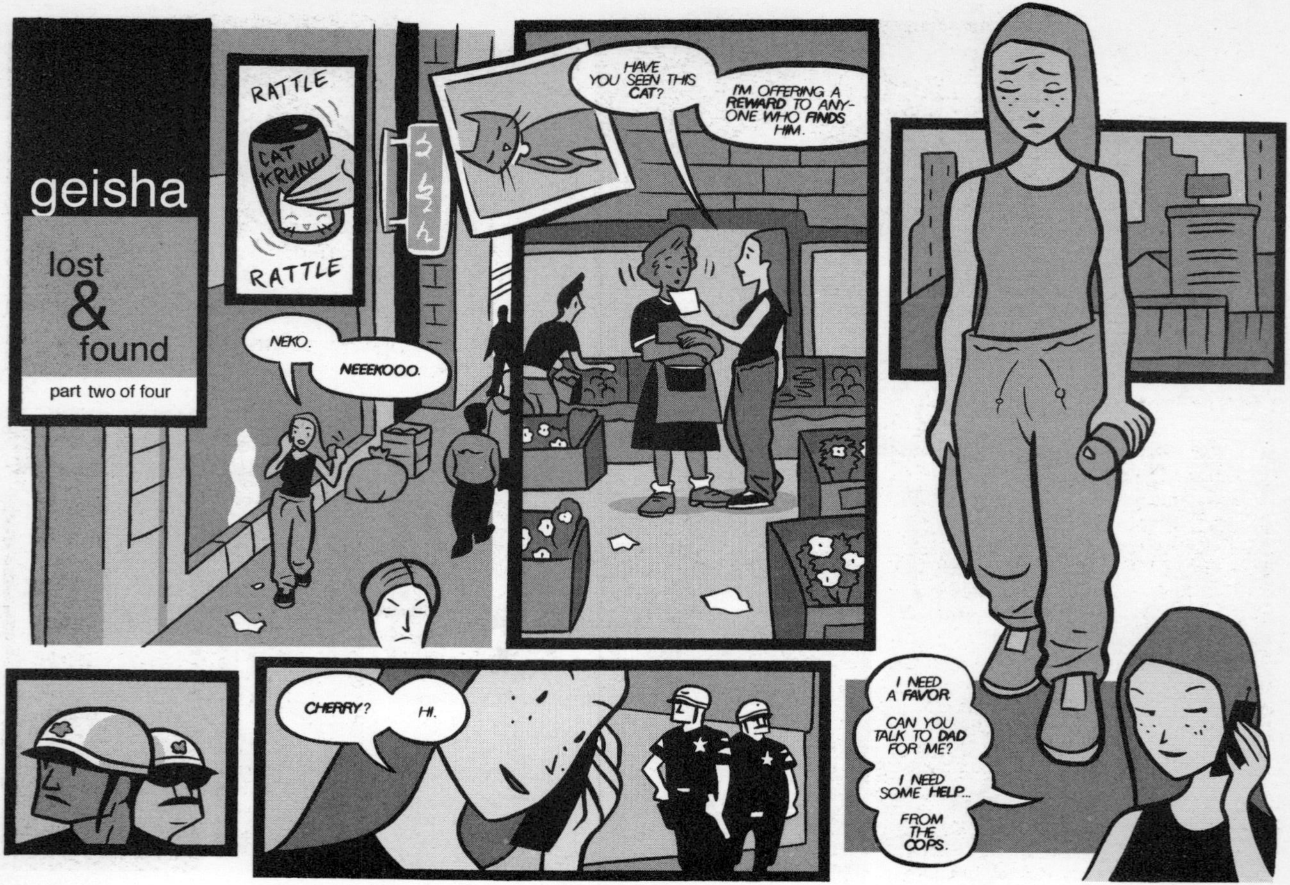
geisha
lost & found
part two of four
RATTLE
CAT KRUNCH
RATTLE
NEKO.
NEEEKOOO.
HAVE YOU SEEN THIS CAT?
I'M OFFERING A REWARD TO ANYONE WHO FINDS HIM.
CHERRY?
HI.
I NEED A FAVOR.
CAN YOU TALK TO DAD FOR ME?
I NEED SOME HELP...
FROM THE COPS.

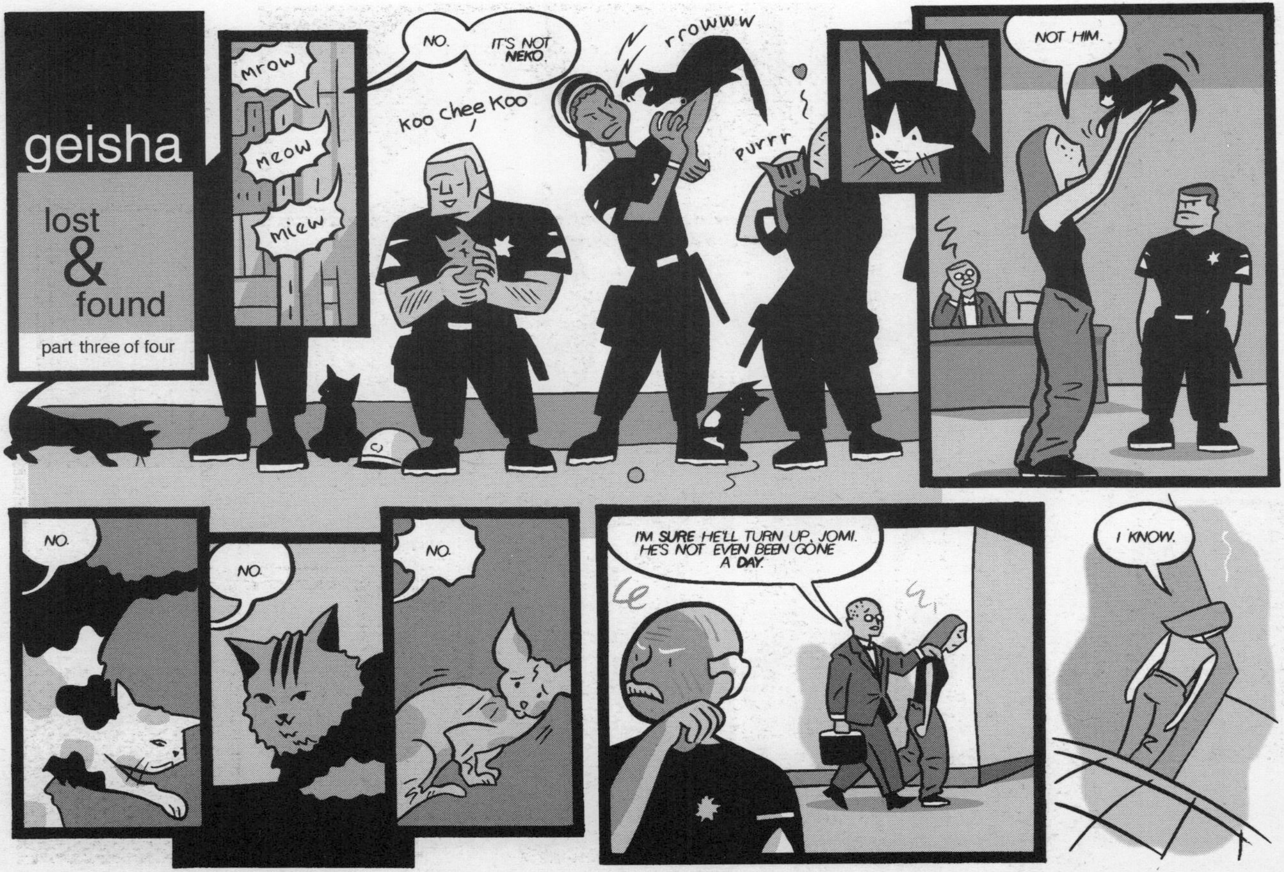
geisha
lost & found
part three of four
mrow
meow
miew
NO.
IT'S NOT NEKO.
koo chee koo
rrowww
purrr
NOT HIM.
NO.
NO.
NO.
I'M SURE HE'LL TURN UP, JOMI. HE'S NOT EVEN BEEN GONE A DAY.
I KNOW.

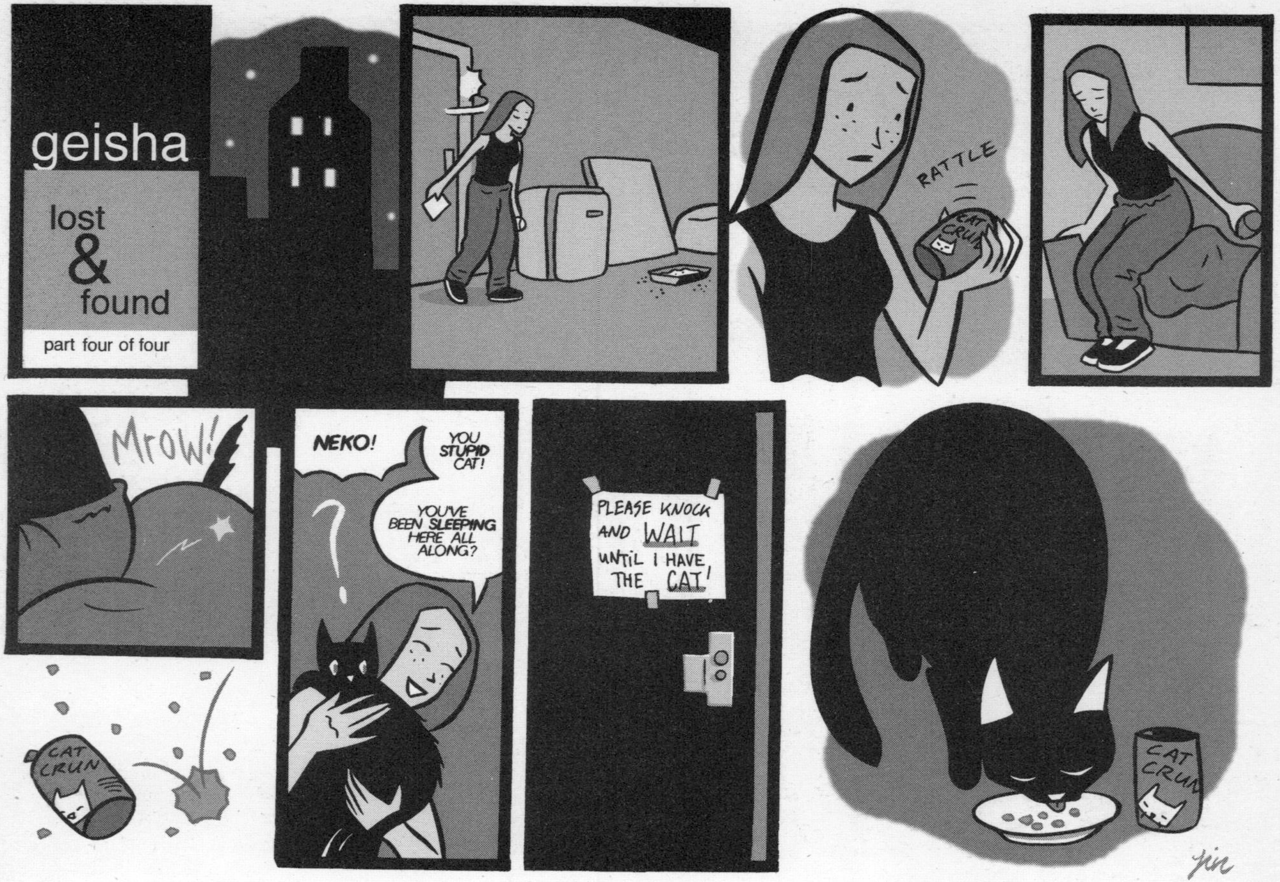
geisha
lost & found
part four of four
RATTLE
CAT CRUN
Mrow!
CAT CRUN
NEKO!
YOU STUPID CAT!
YOU'VE BEEN SLEEPING HERE ALL ALONG?
PLEASE KNOCK AND WAIT UNTIL I HAVE THE CAT!
CAT CRUN
jin